P9-CCP-599

ALSO BY BETTE HAGMAN

The Gluten-free Gourmet

More from the Gluten-free Gourmet

The Gluten-free Gourmet Cooks Fast and Healthy

The Gluten-free Gourmet Bakes Bread

The Gluten-free Gourmet Makes Dessert

The Gluten-free Gourmet Cooks Comfort Foods

BETTE HAGMAN

The
Gluten-Free Gourmet
Cooks Comfort Foods

More Than 200 Recipes for Creating
Old Favorites with New Flours

A Holt Paperback
Henry Holt and Company | New York

Holt Paperbacks
Henry Holt and Company, LLC
Publishers since 1866
175 Fifth Avenue
New York, New York 10010
www.henryholt.com

A Holt Paperback® and ® are registered
trademarks of Henry Holt and Company, LLC.

Copyright © 2004 by Bette Hagman
All rights reserved.
Distributed in Canada by H. B. Fenn and Company Ltd.

Library of Congress Cataloging-in-Publication Data
Hagman, Bette.
    The gluten-free gourmet cooks comfort foods : more than 200 recipes
for creating old favorites with new flours / Bette Hagman.—1st ed.
        p.   cm.
    ISBN-13: 978-0-8050-7808-4
    ISBN-10: 0-8050-7808-8
    1. Gluten-free diet—Recipes. 2. Comfort food.   I. Title.
    RM237.86.H3377   2004
    641.5'638—dc22   2003056649

Henry Holt books are available for special promotions and
premiums. For details contact: Director, Special Markets.

Originally published in hardcover in 2004 by
Henry Holt and Company

First Holt Paperbacks Edition 2005

Designed by Kelly S. Too

Printed in the United States of America
7   9   10   8

*This book is dedicated to the memory of three friends,
pioneers in celiac awareness when it was still considered a "rare" disease:
Pat Garst, author of some of the first layman's writings about the disease;
Elaine Hartsook, founder of the Gluten Intolerance Group; and
Mary Alice Warren, who took celiacs on the first gluten-free cruises.*

Contents

Foreword

Celiac disease is a syndrome characterized by damage to the lining of the small intestine, caused by the gluten in wheat and similar proteins of barley and rye. The presence of gluten in people with celiac disease leads to mucosal damage, while the elimination of gluten results in full recovery for the patient. In the continued presence of gluten, the disease is self-perpetuating. It is the interplay between genes and environment (gluten) that leads to the intestinal damage typical of the disease.

Celiac disease is one of the most common lifelong disorders in Europe and in the United States. This condition can be found in patients with a range of symptoms, including chronic diarrhea, weight loss, and abdominal distention or a range of symptoms potentially affecting any organ or part of the body system. Since the disease is often atypical or even silent, many cases remain undiagnosed and thus expose the patient to the risk of long-term complications such as osteoporosis, infertility, or cancer. There is growing interest in celiac disease since the burden of the illness related to this condition is doubtless higher than previously thought.

In countries where individuals are mostly of European origin the prevalence of this disease ranges between 0.25 and I percent in the general population. The first mass studies were performed in Europe, but recently this finding has also been confirmed in the United States, South America (Brazil, Argentina), and Australia.

It is increasingly clear that celiac disease is also a common disorder in many areas of the developing world such as North Africa, the Middle East, and India. The highest frequency of the disease in the world has actually been reported among the Saharawi refugees, an inbred population of Berber-Arabic origin.

While in the past celiac disease was typically considered a pediatric condition, we are now aware that the disease may appear after years of silent intestinal damage following exposure to gluten. Therefore, its diagnosis can be extremely challenging and currently relies on sensitive and specific tests that allow the identification of different manifestations of the disease.

Most celiacs are diagnosed following a small intestinal biopsy that shows damage to the mucosa. In the last few decades, however, a number of other diagnostic tests have been developed that are also useful in the patient's follow-up. Besides the antigliadin (AGA) and the antiendomysium (EMA) tests, both in use since the 1980s, the anti-tissue transglutaminase (tTG) antibody test is increasingly used. Several studies conducted in both children and adults have recently shown that the IgA anti-tTG ELISA test is an especially valuable and reproducible tool for diagnosis and follow-up. New genetic tests are also now available to establish whether celiac disease can be excluded, with a 99 percent accuracy in patients who do not carry the DQ2, DQ8 genes.

The treatment of celiac disease requires a lifelong diet eliminating all food products containing gluten. In principle, the treatment appears simple and straightforward, but embracing a gluten-free diet is not an easy enterprise. There are things in life that we do automatically without paying attention to them. How many times do we drive back home from work thinking about something else and find ourselves at the garage door without recalling how we got there? How often do we perform routine tasks such as tie our shoes, brush our teeth, listen to the sounds of nature, and yet, don't have distinct memory of these acts?

For the vast majority of human beings eating is another automatic activity. Celiacs, however, must devote a great deal of mental, physical, and social energy to what should be one of the most natural and enjoyable activities in life. In the United States this task has, in the past, been aggravated by the limited alternatives to gluten-containing food. Bette Hagman experienced firsthand the journey from the dark times of the rice and banana diet to a more humane way of eating. Not only was she a spectator of this evolution, but she also played a key role in paving the way to a more palatable lifestyle for celiac patients. For more than a decade, thousands of American celiacs have enjoyed her groundbreaking and creative recipes.

With this new book on comfort foods, Bette is closing the gap between celiac and non-celiac cuisine to reach the holy grail of handing to the celiac community the pleasure of eating as a routine activity.

Alessio Fasano, M.D.
Center for Celiac Research
University of Maryland School of Medicine

Acknowledgments

I cannot take credit for this book as my work alone; it is the result of the work of many people who helped me to create the comfort foods in the recipes and added to my knowledge of celiac disease.

First, although I shall not name them, were the wonderful celiacs who answered the questionnaire I sent out. All answered in great length to give me a real picture of what it was like to live on a gluten-free diet and told in depth how it affected them. And each, without knowledge from others, gave me permission to call or write them to gain more information. I owe the chapter "Growing Up Celiac" to this vast array of information.

I owe the chapter "Autism and the GF/CF Diet" to Laurie K. Mischley, N.D., for her medical knowledge and special research on autism and children's behavior patterns. I also thank Lisa Lewis for added information and her books written for parents of the autistic child.

My testers not only tested the recipes and added ingredients but sent me others to add to the book. They also nixed some recipes that I now see were not good enough. I want to thank them sincerely for their time and all their efforts: Norma Bartlett, Carol Becker, Minika Bradley, Adele Fosser, Keri Fosser, Bert Garman, Marlene Kier, Nancy Kloberdanz, Diane Lane, Mike Lodico, Jan Meeling, Karen Meyers, Jean Nichols, Pat Peckham, Genevieve Potts, Virginia Schmuck, Terry Tangen, Mary Lou Thomas, and Reesa Zuber.

Finally I want to thank Alessio Fasano, M.D., who, in spite of a busy schedule, took time to write the foreword to this work.

I could not close without giving credit and many thanks to my editor Deb Brody, who caught me mid-book a few years ago and has since constantly championed my work and created readable books from chaotic manuscripts.

The Gluten-free Gourmet Cooks Comfort Foods

Introduction

Living gluten free can seem a terrible hurdle to the beginning celiac, can't it? When the doctor tells you that you have gluten intolerance and assures you the diet can cure your problems, you may rejoice, but only until you realize that most of the foods you crave seem to have gluten in them. You think "no macaroni and cheese," "no chicken and dumplings," "no pizza"; the list seems to stretch on forever.

It's even worse when you first browse the grocery shelves and see that even tomato soup and your favorite chili have modified food starch in the form of wheat thickening. The cookie and cracker aisle, as well as the in-house bakery, might as well be marked off-limits.

Cheer up! This lack of your favorite foods is all in the past; gone are the days of the banana and rice diet for the gluten intolerant. Medical science has come a long way since 1945 when a doctor first suspected that not all grains caused the damage to the intestine and the distress symptoms of celiac disease or gluten enteropathy.

When I was diagnosed in the early 1970s, celiacs could only have two grains that didn't contain the toxic gluten: corn and rice. But we could have flourlike substances made from roots, lentils, and seeds. That left us with the flours from rice, corn, tapioca, and potato. Later we added the more nutritious bean flours. In my earlier books I gave substitutions for everything from pizza to pasta using these flours.

So why write another book? I didn't start out to, but like my first book, I just started writing down, for my own files, recipes of some of my favorite foods, automatically

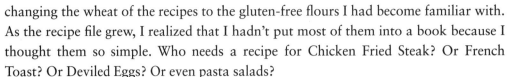

changing the wheat of the recipes to the gluten-free flours I had become familiar with. As the recipe file grew, I realized that I hadn't put most of them into a book because I thought them so simple. Who needs a recipe for Chicken Fried Steak? Or French Toast? Or Deviled Eggs? Or even pasta salads?

A lot of celiacs probably did, including those noncooks (as I was originally) who'd been diagnosed and had decided that cooking was better than starving to death, and were now trying to eat at home. I'd also added new twists to recipes I'd already published, making them tastier and often more nutritious. As an example, try one of the new breads created when I accidentally dumped some sorghum (with more protein, fat, and fiber) into a Featherlight Mix bread batter, making it even tastier, thus creating a new line of more nutritional breads for those who, unfortunately, can't tolerate the bean flours.

I talk of all this blithely, as if it happened overnight. Believe me, that is nowhere near the truth. In the beginning, it took me nine long years working with a friend who knew how to cook to come up with a gluten-free egg noodle that tasted like the ones I recalled from my childhood. Remember, at the time I was diagnosed in the early 1970s, there were no pastas to be purchased at the local health food store as there are today. We had to mail order from the only company that imported from Germany so pasta was high on the list of cravings.

Even more important, if you read a recent magazine article you'll realize that the title "What's Old Is New Again" holds true for food as well as for the toys mentioned in the article. Years ago (so long ago some of you won't even remember it) every recipe seemed to start with "Take a can of mushroom (or chicken) soup. . . ." In my third book, *The Gluten-free Gourmet Cooks Fast and Healthy,* I published a recipe for a cream soup base that I keep on the counter next to my stove. Today these "quick cream soup" recipes have come back into style and I've included many, hoping you, too, will keep that cream soup mix handy. Since we still can't buy cream soup without gluten, I've repeated the recipe here.

New celiacs may groan about the restrictions on what they can eat, but they don't realize that every year our diet has expanded. While we in the United States and Canada maintain a "zero" tolerance to gluten, celiacs have turned to scientists and cereal chemists to certify that the once forbidden distilled vinegars and spirits made from gluten grains do not contain toxic proteins as they cannot pass through the distillation process. So we've added more vinegars and liquors to our diet in the United States. Canada was ahead of us for they have always accepted them.

In very recent years, it was scientifically confirmed that other, even more exotic, seeds and grains that Canada allowed while we debated also were gluten free and were admitted to the U.S. diet: amaranth, millet, quinoa, and teff. The only trouble was that no one had developed recipes for us using these almost unknown grains. I was already using buckwheat and sorghum when I began to experiment with these other flours. Although I find each is different, all of them have more nutrition than rice and by using these grains we get a lot more variety.

This led me to realize that I had recipes that were different but were of familiar foods, many of them foods we craved but couldn't eat out. Not yet anyway. Although there are more suppliers of gluten-free items every year, for most of us, our food is still cooked at home and eaten with the family. And many celiac cooks have found that the whole family will gobble up their favorite recipes even when made with substitute flours. In fact, a lot of them don't know they are doing so. Many foods will be made of the rice or bean mixes with which you are familiar. Only in special cases have I baked with the exotic flours just to give you suggestions on how you, too, can be daring and add a little of the new grains to the old diet.

Use these recipes and eat well. It may seem awkward at times but do as I do, just tell anyone who asks that you are eating all your old favorites with new flours.

A History of Celiac Disease

The story of celiac disease is both old and new. It was first mentioned over two centuries before Christ but it took two more millenniums before anyone tried to do something about curbing the effects. After that slow start, the disease began snowballing with recognition, control, easier diagnosis, and research. It is hoped that somewhere in the next ten years there may also be a "cure" or a simpler method of control than the lifelong diet free of gluten in wheat, rye, and barley. The sad part is that, although scientists have proved that one in one hundred fifty people may have celiac disease, only one out of ten has been diagnosed so far. The others are living with this condition, unaware that they could have a far healthier life.

This disease—the autoimmune reaction to gluten in our food leading to malnutrition—may have its roots in the agricultural revolution 10,000 years ago when man stopped chasing prey for his only food to settle down to raise seeds as well. Who knows what intolerances developed in the people unused to grains in their diet? But the first known writing of the suspected disease was in the third century.

250 A.D.: Artaeus of Cappadocia first wrote of the symptoms but it wasn't until 1856 that his work was translated into English.

1880: Samuel Gee, M.D., in an article in the medical magazine *St. Bartholomew's Hospital Reports,* Vol. 24, identified food as the probable cause of the debilitating symptoms of the malady later to be called celiac disease. He suggested cow's milk be removed from the diet and that other foods be introduced in small portions. He also was astute enough to recognize that the symptoms probably arose from some foods but didn't specify which ones. He suggested patients remove from their diet foods that caused symptoms.

1924: Scientists felt that celiacs should be on a rice and banana diet. It worked, because it removed all grains, meats, vegetables, and milk from the patient. As the children improved (only children were thought to have the disease), they were introduced to other foods. The improvement suggested to the doctors that they were "cured." We know now that the doctors were wrong.

1946–1950: During World War II celiacs in Holland were unable to get wheat for their bread and surprised their doctors by their return to good health. W. K. Diecke wrote his doctoral thesis on the subject, identifying wheat as a source of the symptoms. It was the first definitive suggestion that a certain grain contained toxicity to those with celiac disease.

1958: Introduction of the Rubin Tube. Up until this time diagnosis for celiac disease had to be made from a description of the symptoms—diarrhea, vomiting (in infants), malnutrition, and protruding stomach. Although barium X rays were used to diagnose some internal ailments, they failed to show celiac disease. There was no way of actually viewing the upper intestine without surgery until Dr. Cyrus B. Rubin and his associates at a Seattle hospital created the first crude tube with rotating blades to take a biopsy of the damaged area when swallowed by the patient. This tube has been improved over the years from the original tests with the patient awake and conscious; now the endoscopy is practically painless with the patient medicated and asleep throughout the examination. At this time it was known that children had celiac sprue but few recognized the fact that the adult disease, nontropical sprue, was the same. The Rubin Tube showed that, in biopsy, they were identical. Doctors still stuck to the separate names while patients were beginning to suspect that they were the same. Adults suffered much longer before being diagnosed, often being told it was "all in their heads" or to "just take a stomach settler and they would feel better."

1973–1974: Start of celiac support groups. Until this time, each diagnosed patient felt alone while the doctors had little knowledge and no time to help him/her cope with the diagnosis of a "rare" disease that had no cure except a strict diet. In fact, the disease was so little known that few people had heard of it, and dieticians were of no help because they had received little information about it.

Five support organizations started at about the same time, each begun because the founder found a fellow sufferer and realized she was not alone and that others out there must need help, too. On the east coast of the United States, the American Celiac Society was started by Annita Garrow for research; in Seattle, the Gluten Intolerance Group was founded by Elaine Hartsook for research, support, and diet instruction. A few years later, in the Midwest, the Midwestern Celiac Sprue Association (later to be called CSA/USA) was begun by Pat Garst for support and diet instruction. At the same time, in Canada, Kay Ernst, the mother of a celiac child, joined with another to begin what became the Canadian National Association. Later, the organizations in the United States were joined by the Celiac Disease Foundation in Los Angeles, organized by Elaine Monarch. These groups are all still active and several have joined together to provide support and educate the public.

These groups, working alone or with others, have been responsible for better labeling laws. We can now tell by the new ingredients list if a product contains gluten or milk products, although they may be hidden under the term "modified food starch" or some other terms for gluten, while milk may hide under such terms as "whey" or "casein." The groups, whether alone or in conjunction with others, are constantly working to improve the wording of labels.

1978: The toxic part of the grain found! Although doctors were aware that certain grains were responsible for the disease, it wasn't until Donald Kasarda, Ph.D., identified the particular proteins in gluten that caused the toxic reactions from the grains of wheat, rye, barley, and, possibly, oats.

1992: The first all-celiac cruise. Mary Alice Warren of Florida arranged a Caribbean cruise with all gluten-free meals for celiacs across the nation and Canada. She had chefs and helpers in a separate gluten-free kitchen prepare all meals. Between stops, the celiacs were treated to seminars on eating, cooking, and living gluten-free. She also arranged for cruises in 1993 and 1994.

1998: Blood testing could show celiac disease. This was the beginning of the discovery by scientists that several different sereological studies could discern celiac disease, but physicians continued to rely on the physical symptoms and the endoscopy for diagnosing patients.

1998–2001: Alessio Fasano, M.D., working in Maryland at the Center for Celiac Research, realized that the number of celiacs reported in the United States was far lower than the numbers reported in Europe and wanted to know why. Was it our way of living? Our heritage? Or the fact that doctors here were not diagnosing the illness?

He started a nationwide project of blood testing using the help and facilities of various celiac organizations nationwide at their meetings, conventions, and other gatherings. He discovered that the ratio, which formerly was thought to be 1 in 3,000, was actually closer to 1 in 150! Celiacs were not being diagnosed in the United States. He started an active campaign for celiac awareness with the Walk.

2002: First International Walk for Celiac Disease. This walk was to raise awareness of the disease around the world and was so successful that others followed.

In conclusion, take heart, the activities surrounding celiac disease—support awareness and research—have never been more active. You are not alone now. There are many out there with the disease and many more working to make it easier and easier to live, whether it be on the diet for life or eventually finding some type of medicine that may curb the toxicity of the proteins.

Today's celiacs are fortunate to find themselves the focus of so much research that it can be mind-boggling. Some medical scientists are attempting to find a simple pill that can be taken to offset the toxic effects of gluten. Others are attempting to create a wheat that will not contain any toxic particle. And across the nation even suppliers are aware that wheat, as well as other products, can cause extreme illness and are now considering labeling foods that contain allergens. There are dreams of a better future for all of us.

But until some of these dreams come true, we will have to settle for making or buying products we can tolerate and sticking to the diet. It's difficult for one person to keep up with all the scientific work, but the large celiac organizations have conferences that invite the top doctors to bring insight on the latest discoveries as well as keep us aware that this disease, unresolved, can lead to more chance of having another or several of the autoimmune diseases.

To join a support group near you and become part of a larger organization, write or call one of the following:

American Celiac Society Dietary Support Coalition, P.O. Box 23455, New Orleans, LA 70183-0445; phone (504) 737-3293; e-mail: AmerCeliacSoc@netscape.net.

Canadian Celiac Association, 5170 Dixie Road, Suite 204, Mississauga L4W 1E3, Ontario, Canada; phone (905) 507-6208, fax (905) 507-4673, toll free (800) 363-7296.

Celiac Disease Foundation, 13251 Ventura Blvd., Suite 1, Studio City, CA 91604-1838; phone (818) 990-2354, fax (818) 990-2397, e-mail: cdf@celiac.org. Web site: www.celiac.org.

Celiac Sprue Association/United States of America (CSA/USA), P.O. Box 31700, Omaha, NE 68131-0700; phone (402) 558-0600.

Gluten Intolerance Group (GIG), 15110 10th Avenue, SW, Suite A, Seattle, WA 98166; phone (206) 246-6652, fax (206) 246-6531, e-mail: info@gluten.net. Web site: www.gluten.net.

REFERENCES

Annette C. Bentley, "Evolving Celiac Organizations in the United States." Paper delivered at CSA/USA convention in Omaha, Neb., October 2001.

Alessio Fasano, M.D., "Celiac Disease: the Past, the Present, the Future." Paper delivered at Canadian/Celiac Conference, Ottawa, Canada, May 16, 2001, and at the Gluten Intolerance Group national convention, Winston-Salem, N.C., 2001.

Stefano Guandalini, M.D., and Michelle Melin-Rogovin, "The History of Celiac Disease and of Its Diagnostic Practices." Paper delivered at Living Free national convention, Philadelphia, Pa., 2001.

Growing Up Celiac

Have you ever wondered if celiacs who have lived gluten free as long as they can remember find the diet easier? What problems do they confront when they've never tasted store-bought bread or ordered a sandwich sent up to the hotel room when traveling? Do they resent the diet? And how have eating restrictions shaped their lives?

I wondered, too, and, being curious, conducted a survey of those adults who could answer these questions by offering a questionnaire through the Internet and numerous celiac newsletters for one year. I was aware there might be very few who could answer, for most patients diagnosed more than twenty-one years ago were usually considered "cured" and taken off the diet by their doctors. But I never guessed it would be so few.

I received letters from many celiacs admitting they had been on the diet, taken off, and later rediagnosed. Some of you, I suspect, know celiacs with the same story. Other letters drifted in slowly; as few as I anticipated. As these celiacs had all been less than four years old when diagnosed, none could remember eating wheat.

To establish a base I asked other questions about their lives, their feelings, and their diet.

How were you diagnosed? Here the answers varied but the largest number were found by their doctors. Others gave credit to research by family members or the naturopathic community.

Do you have relatives (first or second degree) with celiac or other autoimmune diseases? Some replied they didn't know of any. Almost half of them had first-degree relatives with celiac disease. Others listed Sjögren's syndrome, thyroid disease, or diabetes. From the numbers, it was easy to recognize that the proportion of auto-immune diseases represented here was higher than the average norm.

At what period in your life has the GF diet been hardest to maintain? The answers here were predictable. All admitted the hardest was when they were making a big change, such as first going to school and missing out on treats because the teacher had nothing to substitute. Others felt the full brunt of the disease on entering college or leaving home to finally shop and cook for themselves. Other answers included the first awareness of eating differently when the celiac so much wanted to be the same. In these cases it seems that peer pressure was harder than actually missing the wheated food.

Do you feel living on a GF diet has any effect on your social life? There were definite answers here. One woman with a sense of humor wrote that it was easy to tell who were her friends: they were the ones willing to drive long enough to find a place where she could eat. She also added that one time she dared her friends to go on her diet, and not one lasted a full day. One thing all agreed on was that having to eat gluten-free caused them to avoid accepting some social engagements revolving around food. One admitted that she had become rather shy because of this. Almost all said that eating out was more a duty than a pleasure, and some wondered when restaurants would become aware of this large segment of the population.

Actually, a restaurant awareness program has been in progress for several years on the East Coast and now is being carried out in Seattle and many food establishments can now offer a gluten-free menu.

Does it affect your business life? Definitely! The answers ranged from changing an occupation to avoid the food side of business to confessing problems with client lunches, staff lunches, company conferences, meetings, and traveling. Some offered solutions that weren't as drastic as changing jobs: keeping a food box in a carry-on bag, purse, and car, and learning which restaurants were celiac friendly.

Does it affect your religious life? As expected, the answers here were varied. Some admitted to accepting a "crumb" of the host; others took only the wine while others made or brought their own host to the church. It was interesting to me that those who answered were aware that even as much as the host once a week could be harmful to a celiac. I was glad to see this, for in the early years, I had never heard it even considered.

Do you deliberately cheat on the diet? And if you do, what are the symptoms? No! Never! Not if I can help it! Only once; never again. Every respondent articulated.

I expected the symptoms of the disease to vary since we now know that there are a variety of them, not all pertaining to the intestines. In this case I was surprised when all answered that they had severe intestinal distress, often lasting for days. Some reported vomiting, most with diarrhea, cramping, bloating, and all with pain. A few of them indicated they also felt mental fatigue and recognized a loss of focus.

Before 1980 celiac disease was basically considered to be a disease of the intestine and diagnosed because of the complaint of overwhelming stomach distress with varying symptoms. As I read the answers to the questionnaire, I felt that the celiacs who responded might have been the children most seriously ill when diagnosed and who were still suffering symptoms if they got any gluten. There may have been many who become nonsymptomatic to gluten after a few years on the diet. Maybe these were taken off in those days—only to be reconfirmed with the disease when they started showing distress symptoms later, in adulthood. We'll probably never know but it is something to think about.

Have things changed since your diagnosis? How? (In medical awareness?) (In social attitudes?) (In foods available?) Yes! In every way. There's more knowledge about the disease. One respondent said that she has never had a doctor admit that he didn't know what celiac was, but she sometimes wondered if after she left the office he'd go look it up. Others said that now they didn't have to spend so much time explaining the disease, for many of their friends had heard of it or even knew someone with it. Most still tried to avoid situations where they would have to embarrass the cook by having to refuse food. Some said they offered to cook instead.

As for available food, everyone remembered when pasta turned to mush in the pan, pretzels were unavailable, and the cashier wouldn't know how a hamburger without the bun could be done. Now, foods can be and often are as good (or better) than the wheat-filled equivalents. There are more mail-order and Internet food suppliers, and they carry far more variety. In addition, health food stores have often responded to the call by setting up a separate section for gluten-free foods. Almost all offer some semblance of bread, whether in the freezer or wrapped in air-proof packets. One big factor noted by several respondents is that ethnic cuisines have become trendy and many of them have more gluten-free items than the standard American diet. Yes, the celiac life has improved, but one woman put it well: "not to the point I would like it to be."

Is there anything you have missed by having to adhere to the diet? Yes! Of course! Only about a fourth of the respondents were satisfied and content with their way of life. The others responded with missing pizza parties, ordering out for Chinese, soup in a bread bowl, Wonder bread—all typical American cultural experiences.

One wrote that most of the time she has had to fight her friends off because they like her food better than theirs. Another wrote that she grew up having favorite foods and desserts like everyone, only hers were gluten free. It looks as if these celiacs have good cooks at home.

Have you, at any time in your life, ever felt anger, rage, or denial about the medical need for the strict diet? The answers surprised me in their variety. They swung from a definite "No, because I value my health" to a big YES, to all of the above at one time or another. One said, "In my teens, I didn't want to be different." Another wanted to be normal. But most of them wrote that what they felt was more like frustration and annoyance. The answers don't seem to be much different from any in the celiac society no matter when diagnosed. Some people take the strict dieting with grace because they know their health is better; others kick and fight against becoming gluten free the same way they might against any restrictions.

Where do you get most of your information about the disease? Only one listed a doctor but added that that was in the beginning; now it is the Internet. All the others listed support groups, conferences, newsletters, and gluten-free cookbooks, a few adding that they use the Internet for seeking food. No one listed a dietician or nurse.

How do you obtain baked gluten-free foods? This was a question I asked purely for my own information. After all, I've always said I want to be able to go into my neighborhood grocery and purchase my bread, cake, cookies, and crackers off the shelf, and I want them to taste as good as any I bake. I don't want to settle for bread that has to be toasted to be palatable, cookies that taste like dry cloth, and crackers made only of rice. I was surprised by the answer. There was a wide variety of answers, from some who hardly baked at all, to one who baked 90 percent of her own products. Averaged out, home baking created 44 percent of bakery products; purchased goods 56 percent. Even though I am a cookbook writer, I'd like to see a higher percentage of purchased baked goods; and, I hope, as the number of suppliers increases and the products improve along with availability, so may the purchases.

The above survey may not have been scientific, but it was enlightening. The problems of living on the diet are the same, whether from infancy or a later diagnosis. The diet has proved to be inconvenient, frustrating, and expensive, but not impossible. The most information about the disease and the diet still reaches the dieter from support groups and their writings. And of the respondents, only a small percent felt much aggression about the handicaps of the diet.

Every year the conditions for celiacs improve. We have more books on the disease, and with the First International Walk of 2002, we're seeing a lot more awareness. It's not a rare disease anymore; not when Dr. Alessio Fasano can state that through scientific testing he's proved there may be as many as 1 in 139 people with the disease. The tragic part is that probably nine out of ten of them don't show the "typical" symptoms of severe intestinal distress. As the medical profession catches up, the years ahead can only get better.

Autism and the GF/CF Diet

When I speak to audiences about the value of the gluten-free diet in relieving celiacs of their symptoms I'm happy to see the audience nodding agreement. But I was utterly surprised several years ago when a group of mothers of autistic children came up after the speech and said they also used the diet for their children, but they had to augment it with a casein-free one also. Casein is the protein in dairy products just as gluten is the protein in wheat, rye, and barley.

Since many celiacs have problems with dairy products (lactose intolerance) when they are first diagnosed and about twenty percent remain intolerant, I try to offer a substitute for dairy whenever possible. This has made many of my recipes also suitable for the diets of autistic children.

This disease interested me. On reading more and asking questions I found that there seems to be more than one form of autism. While the genetic form (diagnosed at birth) may not be seen any more frequently than before, it seems that a recessive form of autism has grown to almost epidemic proportions in today's society. The symptoms are abnormalities in the social behavior of the child (autism, aggression, dyslexia, poor eye contact).

In this form of the illness the child develops normally during the first few years of life and then suddenly regresses. In only a few weeks, a child can lose his or her ability to communicate and begin to withdraw socially. Many consider this sudden onset to be suggestive of an environmental trigger rather than a purely genetic one, which would be more likely to be evident at birth.

I found that these autistic symptoms can begin after some shock to a child's system such as a vaccination, an infection, and/or a course of antibiotics, which can damage the immune system. This often leads to gastrointestinal symptoms such as foul smelling stools, diarrhea, constipation, gas, bloating. These gut problems sound just like the symptoms many celiacs have, don't they?

When I consulted Dr. Laura Michley, a Seattle specialist working with autistic patients, she suggested that the combination of the gluten and dairy proteins seemed to result in "increased formation of substances toxic to the brain." This wasn't only her idea. Many others had suggested this. She strongly recommended that parents try the diet for their autistic child, saying, "Although, at first, only a small minority of doctors looked beyond treating these children with drugs, there is a growing group of mothers who have found that their children can improve when they stay on the gluten-free/casein-free diet as a treatment. Although the medical field is hesitant to admit it, some children seem to have complete recovery with no sign of either the distress symptoms of the gut or with the autism."

WHY A GF/CF DIET?

The gluten-free diet of eliminating wheat, rye, and barley has proved to eradicate the distress symptoms from celiacs but autistic children seem to also have an addiction to the combination of the gluten proteins and dairy casein. Many of these children insist on surviving on grilled cheese, cereal with milk, pizza, and macaroni and cheese, and behave like an addict when these foods are taken away.

As with other opiates, the addicts must detoxify. This is a difficult process for the entire family and miserable for the autistic child. It makes keeping to a strict diet ever harder since it is often impossible to control what some of the children eat while away from home. They may go so far as to fight, lie, or steal for a slice of pizza.

HOW DO I KNOW IF MY CHILD WILL BENEFIT FROM THE GF/CF DIET?

You don't know until you try. Although many blood and urine tests are available to help guide treatment, these tests may be expensive and do not always reveal the underlying problems. Trying the diet, though, will cost little except energy on the part of the cook and has been praised by scores of parents.

HOW DO I START THE DIET?

Our standard American diet is typically loaded with wheat and dairy. These foods may be all your children know and may be all you, the caregiver, know how to cook and shop for. Where do you start? Begin with a cookbook like this, which eliminates gluten, replaces it with some of the many "safe" flours, and gives substitutes for dairy products. You may have to go further and read all the labels on dairy substitutes, for some of them still contain some trace of casein hiding under a different name, such as whey.

For the first few weeks, experiment with new recipes and try to find ones your child enjoys. Having a freezer full of GF/CF replacement foods on hand will make the process easier but your child may still have a withdrawal phase, which you will both have to suffer through.

Here are suggestions to eliminate gluten and casein from the diet:

- The earlier you begin, the easier and more effective the results.
- Do not attempt to go "cold turkey." Try one-half the diet first; add the other half the next month.
- Find substitutes for the favored food; don't just eliminate. For example, use gluten-free pastas and tofu cheeses. Bread, crackers, cakes and cookies can be made gluten/casein free.
- Stop buying the foods you are trying to restrict.
- Recognize withdrawal symptoms. Sympathize but don't break down and feed the child the toxic proteins.
- Involve the family as much as possible. This is a lifestyle, and it will be easier if you try to feed everyone the same food.
- Keep some GF/CF foods in the freezer to substitute when serving a meal not gluten/casein free.

For many, especially children with limited tastes, a restricted diet may lack some of the enzymes and vitamins necessary for the best health, so work with a dietician or nutritionist to supplement the nutritional quality of the food. Some children, just as some celiacs, may need pancreatic enzymes for digestion as well as vitamins.

This may sound like oversimplification, and mothers may still wonder, are there any studies on just how many autistic children are better because of the diet, or did they improve because of other ways of intervention? The books written by mothers who went through the difficult diet drill admit it isn't always easy but suggest that about 80 percent of the children are helped, some to the point where doctors have declared them to have complete remission of all autistic symptoms. Jaquelyn McCandless, M.D., writes in her book *Children with Starving Brains,* that the "clinical experience of many . . . physicians ha[s] identified the GF/CF diet as the single most effective move you can make on your own to begin to help your child."

REFERENCES

Lisa Lewis, Ph.D., *Special Diets for Special Kids: Understanding and Implementing Special Diets to Aid the Treatment of Autism and Related Developmental Disorders* (Arlington, Tex.: Future Horizons Inc., 1988).

Lisa Lewis, Ph.D., *Special Diets for Special Kids Two* (Arlington, Tex.: Future Horizons Inc., 2001).

Jaquelyn McCandless, M.D., *Children with Starving Brains: A Medical Treatment Guide for Autism Spectrum Disorder* (Paterson, N.J.: Bramble Books, 2002).

Karyn Seroussi, *Unraveling the Mystery of Autism and Pervasive Developmental Disorder: A Mother's Story of Research and Recovery* (New York: Simon and Schuster, 2000).

Exotic Flours and How to Use Them

To call some of the flours we celiacs are now learning to use exotic may seem too assuming. Orchids are exotic, but are amaranth, buckwheat, millet, quinoa, and teff? Yes! If we accept the true meaning of exotic as "of foreign origin, introduced from abroad," then most of these are truly exotic. They may not be orchids but just flours ground from seeds or grains as are corn and rice. Where they come from is not as important to the celiac as the fact that these handle more like wheat, have more nutrition without the gluten, and are far better for health than most of the ones we've baked with before. They also add new tastes to our baked goods.

We've been using "exotic" sorghum for several years without questioning its background so we should be able to incorporate the others as easily into our diet if we remember that each flour has a different family, so some people may be sensitive (or even have allergic reactions) to one or more but not to all of them. For example, a person with sensitivities to rhubarb may be able to tolerate amaranth, but not buckwheat, for amaranth is of the pigweed family while buckwheat is a close relative of rhubarb.

When working with these flours, I've discovered that, like rice flour, they bake better when mixed with other flours. With some, only a tiny bit can flavor the baked goods wonderfully; with others, the flavor is mild and other flavorful additions (banana, spice, nuts) are needed to make the goods the most edible. Either amaranth or quinoa cereal can be cooked, cooled, and used as replacement for rice in the salad on page 114.

A quick look at the chart below will show you that all of these flours are relatively close to (or even higher than) wheat in proteins, which is not true of rice with only 6%, tapioca with 1%, and cornstarch with only a trace. Thus you can easily replace some of the rice flour mix with any one of the exotics and get more nutrition and sometimes more fat. As you work with them, you'll find that they often complement the flour mixes you are using but many can only be used as 15 or 20 percent of the whole flour amount.

As usual, to avoid contamination with gluten, try to procure your exotic flours from suppliers (listed on page 291) who only mill and/or sell gluten-free flours and cereals.

AMARANTH

From this plant, once grown in Mexico and south and central America, the seeds can be ground into flour or puffed into snacks. It is claimed that the Aztec culture was sustained by amaranth but that when the conquistadors came in the 14th century, they banished it as a crop and it almost disappeared. The plant can be grown in gardens as it requires little attention and produces leaves that can be used all season as they grow back when stripped for eating. The seeds are extremely tiny, so harvesting requires special equipment.

TABLE 1: A COMPARISON OF GLUTEN-FREE FLOURS TO WHEAT

| | Food Value | | | | |
Flour	Carbohydrates %	Protein %	Fat %	Fiber %	Additional Trace Elements
Amaranth	66	13	6	15	Balanced protein
Buckwheat	72	11.5	0	1.6	B vitamins
Millet	73	10	3	3	Magnesium
Montina	68	16	3	23	High fiber
Quinoa	66	12	5	7	Potassium, calcium
Sorghum	75	10	4	2	Iron, B vitamins
Teff	71	11	4	3	Iron, some thiamin
Wheat	76	10	1	3	

Amaranth is sold both as a cereal grain and flour. As a flour it has a strong nutty branlike taste so a little goes a long way. It is used in some commercial products already on the market, such as waffles. As it contains slightly more protein than wheat and one-third more fat, it should be bought as fresh as possible and stored in the refrigerator. In baking I find that for best results no more than 15 to 20 percent of the total flour should be amaranth. The flakes, sold as cereal, can replace rolled oats in some recipes. For those with allergies: *Amaranth is closely related to pigweed.*

BUCKWHEAT

The seeds of this plant, once raised in China, came to the United States through Europe. It was more important as a grain and flour in the mid-1800s and has since faded in popularity, but it's now making a small comeback as a gluten-free alternative flour. As most buckwheat flours don't contain fat, it keeps well, which may be why so many miners used it in the gold fields of Alaska.

This seed, too, can be cooked as a cereal as well as ground into flour. But by far the most common use is in breakfast pancakes and waffles. Buckwheat flour is a dark tan that colors the baked product and has a slightly astringent flavor, just as does its *closest relative: Rhubarb.*

MILLET

This grain, of the grass family (rice and corn), was originally brought to the United States to feed animals (but not horses). In large areas of Europe and Asia, millet is grown for human food. Millet raised for human consumption has a far higher nutritional value than rice and, some growers claim, even higher than wheat. It makes a mild tasting flour that can be used in far larger proportions in the recipes than more highly flavored ones used in baking for the gluten-free diet. Millet contains approximately the same fat as wheat so it stores well.

For those who want to try millet flour, you can replace your regular flours with up to one-half millet since it is so mild and light colored. It won't change the flavor or appearance much but it definitely will give it more of the protein stretch factor. *Millet is in the same family as corn, rice, and sorghum.*

MONTINA

This is the only grain in this section native to the United States. It was discovered as a grass growing wild in Montana when the research council of the state university was looking for a crop that would grow in that harsh climate. When the grain of this Indian rice grass was ground and tested as a flour it was found to work well as a baking flour and, even more exciting, it tested gluten free.

At this time, the flour I have used has not been as finely ground as the others in this category (amaranth, teff, etc.). The color is a dark gray-brown so it looks like a bran flour; but it is extremely bland tasting, like rice. Unlike rice, Montina is high in unsoluble fiber. It was best used in baking with a lot of flavors (banana, nuts, seeds, chocolate, coffee). For those who like more color in their rice baking, this should be a good addition. As with other rice-like flours, this seems to need liquid adjustments depending on the humidity. During rainy weather the flour has already absorbed some liquid from the atmosphere so, if using large amounts, you might need to reduce fluids. In the addition of small amounts, this is unnoticeable. *Montina appears to be close to wild rice and the corn family.*

QUINOA

This is another seed rather than grain plant that is used both as cereal and as flour. It originally came from high in the Andes and was the miracle food of the Inca Indians. The seed has a bitter coating that must be washed either at the production plant or in the home. If cooked, it has a nutritional value far above the starch filled rice.

When used in addition to other flours, as I have done in my recipes, it adds more protein as well as flavor to the final product without changing color for it is creamy white. It can replace the rice mix, in small quantities, as desired in baking whenever desired without changing the rest of the formula. Use it in breads and muffins. Because growing it requires a high altitude with hot days and cold nights, this has not been as common in the markets here as some of the other flours. Still, it has been incorporated into a few products on the natural food shelves.

Quinoa comes from the goosefoot family (spinach, beets, chard).

SORGHUM

This grain, once used here only for animal feed, came to the United States from Africa in the middle of the 1900s. Only recently have cereal chemists bred a more refined grain to make flour for human consumption. The flour from this grain is more ivory in color than wheat so it doesn't color the baked product.

This was the first of the exotics to be well accepted and used regularly in gluten-free baking. Like the other grains, it needs to be combined with other flours for the best product. We already know that sorghum, with its mild, sweet flavor, is a wonderful complement to our bean flours, which originally needed molasses and brown sugar to be the most palatable. I've included it as a little over 10% of the Four Flour Mix. It also teams well with the rice flour mixes, giving them more sweetness, flavor, and body.

Sorghum is of the same family as sugar cane, rice, and corn.

TEFF (TEF)

One of my favorite "exotic" flours, teff is grown in several colors: ivory, red, or brown (called dark by teff growers). All teffs have the same wheatlike taste for they are all ground from the whole grain. The original teff plants now grown in the United States came from Ethiopia, where it is made into flatbread (injera), one of their staple foods. It grows under harsh conditions where wheat would not, and teff growers regret that the Ethiopians now consider it a "poor man's food" while Americans have found it more nutritious than wheat. In Ethiopia scientists found that the high iron content of this grain led to an absence of anemia until wheat was introduced.

Dark teff, which is slightly more robust, makes a wonderful "graham" bread, while the ivory teff can give a delicate toasty flavor to spice cakes and other baking. Either one combines well with and gently flavors rice flour products. Teff has a higher fat content than wheat and should be stored in the refrigerator or freezer for best taste. In spite of coming from Ethiopia, this grain is grown in the states in America where the growing season is short and other grains would not do well. Like the other exotics, teff grain can be used as a cereal as well as flour.

Teff is related to the rice family, corn, millet, and sorghum.

For a complete list of all the recipes in the Gluten-free Gourmet series using one of the exotic flours as a basic ingredient, see pages 26–27.

REFERENCES

Susan E. Gebhardt and Ruth H. Matthews, *Nutritive Value of Foods* (Washington, D.C.: U.S. Department of Agriculture, Home and Garden Bulletin No. 72, 1981 and 1988).

National Research Council, *Lost Crops of Africa,* Vol. I (Washington, D.C.: National Academy Press, 1996).

Marjorie Hunt Jones, R.N., *Super Foods: Six Best Alternatives to Wheat* (Coeur d'Alene, Idaho: Mast Enterprises, 1998).

Donald Kasarda, Ph.D., "Plant Taxonomy in Relation to Celiac Toxicity," presentation at the International Celiac Symposium, Dublin, 1992.

———, "Celiac Disease," presentation at North American Society for Pediatric Gastroenterology and Nutrition, Toronto, Canada, October, 1997.

Gayla J. Kirshman, *Nutrition Almanac,* 4th ed. (New York: McGraw-Hill, 1996).

Montana Agriculture Development Council, *Montina Recipes* (Bozeman, Mont.: Montana State University Agricultural Experiment Station, 1997).

TABLE 2: RECIPES USING AN EXOTIC FLOUR AS A BASIC INGREDIENT			
NAME OF RECIPE	FLOUR	BOOK	PAGE
Amaranth or Quinoa Waffles	amaranth	Comfort Foods	130
Banana Pineapple Cake	teff	Comfort Foods	236
Banana Bread Deluxe	teff	Comfort Foods	219
Banana Nut Montina Muffins	montina	Comfort Foods	225
Basic Millet Bread	millet	Bakes Bread	82
Bette's Best Hamburger Buns	sorghum	Comfort Foods	213
Buckwheat Pancakes	buckwheat	Comfort Foods	128
Chewy Quinoa Cookies	quinoa	Comfort Foods	250
Chicken Rice Salad (variation)	amaranth/quinoa	Comfort Foods	114
Chocolate Pecan Cupcakes	quinoa	Comfort Foods	240
Christmas Cherry Fruit Drops	sorghum	Comfort Foods	252
Cream Cheese Pound Cake	sorghum	Comfort Foods	239
Devil's Food Cake	teff	Comfort Foods	238
Frosted Fudge Fingers	teff	Comfort Foods	255

Name of Recipe	Flour	Book	Page
Frosted Mincemeat Cookies	teff	Comfort Foods	253
Gingerbread Waffles with Teff	teff	Comfort Foods	131
Honey Graham Crumpets	teff	Comfort Foods	214
Hot Cross Buns	teff	Comfort Foods	135
Kasha (Buckwheat) Muffins	buckwheat	The Gluten-free Gourmet (rev.)	80
Light Graham Bread	teff	Comfort Foods	198
Montina Bread with Seeds and Nuts	montina	Comfort Foods	204
New Oatmeal Cookies with Quinoa Flakes	quinoa	Comfort Foods	249
Nut and Raisin Bread	teff	Comfort Foods	199
Nutty Graham Crackers	teff	Comfort Foods	227
Potato Patties with Apple	sorghum	Comfort Foods	173
Pecan-Pumpkin Roll	teff	Comfort Foods	273
Pineapple Zucchini Bread with Teff	teff	Comfort Foods	221
Quinoa Bread	quinoa	Bakes Bread	70
Quinoa Buns	quinoa	Bakes Bread	168
Seattle Coffee Bread	montina	Comfort Foods	202
Sesame Teff Bread	teff	Comfort Foods	209
Sorghum Bread	sorghum	Comfort Foods	197
Sweet Potato and Cranberry Loaf	teff	Comfort Foods	220
Sweet "Rye" Sourdough	teff	Comfort Foods	210
Three Gingers Pound Cake	teff	Comfort Foods	237
Three-Layer Lemon Bars	teff	Comfort Foods	246
Teff Muffins	teff	Comfort Foods	222
Touch-of-Honey Millet Bread	millet	Comfort Foods	201
Walnut Bread	teff	Comfort Foods	218

Supplies Used in Gluten-free Baking

If you haven't tried it before, baking with gluten-free flours and additives is going to be an education. Yes, you can turn out wonderful products, but a lot of times the methods of making them and the disposition of the batters may be very different from what you are used to with wheat flour. The end result often is very close in texture to the wheat product so don't believe anyone who tells you that gluten-free has to taste gritty.

If you haven't used these flours before, here's a short explanation of each, along with some of the more unusual supplies used in baking. At the end of the section, I've included a few paragraphs on the flours made from seeds and grains that have just been accepted here in the United States although they are familiar to Canadians.

At the end are the formulas for all the flour mixes used in this book. The most inexpensive way is to buy the flours separately and make them up in large quantities to have handy for baking. If you prefer, you may buy them in smaller quantities as sold by celiac support groups and in some health food stores, and always by mail order.

ARROWROOT

This white flour is ground from the root of a West Indian plant and can be exchanged measure for measure with cornstarch in recipes and mixes if you are allergic to corn. I do not call for this in any recipe in this book.

GARBANZO BEAN FLOUR

Ground from garbanzo beans (sometimes called chickpeas or cici beans), this flour may be used in combination with Romano bean flour (equal parts) to make a flour similar to the Garfava flour. Do this if you are allergic to fava beans.

GARFAVA FLOUR

This is the registered trade name of a smooth combination of garbanzo and fava beans produced by Authentic Foods (see page 292). It is a staple in many of my recipes. High in protein and nutrients, it makes a better-textured baked product than many rice flours. The flour is very stable and may be stored in the pantry. See "Garbanzo Bean Flour" above if you are sensitive to fava beans.

Warning: There are some flours now being sold that claim to be compounded like this but often are not the same formula. They may not produce equally good results in these recipes. Look for the name Authentic Foods on the label.

ROMANO BEAN FLOUR

A dark, strong-tasting bean flour milled from the Romano or cranberry bean. The flour is high in fiber and protein and can be used successfully in combination with garbanzo bean flour to make up a mix similar to Garfava flour (see "Garbanzo Bean Flour" above). It can be purchased in health food stores in Canada and from mail-order suppliers in the United States.

CORNSTARCH

This refined starch from corn is used in combination with other flours to make some of my baking mixes. Some people are allergic to corn. If so, either replace this with arrowroot in mixes and recipes or use one of the cornstarch-free mixes on page 36.

CORNMEAL

This meal, ground from corn, may be obtained in yellow and white forms. Combine this with other flours for baking or use it alone in Mexican dishes.

POTATO STARCH FLOUR

Made from potatoes, this fine white flour is used in the Gluten-Free Mix and in the new Potato Flour Mix. This keeps well and can be bought in quantity.

POTATO FLOUR

Do not confuse this with potato starch. This is a heavy flour. Buy it in small quantities because you will need very little of it in the Featherlight Mix. Store this in the refrigerator.

WHITE RICE FLOUR

This very bland (and not very nutritious) flour, milled from polished white rice, doesn't distort the taste of any flavorings used. It has long been a basic in gluten-free baking but the more nutritious bean flours are now gaining popularity. This can be stored in the pantry and has a long shelf life.

There are several blends of this flour: fine (found in Asian groceries and some suppliers), medium (some suppliers), and coarse (home milled). My recipes are based on the fine grind and may take slightly more liquid than the other blends.

BROWN RICE FLOUR

This flour, milled from unpolished brown rice, contains bran so is higher in nutrient value than white rice flour. Use it for breads, muffins, and cookies where a bran (or nutty) taste is sought. If desired, you can replace the white rice in the mixes for brown rice in breads and muffins. Because there are oils in the bran, it must be kept refrigerated, as it has a much shorter shelf life and tends to become stronger tasting as it ages. Always purchase fresh flour and store in the freezer if not using frequently.

SWEET RICE FLOUR

This flour, made from a glutinous rice often called "sticky rice," is an excellent thickening agent. It is especially good for sauces that are to be refrigerated or frozen, as it inhibits separation of the liquids. I also use it by the tablespoon to add to bread when the dough is too thin or to batters when they seem too runny. I've found this in many grocery stores under the label Mochiko Sweet Rice Flour, but it can be found in Asian markets and ordered from several of the suppliers of GF products. Do not confuse this with plain white rice flour.

SORGHUM FLOUR

This new flour, ground from specially bred sorghum grain, is available from several suppliers and should be on the shelves of some health stores. This combines with the bean flours to make my Four Flour Bean Mix, used in a lot of recipes in this book. Sorghum is distantly related to sugar cane and, although it stores well on the pantry shelf, if bought in quantity, will keep better in the refrigerator. Sorghum flour is seldom used alone but also combines to give more taste, nutrients and body to many of my rice bread recipes. Replace about one-quarter of the rice mix with sorghum flour. See page 197 for an example.

SOY FLOUR

A yellow flour with high protein and fat content, this has a nutty flavor and is most successful when used in combination with other flours in baked products that contain fruit, nuts, or chocolate. Purchase it in small quantities and store in the freezer or refrigerator as it, too, has a short shelf life. Some celiacs may be sensitive to this flour. Bean flour can be substituted in many recipes that call for soy.

TAPIOCA FLOUR

Made from the root of the cassava plant, this light, velvety white flour imparts "chew" to our baked goods. I use it in all my mixes. It can be stored at room temperature for a long time.

FLOURS ON THE RESTRICTED LIST

Spelt, Kamut, Club, Durum, Bulgur, Einkorn, and Semolina

These are all different species of wheat and should be eliminated in any form from the gluten-free diet.

Triticale

This is a hybrid of rye and wheat. Not for a gluten-free diet!

Oats

The question of whether people on a gluten-free diet can safely eat oat products remains the subject of scientific debate. Some medical experts are now listing oats as only "possibly" containing toxic gluten, but most doctors in the United States admit that they don't want to commit their patients to oats in the diet at this time. Difficulties in identifying the precise amino acids responsible for the immune response, the chemical differences between wheat and oats, and the high possibility of contamination have all contributed to the controversy.

OTHER BAKING SUPPLIES

Dough Enhancers

These powdered products are used in bread making to substitute for the vinegar that balances the pH in most waters. They also tend to make the bread stay fresh longer. Dough enhancers are produced by many companies and can be found in baking supply stores and some health food stores. *Always read the ingredient labels to find one that's gluten free and doesn't contain anything else to which you may be sensitive.* Several suppliers listed on pages 291–98 carry dough enhancers.

Egg Replacer

This powdered substitute for eggs in cooking contains no egg product and is also free of dairy, corn, soy, and gluten. I use a little of this for extra leavening in many recipes. Egg replacer can be ordered from some suppliers or found in most health food stores. A similar product is also available in Canada.

Guar Gum

Derived from the seed of the plant *Cyamopsis tetragonoloba,* this powder can be purchased in health food stores or ordered from suppliers. Its cost is less than xanthan gum but because it has a high fiber content and is usually sold as a laxative, it should be avoided by anyone whose symptom of the disease is diarrhea or stomach distress. For others, this can substitute for xanthan gum in baking.

Liquid Egg Substitutes

These cholesterol-free liquid substitutes for whole eggs are made from egg whites plus coloring and flavoring ingredients. They may be found in the dairy section and freezer cases of most grocery stores. *Always read the ingredient label to be sure the one you choose doesn't contain gluten or some other ingredient to which you are allergic.*

Nondairy Powdered Milk Substitute

There are now many more substitutes for milk than there were a few years ago. Some powdered examples are Lacto-Free, Tofu White (both contain soy), Nutquik (made from almonds), or DariFree (potato based). Another choice could be one of the powdered baby formulas from the supermarket or drugstore: some are soy based and others corn based. *Always check to be sure the one you choose is gluten free.*

Xanthan Gum

This is a powder milled from the dried cell coat of a microorganism called *Xanthomonas campestris* grown under laboratory conditions. It replaces the gluten in baking with our gluten-free flours. It is available in some health food stores and by order from some of the suppliers listed on pages 291–98. Recently I've noticed that some companies are producing a xanthan gum that is lighter in weight, so it seems you get more for your money but, because of its lighter weight, it takes about one fourth more in a recipe to achieve the same texture of batter. If you find your batter is too thin, check the xanthan gum and try adding slightly more.

Flour Mixes

In baking with the many gluten-free flours now available, we find that none is very successful when used alone. A combination of several flours in differing amounts seems to create the tenderest and most tasteful baked goods and makes the smoothest gravies and sauces.

Through experimentation, I've created several mixes for the gluten-free baker. Because of the many differing allergies celiacs have, I created two that are corn free and two that are potato free. You may use these all (except the Light Bean Mix) interchangeably. There will be differences, and in the recipes I suggest which is best, but if you have an allergy to one of the components in a mix, naturally you will want to use another even if it doesn't make the perfect product.

Some of these mixes are now being sold by health food stores and by mail or on order from suppliers. These are handy for those who bake seldom or just for another celiac friend or neighbor, but will be far more expensive than buying the flours separately and mixing your own if you bake a lot.

TABLE 3: FLOUR MIXES

FORMULAS	FOR 9 CUPS	FOR 12 CUPS
GLUTEN-FREE MIX (Called GF Mix in recipes)		
Rice flour (2 parts)	6 cups	8 cups
Potato starch (⅔ part)	2 cups	2⅔ cups
Tapioca flour (⅓ part)	1 cup	1⅓ cups
POTATO FLOUR MIX (For corn-intolerant people)		
Rice flour (1¼ parts)	3¾ cups	5 cups
Tapioca flour (1 part)	3 cups	4 cups
Potato starch (I part)	2¼ cups	3 cups
FEATHERLIGHT RICE FLOUR MIX (Called Featherlight Mix in recipes)		
Rice flour (1 part)	3 cups	4 cups
Tapioca flour (1 part)	3 cups	4 cups
Cornstarch (1 part)	3 cups	4 cups
Potato flour* (1 teaspoon per cup)	3 tablespoons	4 tablespoons
LIGHT BEAN FLOUR MIX (For breads only)		
Garfava† bean flour (1 part)	3 cups	4 cups
Tapioca flour (1 part)	3 cups	4 cups
Cornstarch (1 part)	3 cups	4 cups
FOUR FLOUR BEAN MIX (Called Four Flour Mix in recipes)		
Garfava† bean flour (⅔ part)	2 cups	2⅔ cups
Sorghum‡ flour (⅓ part)	1 cup	1⅓ cups
Tapioca flour (1 part)	3 cups	4 cups
Cornstarch (1 part)	3 cups	4 cups

*This is potato flour and not potato starch.
†Garfava flour is available from Authentic Foods.
‡Sorghum flour can be obtained from Red River Milling.

Appetizers

Over the years, appetizers have become part of some people's daily routine. A few may settle for just the simple drink before dinner, but many expect something more. It isn't often you can please with just cheese and nuts. The recipes in this chapter present "that something extra" from the days of the "blue laws" to the baked green chilies and cheese of the present.

Cheese Wafers

400°

An easy to make and keep–handy appetizer cracker for anytime. This can be made ahead and stored in the refrigerator to slice and bake for drop-in guests.

1 pound sharp cheddar cheese, grated	¾ teaspoon xanthan gum
1 cup (stick butter)	1 cup finely chopped nuts (pecan, walnut, or other)
2 cups Featherlight Mix	⅛ teaspoon cayenne pepper

Process the cheese and butter in a food processor until creamy. Add the flour mix and xanthan gum, nuts, and cayenne pepper. Continue processing until thoroughly mixed and forms a ball.

Divide into 4 parts. Roll each part between your hands into a log-shaped roll about 1 inch in diameter. Wrap in waxed paper and refrigerate at least 30 minutes to firm up to slice.

Preheat oven to 400°. Cut each roll into approximately ¼-inch slices and place on ungreased baking sheets. Bake 10 to 13 minutes until light brown at edges. Cool and store for up to a week or freeze to keep longer.

The dough can also be frozen to be thawed, cut, baked, and served later. *Makes about 10 dozen wafers.*

Nutrients per wafer: Calories 39, Fat 3g, Cholesterol 7mg, Sodium 31mg, Carbohydrates 2g, Protein 1g, Fiber 0g.

Deviled Ham and Cheese Spread

This quick and easy spread will make even rice crackers taste good, but it is especially tasty on toasted or dried triangles of some of the rye or bean bread slices.

Note: Some of the fat-free cream cheeses are not gluten-free. Always read the ingredients lists.

One 8-ounce package cream cheese (regular, light, or fat-free), softened

One 6.75-ounce can deviled ham spread (or honey ham)

½ cup crushed pineapple, drained well

2 green onions, sliced thin

1 tablespoon mayonnaise (optional)

In a medium bowl, combine the cream cheese and ham spread. Beat until smooth. Add the pineapple and green onions, mixing well. If needed, add mayonnaise for a more spreadable consistency. (May be made a day ahead.) *Makes 2 cups.*

Nutrients per tablespoon: Calories 45, Fat 4g, Cholesterol 10mg, Sodium 95mg, Carbohydrates 1g, Protein 1g, Fiber 0g.

Creamy Crab Quiche

325°–350°

Cut this rich quiche into tiny wedges and watch your guests enjoy a delicious treat. It's easy to make with the crumb crust in a springform pan. The final topping of fat-free sour cream makes a perfect finish.

CRUST:
1 cup crushed GF crackers
  (any kind but graham)
3 tablespoons margarine or
  butter, melted
¼ teaspoon seafood seasoning

FILLING:
Two 8-ounce packages
  ⅓-reduced-fat cream cheese
¼ cup fat-free sour cream
3 eggs

1 tablespoon grated onion or
  3 green onions, sliced fine
2 teaspoons lemon juice
¼ teaspoon seafood seasoning
4–5 drops hot pepper sauce
½ teaspoon salt
1 cup cooked crabmeat

TOPPING:
½ cup fat-free sour cream
Additional seafood seasoning
  (optional)

Preheat oven to 325°. Grease a 9" springform pan on bottom and up sides.

Place crushed crackers, melted margarine, and seafood seasoning in a plastic baggie and work together with hands until margarine is incorporated. Press onto bottom of the prepared pan. Bake for 10 minutes. Remove the crust and raise oven temperature to 350°.

In a large mixing bowl, beat the cream cheese and sour cream until smooth. Add the eggs and beat on low until combined. Add the grated onion (if using), lemon juice, seafood seasoning, pepper sauce, and salt. Beat smooth. Gently fold in the crabmeat and green onion bits (if using). Pour over the crust. Bake for 35–40 minutes or until the center is almost set. Cool for about 1 hour before topping with the sour cream and the additional seafood seasoning (if used). Refrigerate from 4 hours to overnight before serving. *Makes 20–24 servings as appetizer.*

Nutrients per serving: Calories 80, Fat 6g, Cholesterol 45mg,
Sodium 250mg, Carbohydrates 3g, Protein 4g, Fiber 0g.

Amanda's Artichoke Dip

350°

This recipe will bring raves when served on GF crackers or toasted GF bread cut into triangles. I've given you a choice for the amount of cheese. More cheese provides a richer flavor, while less cheese saves calories.

1 cup mayonnaise
1–2 cups Parmesan cheese, grated
One 4-ounce can diced green
    chilies with juice

One 14-ounce can artichoke
    hearts, drained and coarsely
    chopped

Preheat oven to 350°. Butter an 8" square casserole.

    Mix all ingredients together and spoon into the casserole. Cover with lid or foil and bake for 30 minutes. Serve warm. *Makes 12–15 servings.*

*Nutrients per serving (1 cup): Calories 150, Fat 15g, Cholesterol 10mg,
Sodium 26mg, Carbohydrates 4g, Protein 4g, Fiber 1g.*

Layered Salsa Dip

A dip with the flavor of Tex-Mex that has moved up from the southern states to infiltrate even our northern parties. This can be prepared ahead and refrigerated several hours or overnight until 30 minutes before serving.

One 8-ounce package cream cheese

One pound ground beef, cooked and drained

One 2.5-ounce package taco seasoning

¾ cup salsa

1½ cups shredded cheese

In an 8" × 8" baking pan place the ingredients in layers starting with a cream cheese layer. Spread on the meat and sprinkle with the taco seasoning. Spoon on the salsa, covering the whole dish. Sprinkle on the cheese.

Bake for 30 minutes in a preheated oven at 350°. Serve with gluten-free tortilla chips. *Serves 12 as an appetizer.*

Nutrients per serving: Calories 250, Fat 18g, Cholesterol 70mg, Sodium 680mg, Carbohydrates 5g, Protein 15g, Fiber 1g.

Crockpot Chicken Wings

Wonderfully easy! Delightfully delicious! The drumettes are the largest part of the chicken wing and are often sold separately from the rest of the wing.

3 pounds chicken drumettes
Salt and pepper to taste
½ teaspoon minced garlic
2 tablespoons ketchup

2 tablespoons vegetable oil
1 cup honey
½ cup GF soy sauce

Place the drumettes in your slow cooker. Season with salt and pepper.

In a medium bowl, combine the garlic, ketchup, oil, honey, and soy sauce. Pour over the chicken. Cover and cook 6–8 hours on low, stirring to rearrange chicken in the sauce at least once. *Makes 8–10 servings as an appetizer.*

Nutrients per serving: Calories 290, Fat 13g, Cholesterol 45mg, Sodium 910mg, Carbohydrates 20g, Protein 15g, Fiber 0g.

Ham Balls

350°

An appetizer that's filling as well as tasty. These ham balls can be made ahead and frozen; simply thaw and reheat them on the day of the party.

MEAT BALLS:
1 pound ground pork
1 pound cooked ham, ground
2 eggs, beaten slightly
¾ cup milk
⅔ cup quinoa flakes or crushed
   GF cereal

SAUCE:
1½ cups brown sugar
⅔ cup water
⅓ cup vinegar
¾ teaspoon ground mustard

Preheat oven to 350°. Grease a 9" × 13" baking pan.

In a large mixing bowl, combine the pork, ham, eggs, milk, and quinoa flakes. Mix well. Shape into 1" balls and place in the prepared pan.

In a 2-quart saucepan, combine the sauce ingredients and bring to a boil over medium heat. Simmer, uncovered, for 4 minutes. Pour over the ham balls and bake, uncovered, for 1 hour. *Makes 55–60 balls.*

Nutrients per serving (3 balls): Calories 190, Fat 10g, Cholesterol 50mg, Sodium 560mg, Carbohydrates 16g, Protein 10g, Fiber 0g.

Deviled Eggs

Don't forget this popular appetizer when planning a party. It is making a comeback on buffet tables at many special occasions. The simple ingredients can usually be found right in your refrigerator.

6–9 hard-cooked eggs	Salt to taste
2–3 tablespoons mayonnaise	Paprika
2–3 tablespoons sweet pickle relish	Parsley for garnish (optional)

Shell eggs when cold. Cut them in half lengthwise and remove the yolks carefully so as not to damage the whites. Crush the yolk and moisten with enough of the mayonnaise and pickle relish to form a creamy consistency when blended. Salt to taste.

Spoon the filling back in the whites, mounding the centers. Sprinkle on paprika for color. Put the eggs on a plate and garnish with parsley. They may be refrigerated for up to 24 hours covered in plastic wrap. Be sure to remove them from the refrigerator about ½ hour before serving. *Makes 6–9 servings.*

Nutrients per egg: Calories 90, Fat 6g, Cholesterol 170mg, Sodium 90mg, Carbohydrates 2g, Protein 4g, Fiber 0g.

Nondairy Stuffed Celery

The appetizer table usually offers few foods the lactose-intolerant celiac can eat. There may be some plain fruit and vegetables, but we eat them without crackers or dip. Even cheese and cream cheese–stuffed celery are off-limits. But this celery is one any celiac can enjoy because Tofutti (cream cheese substitute) contains no dairy, cholesterol, or butterfat.

One carton (8 ounces) Tofutti

½ tablespoon Worcestershire sauce

1¼ cups chopped walnuts or pecans

½ teaspoon onion salt

½ teaspoon black pepper

½ bunch celery, cleaned, trimmed, and separated into ribs

In a medium bowl, with a fork or spoon, beat the Tofutti until creamy. Add in the Worcestershire sauce, walnuts, onion salt, and black pepper.

Cut the celery ribs into 3" sections and fill. Arrange on platter, cover with plastic wrap, and chill until serving. *Makes about 2 dozen pieces.*

Nutrients per serving: Calories 67, Fat 4g, Cholesterol 12mg, Sodium 77mg, Carbohydrates 2g, Protein 2g, Fiber 1g.

Casseroles

Rice

Curried Chicken-Rice with Almonds
    (p. 51)
Fruited Brown Rice and Chicken (p. 52)
Rice and Sausage Casserole (p. 53)
Brown Rice with Cranberries (p. 54)
Fried Rice with Ginger (p. 55)
Curried Rice Pilaf (p. 56)
Risotto with Sausage and Apple (p. 57)
Mushroom Risotto (p. 58)
Top-of-the-Stove Rice Casserole (p. 59)
Turkey Casserole Oriental (p. 60)
Saffron Rice (p. 61)

Beans

Five-Bean Casserole (p. 62)
Southwest Bean Stew (p. 63)
Baked Beans with a Nip (p. 64)
Crazy-for-Chili Chili (p. 65)
Four-Star Chili (p. 66)
Crockpot Chili (p. 67)

Cornmeal

Tamale Pie (p. 68)
Chicken Spoon Bread (p. 69)

Bread or Bread Crumbs

Hot Chicken Salad (p. 70)
Quick Chicken Pot Pie (p. 71)
Bette's Best Chicken Pot Pie (p. 72)
Soup 'n' Dumplings (p. 73)
Turkey 'n' Dressing (p. 74)
Chicken Casserole with Ham and Cheese
    (p. 75)
Apple-Celery Dressing (p. 76)
Fruited Dressing for Pork or Chicken
    (p. 77)

Potato

Pork and Sweet Potato in Foil (p. 78)
Poor Man's Pie (p. 79)
Bette's Best Baked Stew (p. 80)

Although baked foods for celiacs have improved considerably in the last twenty years, there are still very few casseroles we can buy either at a restaurant or through the gluten-free suppliers. And we often have to pass up casseroles at the homes of friends and even relatives. (You have to ask, "What's the thickening?" The answer is usually, "Just flour." Gluten! you think—and you know you have to desist.)

Even most chili in cans has a thickening of modified food starch, which is usually wheat flour; and I've found only a few brands of pork and beans that are gluten free. As for recipes that include bread crumbs, cubes, biscuits, or dumplings, you can be sure they will be off-limits.

I love mixed dishes with their blend of flavors, their crunchy textures, and the fact that they often taste better the second day, which means a night off for the cook. I've discovered that most of you, like myself, miss those foods in the gluten-free diet. Oh, sure, you can exist on plain meats, vegetables, and a baked potato—which we have to order when dining in a restaurant. But who wants to be so handicapped at home?

Among the casseroles in this chapter are those that many generations remember: Soup 'n' Dumplings, Chicken Pot Pie, rice and bean dishes. Make them now and enjoy some of the foods you'd come to love before celiac disease tried to deny them to you.

Curried Chicken-Rice with Almonds 350°

If you like curry and ginger, try this quick-fixing casserole when you don't want to take the time to make the sauce and boil the rice. Top the dish with sliced green onions, raisins, and coconut, or serve it with your favorite chutney. Add a green salad for a complete meal.

¾ cup long-grain white rice
¾ pound boneless, skinless
   chicken, cut in bite-sized pieces
⅓ cup slivered almonds
Salt and pepper to taste
2 tablespoons margarine or butter
¼ large onion, minced
2 tablespoons grated fresh
   gingerroot

1½ teaspoons curry powder
2 tablespoons GF powdered soup
   base dissolved in ¼ cup water
   (optional) (see page 277)
1 cup chicken broth
1 cup milk or nondairy substitute
1 teaspoon sugar (optional)

Preheat oven to 350°.

In a 2½-quart casserole, place rice and chicken. Toss in the almonds and stir. Season with salt and pepper.

In a 2-quart saucepan, melt butter. Stir in the onion, gingerroot, and curry powder. Add the soup base dissolved in the water (if used) and the chicken broth. Cook, stirring, until the sauce comes to a boil. Add the milk and sugar (if used) and pour the warm sauce over the chicken and rice. Cover and bake for 1 hour. Serve hot. *Makes 4–5 servings.*

*Nutrients per serving: Calories 360, Fat 14g, Cholesterol 65mg,
Sodium 150mg, Carbohydrates 29g, Protein 28g, Fiber 1g.*

VARIATION:

For a different taste, replace almonds with pine nuts.

Fruited Brown Rice and Chicken

400°

Try this rice-and-chicken casserole for a sweet change. Serve it with a green salad for a contrast in taste and texture.

1 cup brown rice, uncooked
1 small onion, diced
⅓ cup dried cranberries
⅓ cup dried fruit bits
1¾ cups chicken broth (14-ounce can)
½ cup orange juice

8 skinned and boned chicken thighs
2 tablespoons orange juice concentrate, thawed
1 tablespoon honey
1 teaspoon prepared mustard

Preheat oven to 400°. Butter a 9" square casserole or baking pan.

In a medium bowl, combine the rice, onion, cranberries, fruit bits, chicken broth, and orange juice. Pour this mixture into the prepared pan and top with the chicken thighs.

In a small bowl, combine the orange juice concentrate, honey, and mustard. Spread this sauce on the chicken thighs. Cover the casserole or top the baking pan with aluminum foil and bake for 1 hour and 15 minutes. *Makes 4 servings.*

Nutrients per serving: Calories 279, Fat 20g, Cholesterol 87mg, Sodium 810mg, Carbohydrates 56g, Protein 18g, Fiber 4g.

Rice and Sausage Casserole

A hearty main dish with lots of flavor. It can be made up ahead of time and baked just before dinner. This makes a great change for the buffet or picnic table.

1 cup blended wild rice and
   brown rice
2 cups chicken broth, boiling
4 tablespoons butter
1 pound turkey sausage (see page
   289)

1½ cups chopped onion
2 cups chopped celery
½ cup chopped walnuts, toasted
Salt and pepper to taste

Preheat oven to 350°. Lightly coat a 2-quart casserole with nonstick spray.

Place rice in the prepared casserole and pour in the boiling chicken broth. Cover and place in the oven to partially cook while preparing the rest of the ingredients.

In a frying pan, melt 2 tablespoons of the butter and crumble in the sausage. Cook until no pink shows. Remove to a dish and cover with foil. Add the remaining butter to the frypan and sauté the onion and celery until the onion is translucent. Add the sausage, onion, celery, and walnuts to the partially cooked rice. Salt and pepper to taste. Return to the oven and bake for 45 minutes. *Makes 8–10 servings.*

Nutrients per serving: Calories 600, Fat 34g, Cholesterol 65mg, Sodium 1,300mg, Carbohydrates 54g, Protein 19g, Fiber 3g.

Brown Rice with Cranberries

A flavorful top-of-the-stove side dish to serve with meats that have no gravy or sauce. This is especially good with baked chicken.

3 tablespoons margarine or butter
1 cup chopped onion
½ teaspoon minced garlic
¾ cup diced celery
2¼ cups vegetable broth
1 cup brown rice

1 teaspoon salt
Pepper to taste
1 teaspoon dried thyme
1 cup dried cranberries
½ cup chopped walnuts

In a large saucepan, melt the margarine and sauté the onion, garlic, and celery until the onion is translucent. Pour in the vegetable broth. Heat to boiling and add the rest of the ingredients. Bring back to a boil; reduce heat to low. Cover and cook for approximately 45 minutes or until the rice is tender. *Makes 4–5 servings.*

Nutrients per serving: Calories 740, Fat 54g, Cholesterol 0mg, Sodium 870mg, Carbohydrates 50g, Protein 24g, Fiber 5g.

Fried Rice with Ginger

This is not a new recipe but a twist on an old favorite, Chinese fried rice. It makes a little leftover meat go a long way. Or try it with fresh shelled shrimp and start them cooking in the pan with the ginger and onions.

¼–½ cup cooked meat (see
   above)
2 tablespoons butter or margarine
2–3 green onions, sliced thin
1 tablespoon grated gingerroot
2 cups cooked rice

1 large egg
½ teaspoon salt
1½ tablespoons soy sauce
½ cup frozen peas
Minced parsley for garnish
   (optional)

Cut the meat in thin slivers. Or, if using shrimp, be sure they are shelled and deveined.

Heat the butter in a large skillet or risotto pan. Add green onions, gingerroot, and meat (or shrimp). Sauté for about 2 minutes. Add the rice and stir until the ingredients are melded.

Beat the egg with the salt and soy sauce and add to the rice mixture. Stir in the peas. Cook until the egg mixture is absorbed, the peas have thawed, and the mixture seems dry. This takes only a few minutes. To serve oriental-style, press rice into a bowl with a rounded bottom and turn it out onto a shallow dish with the top now rounded. Garnish with minced parsley if desired. *Makes 4 servings.*

*Nutrients per serving: Calories 220, Fat 10g, Cholesterol 70mg,
Sodium 710mg, Carbohydrates 23g, Protein 10g, Fiber 2g.*

Curried Rice Pilaf

By adding a new taste to my regular curried rice, I came up with a whole new dish.

1 tablespoon margarine or butter
¾ cup uncooked white rice
1 tablespoon vegetable oil
1 stalk celery, sliced thin
1 cup diced onion
1½ teaspoons curry powder
   (more or less, to taste)

1¾ cups chicken broth
½ teaspoon salt (if broth
   unsalted)
Pepper to taste
½ cup chopped pecans
½ cup golden raisins

In a 3-quart heavy saucepan, melt the margarine. Add the rice and cook on medium heat for 5 minutes. Remove the rice and add the oil, celery, onion, and curry powder. Cook until the vegetables are translucent (5 minutes).

Stir in the rice, broth, and seasonings. Bring to a boil and lower heat to simmer covered for 20 minutes or until the liquid is absorbed. Add the pecans and raisins and cook, uncovered, for 3–5 minutes. Serve warm. *Makes 6 servings.*

Nutrients per serving: Calories 255, Fat 9g, Cholesterol 5mg,
Sodium 206mg, Carbohydrates 34g, Protein 3g, Fiber 2g.

Curries will get stronger as they age, but they do freeze well.

Risotto with Sausage and Apple

A truly one-dish meal made in twenty minutes on top of the stove. The turkey (or pork) sausage blends well with apple and celery. Serve this dish with a tossed salad for texture and color contrast. Arborio rice, often called rice for risotto, can be found in large markets or specialty food stores.

See page 289 for making your own turkey sausage from ground turkey (or chicken).

1 pound turkey (or pork) sausage
1 cup chopped onion
1 cup diced celery
1 large apple, peeled, cored, and diced

1 cup arborio rice
3–4 cups chicken stock
¾ cup apple juice
Salt to taste

Sauté the sausage, onion, celery, and apple in a large frypan or wok over medium heat until the onion and apple are tender and the sausage is cooked. Add the rice and stir for 1 minute.

Add 1 cup of the chicken stock and the apple juice. Cook on medium-low, stirring frequently, until the liquid has been absorbed by the rice. Add 1 cup more of the chicken stock and continue cooking until absorbed. Continue adding chicken stock, about ½ cup at a time, until the rice is completely cooked. (You will have to taste the rice to be sure the kernels do not have hard centers.) Season with salt. *Makes 4 servings.*

Nutrients per serving: Calories 500, Fat 7g, Cholesterol 50mg, Sodium 1,110mg, Carbohydrates 77g, Protein 34g, Fiber 8g.

Mushroom Risotto

This risotto, with a variety of mushrooms, can be a main dish for a meatless meal or a side dish to serve with meats that have no gravy or juices. Add a light salad or fruit for a complete meal. For the mushrooms, select from the small button mushrooms or the shiitake or other more exotic kinds. Even a small amount of the wild mushrooms will add a lot of flavor to the finished dish.

4½ cups vegetable broth or three 14½-ounce cans
3 tablespoons butter or margarine
3 tablespoons olive oil
5 green onions, sliced thin
1 pound assorted mushrooms, sliced
1 cup arborio rice (or medium-grain white rice)
½ cup dry sherry
½ cup Parmesan cheese

In a medium saucepan, bring the vegetable broth to a simmer and reduce heat. Keep broth warm.

In a large frypan, melt the butter and olive oil over medium heat. Add the green onions and sauté for 1 minute. Add the mushrooms and cook until they are tender, about 8 minutes. Stir in the rice to coat. Pour in the sherry and simmer until the liquid is absorbed, stirring frequently. Turn heat to medium-high and add ¾ cup of the broth; simmer until absorbed, stirring frequently. Continue adding the vegetable broth, ¾ cup at a time, as before, stirring often until each addition is absorbed. The mixture should become creamy and the rice completely cooked and soft. Remove from heat and stir in the Parmesan cheese. Serve immediately. *Makes 6 servings as a side dish with meat or 4 servings as a main course.*

Nutrients per serving: Calories 440, Fat 19g, Cholesterol 25mg, Sodium 1,440mg, Carbohydrates 50g, Protein 13g, Fiber 1g.

Top-of-the-Stove Rice Casserole

If you have 2 cups of leftover cooked rice (white, herbed, brown, or other), you have the beginning of a great casserole to go with meat loaf, ham slices, or fried chicken.

If you have leftover cooked ham, chicken, or roast beef, you can include them in the casserole and just serve a salad on the side.

1½ cups sliced mushrooms
1 tablespoon margarine or butter
One recipe Cream of Chicken
    Soup (page 277), equivalent to
    one 10-ounce can
2 cups cooked rice

3 green onions, sliced
1 cup frozen green peas, slightly
    thawed
Salt to taste
Leftover cooked ham, chicken,
    or roast beef (optional)

In a large frying pan, sauté the mushrooms in the margarine until soft.

Prepare the soup and add it to the cooked mushrooms. Add the rice and onions, then heat, stirring gently. Add the peas, lower heat, and cook 5–10 minutes. Season with salt. Serve with meats that have no gravies. *Makes 4 to 6 servings.*

Nutrients per serving: Calories 330, Fat 8g, Cholesterol 20mg, Sodium 280mg, Carbohydrates 54g, Protein 11g, Fiber 2g.

*K*eep the powdered soup base (page 277) on hand in a container beside the stove to use for a quick cream soup or the equivalent of 1 can of cream soup.

Turkey Casserole Oriental

A lot of turkey, flavor, and crunch in an easy-to-make one-dish meal. For an easy dinner, serve this casserole with my almost-bran muffins (page 224) and a tossed salad.

¾ cup white or brown and wild rice mix, cooked according to package directions
One recipe Cream of Chicken Soup (page 277), equivalent to one 10-ounce can
3 cups chopped cooked turkey
1 cup chopped celery
1 cup sliced mushrooms (optional)

¼ cup diced onion
One 5-ounce can sliced water chestnuts
½ cup slivered almonds
3 tablespoons soy sauce
1 cup water
1½ cups buttered GF bread crumbs

In a 3-quart microwave-safe casserole, combine the rice and the prepared soup. Add the turkey, celery, mushrooms (if used), onion, water chestnuts, almonds, soy sauce, and water. Mix well. Top with the buttered crumbs.

Cook on high for 14 minutes, turning once if your microwave doesn't have a turntable. *Makes 8 servings.*

*Nutrients per serving: Calories 610, Fat 13g, Cholesterol 60mg,
Sodium 840mg, Carbohydrates 94g, Protein 31g, Fiber 11g.*

Saffron Rice

Another 20-minute rice dish with an exotic look and slightly foreign taste. The flavor is mild, but you can increase the amount of coriander to spice it up. This dish goes well with meats that have no gravies or sauces, such as roast chicken, meat loaf, or baked ham.

Note: *The basmati or jasmine rice can be replaced by regular long-grain white rice, but the flavor will be less dramatic.*

2 tablespoons oil	½ teaspoon salt (or to taste)
1 cup grated carrots	¼ teaspoon crushed saffron
3 cups chicken broth	2 cups basmati or jasmine rice
1 teaspoon coriander	¼ cup sliced green onions

In a wok or large frying pan on medium, heat the oil and stir in the carrots. Cook, stirring, until the carrots are slightly tender.

Add the broth and bring to a boil. Add the remaining ingredients except the onions and mix well. Reduce heat to low, cover, and cook until the rice is tender and the liquid is absorbed (14–18 minutes). Stir in the onions and serve. *Makes 5–6 servings.*

Nutrients per serving: Calories 310, Fat 6g, Cholesterol 0mg, Sodium 580mg, Carbohydrates 56g, Protein 7g, Fiber 1g.

Five-Bean Casserole

This bean dish has proved a hit at our family gatherings and potlucks. It's easy to make using canned beans, but your guests will think you slaved over it.

6 slices bacon, diced
2 cups chopped onion
1 teaspoon minced garlic
⅓ cup molasses
¼ cup brown sugar
⅓ cup vinegar
1 tablespoon mustard
½ teaspoon pepper
One 15–19-ounce can red kidney beans

One 15–19-ounce can garbanzo beans
One 15–19-ounce can great northern beans
One 15–19-ounce can pork and beans
One 15–19-ounce can baby lima beans or one 10-ounce package frozen limas, cooked

Preheat oven to 375°.

In a Dutch oven or heavy baking pan, sauté the bacon and onions until the bacon is cooked and the onions are translucent. Stir in the garlic, molasses, brown sugar, vinegar, mustard, and pepper. Bring to a boil.

Drain and rinse the beans. Add them to the pot and bring to a simmer. Cook 5 minutes, stirring frequently. Pour into a 2½-quart bean pot or casserole. Cover and bake 45 minutes, stirring once or twice as the beans bake. *Makes 12 servings.*

Nutrients per serving: Calories 280, Fat 4g, Cholesterol 5mg, Sodium 310mg, Carbohydrates 49g, Protein 14g, Fiber 10g.

Southwest Bean Stew

Beans with 4 stew vegetables make a hearty meal-in-one-dish supper. Serve this tasty stew with cornbread and top the meal with a dish of fruit.

Note: *You can purchase barbecue sauces that are gluten-free, or make your own using the recipe on page 151.*

4 slices bacon, diced
2 cups diced onions
4 cups diced butternut squash
1½ cups chicken broth
One 15-ounce can black beans
One 15-ounce can garbanzo
 beans

One 15-ounce can kidney beans
¾ cup barbecue sauce
1 red bell pepper, diced
One 8-ounce can corn kernels
½ teaspoon black pepper

In a large (5-quart) Dutch oven, cook the bacon until the fat is opaque. Add the onions and sauté until they are clear. Add the squash and sauté for about 2 minutes. Pour in the broth, bring to a boil, and simmer 5 minutes, covered. Drain and rinse the beans; then add them to the stew, along with the bell pepper, corn (drained), barbecue sauce, and black pepper. Simmer until the squash is tender (8–10 minutes). Serve in large soup bowl. *Makes 8 servings.*

Nutrients per serving: Calories 270, Fat 4g, Cholesterol 5mg, Sodium 680mg, Carbohydrates 50g, Protein 14g, Fiber 11g.

Baked Beans with a Nip

I'm repeating this easy recipe, included in the revised edition of my first book, as it is another winner at gatherings and potlucks. It uses some different canned beans and has the added nip of chili for a twist.

5 ounces bacon, cut in ½" pieces

2 cups chopped onions

One 16-ounce can tomato sauce

1 cup brown sugar

6 tablespoons apple cider vinegar

3 tablespoons molasses

1 tablespoon Worcestershire sauce

2 teaspoons chili powder (or to taste)

5 drops hot pepper sauce

One 16-ounce can garbanzo beans

One 16-ounce can kidney beans

One 16-ounce can black beans

One 16-ounce can butter beans

Preheat oven to 375°.

In a large, ovenproof pot, sauté the bacon and onions until the bacon is brown and the onions are translucent. Mix in the tomato sauce, sugar, vinegar, molasses, Worcestershire sauce, chili powder, and hot pepper sauce. Add the beans (after draining and rinsing thoroughly). Cover the pot and bake for about 1 hour and 30 minutes, stirring occasionally. *Makes 8–10 servings.*

Nutrients per serving: Calories 340, Fat 4g, Cholesterol 5mg, Sodium 820mg, Carbohydrates 66g, Protein 13g, Fiber 9g.

Crazy-for-Chili Chili

This recipe makes a huge pot of slightly sweet chili with a barbecue taste. Although good when first made, it is even better on the second day. I freeze the chili in containers holding 2 or 3 servings, to be defrosted and heated up when I'm pressed for time. Thinned down, this recipe makes wonderful Sloppy Joes (see variations).

1½ pounds ground beef
1 medium onion, chopped
2 cloves garlic, finely diced
¼ cup chili powder
1 tablespoon ground cumin
One 16-ounce can stewed
  tomatoes
1 cup ketchup

⅓ cup brown sugar
¼ cup molasses
¼ cup Worcestershire sauce
1 tablespoon dry mustard
One 28-ounce can kidney beans
One 28-ounce can pinto beans
One 15-ounce can chili beans

In a large kettle with a thick bottom or Dutch oven, cook the meat over medium heat with the onion, garlic, chili powder, and cumin.

When the meat is cooked and the onion translucent, stir in the stewed tomatoes, ketchup, brown sugar, molasses, Worcestershire sauce, and mustard. Bring to a boil and simmer on low heat for about half an hour, stirring occasionally. Drain off about half of the liquid from the canned beans and add them to the sauce. Cover and simmer about 30 minutes, again stirring occasionally. Serve immediately in soup bowls or simmer longer for improved taste. *Makes 12–14 servings.*

*Nutrients per serving: Calories 340, Fat 12g, Cholesterol 35mg,
Sodium 670mg, Carbohydrates 43g, Protein 1g, Fiber 5g.*

VARIATIONS:

Ladle into bowls and top with 1 tablespoon finely chopped raw onion and 2 tablespoons grated sharp cheese.

Thin with V8 juice and ladle over split Honey Graham Crumpets (page 214) for GF Sloppy Joes.

Four-Star Chili

This recipe for chili-from-scratch brought so many raves from those who tasted it that I had to include it here. I now keep some packets of chili in my freezer so I can enjoy this dish whenever I want.

1½ pounds pinto beans	1½ pounds leanest ground beef
1 teaspoon baking soda	12 ounces tomato paste
2 tablespoons olive oil	1 tablespoon chili powder
1 cup chopped onion	(or to taste)
¾ to 1 green pepper	1 tablespoon ground cumin
1 teaspoon chopped garlic (in jar)	1 teaspoon salt (or to taste)
1 teaspoon dried oregano	1 tablespoon sugar (or to taste)

Place the beans in a large kettle, sprinkle the baking soda on top, and add water to cover the beans and 1" more. Bring to a boil and cook over medium heat for 1 hour or until the beans are tender. Check often to be sure the beans are covered with water. Drain and rinse.

In a large frying pan, heat the oil over medium-high heat. Add the onion and pepper and cook until the onion is translucent. Add the garlic and oregano and pour the mixture over the beans.

In the same frying pan, cook the ground beef until cooked through, breaking it up into small lumps. Drain off any fat. Add the tomato paste, chili powder, ground cumin, salt, and sugar.

Stir the beef mixture into the beans. If they do not seem to have enough liquid, add water as desired. Place on heat and bring to a boil. Lower to simmer and cook uncovered for about 1 hour or until the tastes have blended. Add more water, as necessary, to achieve the desired consistently. *Makes 8–10 servings.*

Nutrients per serving: Calories 340, Fat 17g, Cholesterol 45mg,
Sodium 530mg, Carbohydrates 29g, Protein 20g, Fiber 8g.

Crockpot Chili

If you are like me, you can never have too many chili recipes. This is a great one to put on the night before the party. Reheating makes it taste even better.

1–2 tablespoons vegetable oil
1½ pounds lean round steak, cut
   into bite-sized pieces
1 large onion, chopped
Two 28-ounce cans chopped
   tomatoes, pureed
1 teaspoon salt

1 tablespoon sugar
¼ teaspoon pepper
½ teaspoon garlic powder
1 tablespoon chili powder
   (or to taste)
Three 16-ounce cans pinto beans,
   drained and rinsed

Heat the oil in a heavy frypan and brown the steak and onions over medium heat until the meat shows no pink and the onion is slightly translucent. Place the steak and onions in a slow cooker and add the rest of the ingredients. Cook on low for 6–8 hours, adding a little beef broth if the mixture seems too thick. *Makes 8–10 servings.*

*Nutrients per serving: Calories 250, Fat 4g, Cholesterol 30mg,
Sodium 1,230mg, Carbohydrates 34g, Protein 24g, Fiber 2g.*

If a dish is a stew, soup, or casserole, make up the full recipe and freeze the leftovers in one or more portions for thawing and reheating later.

Tamale Pie

350°

Since so many canned tamales contain gluten in their sauces, I had to give them up after I was diagnosed. But when I found this recipe, I started enjoying the taste of tamales again. Any leftovers will freeze well in single-serving containers.

Note: *To save time, use purchased polenta instead of the cornmeal crust; slice it to line the bottom and sides of the pan.*

BASE CRUST:
2 cups water, boiling
1 cup yellow cornmeal
1 teaspoon salt
1 cup cold water, milk, or
 nondairy liquid

FILLING:
1 tablespoon vegetable oil
⅓ cup chopped green pepper
½ –¾ pound lean ground beef

⅓ cup finely chopped onion
1 tablespoon GF Mix
One 16-ounce can stewed
 tomatoes
One 1.25-ounce can sliced olives
1 tablespoon chili powder
 (or to taste)
½ teaspoon salt
½ teaspoon garlic salt
½ cup grated sharp cheddar
 cheese

Preheat oven to 350°. Grease a 1½-quart casserole.

To the boiling water, add the combined cornmeal, salt, and cold water. Cook, stirring constantly, until thickened. Cover and cook on low for 10 minutes.

In a frying pan, heat the oil and add the green pepper, beef, and chopped onion. Cook until the onion is translucent. Blend in the flour mix and add the tomatoes, olives, chili powder, salt, and garlic salt. Cook gently until heated through.

Line the bottom and sides of the prepared casserole with the cornmeal crust. Fill with the hot meat-tomato mixture. Sprinkle the top with cheese and bake 30 minutes. *Makes 4–5 servings.*

Nutrients per serving: Calories 600, Fat 26g, Cholesterol 85mg,
Sodium 720mg, Carbohydrates 63g, Protein 30g, Fiber 7g.

Chicken Spoon Bread 375°

The name of this recipe is misleading. It's not a bread but a main-dish casserole. Add your favorite green salad and dessert for an easy meal. If you don't eat the entire casserole at one meal, it makes a great leftover dish for the next day.

¾ cup cornmeal
2 tablespoons GF Mix
1 teaspoon salt
4 cups chicken broth

¼ cup (½ stick) butter or
    margarine
4 eggs, separated
3 cups chopped cooked chicken

Preheat oven to 375°. Grease a 2½-quart casserole.

In a large saucepan, combine cornmeal, flour mix, and salt; stir in the broth. Cook over medium-high heat until thickened. Add the butter and beaten egg yolks. Stir in the chicken. Beat the egg whites until stiff; fold into the mixture. Spoon into the prepared casserole and bake for 40 minutes or until done. *Makes 6 servings.*

Nutrients per serving: Calories 330, Fat 17g, Cholesterol 220mg, Sodium 1,050mg, Carbohydrates 15g, Protein 28g, Fiber 2g.

Hot Chicken Salad

You'll love the wonderfully crunchy taste of this chicken casserole.

1 pound boneless, skinless
    chicken breast
2 cups diced celery
One 8-ounce can sliced water
    chestnuts
4 ounces fresh mushrooms,
    chopped
½ cup slivered almonds
1 tablespoon finely chopped
    onion

One recipe Cream of Chicken
    Soup (page 277)
¾ cup mayonnaise
¾ cup sour cream (fat-free okay)
1 tablespoon lemon juice
½ teaspoon salt
Pepper to taste
½ cup buttered GF bread crumbs
¼ cup grated cheddar cheese
    (optional)

Preheat oven to 350°. Grease a 2½- or 3-quart casserole.

Wash chicken and cook on high in microwave in covered dish until chicken turns from translucent to opaque. Cut into cubes.

In a large mixing bowl, place the chicken, celery, water chestnuts, mushrooms, almonds, and chopped onion. To the prepared soup, add the mayonnaise, sour cream, lemon juice, salt, and pepper. Combine the soup mixture with the chicken mixture and spoon into the prepared casserole. Top with either the bread crumbs or both crumbs and cheese (if used). Bake for 30 minutes. Serve hot. *Makes 6 servings.*

*Nutrients per serving: Calories 480, Fat 37g, Cholesterol 85mg,
Sodium 470mg, Carbohydrates 15g, Protein 26g, Fiber 2g.*

---

*W*hen you cook a casserole or roast the day before, cool it quickly by placing the pot in a sinkful of cold water for 15 minutes, then refrigerate. Ice may be added to the water.

Quick Chicken Pot Pie

350°

Make this chicken casserole in minutes and top with biscuits from the mix recipe on page 279. Add a salad and you have a real comfort dinner with little fuss.

1½ cups chicken broth, seasoned
1 cup diced carrots
¾ cup diced onions
½ cup sliced celery
3 cups cubed cooked chicken
One recipe Cream of Chicken
    Soup (page 277)

1 cup sour cream
1 teaspoon Worcestershire sauce
Salt and pepper to taste
¾ cup frozen peas, thawed
One recipe Biscuit Mix to Top
    Stews or Chicken Pies
    (page 279)

Preheat oven to 350°.

In a medium saucepan, bring the broth to a boil. Drop in the carrots, onions, and celery. Bring back to a boil and reduce heat to simmer. Cook for 20 minutes.

In a casserole place the chicken and top with the prepared soup, sour cream, and Worcestershire sauce. Season with salt and pepper and add the simmered vegetables with their broth and the peas. Stir well. Top with the biscuit dough dropped from a tablespoon. Bake for 40–45 minutes or until the biscuits are golden brown. *Makes 6–8 servings.*

Nutrients per serving: Calories 210, Fat 12g, Cholesterol 60mg, Sodium 260mg, Carbohydrates 8g, Protein 18g, Fiber 2g.

Bette's Best Chicken Pot Pie

I am repeating this recipe because chicken pot pie is the one dish that I literally drooled over when I passed it in the grocer's freezer. This version is almost as easy as that frozen one of the old days, but it's far tastier.

Note: *This recipe can be made ahead and refrigerated, then baked just before serving. The biscuits still rise but may take a bit longer to bake. Watch the oven and check the cooking. The dish is ready when the filling is bubbly and the biscuits are a warm brown.*

1 cup diced cooked chicken
2 cups chicken stock
½ cup diced carrots
½ cup sliced celery
¼ cup minced onion
½ cup frozen peas
3 tablespoons GF Mix

2–3 tablespoons water
¼ cup cream or nondairy
   substitute
Salt and pepper to taste
One recipe Biscuit Mix to Top
   Stews or Chicken Pies (page
   279)

Preheat oven to 350°.

Prepare the chicken and set aside. Place the chicken stock in a large saucepan and bring to a boil; add the carrots, celery, and onions and cook for 15 minutes. Stir in the peas and chicken and cook 5 minutes longer.

Mix the flour mix to a thin paste with a few tablespoons of water. Thicken the stock with the flour paste and cook on low for 1–2 minutes. Add the cream and season with salt and pepper. (If the stock is salted, you probably won't need any more.)

Pour the cooked pot pie mixture into a 2-quart casserole or individual casserole dishes and top with 2½" rounds of biscuit dough. Bake for about 20–25 minutes. *Makes 5–6 servings.*

*Nutrients per serving: Calories 150, Fat 5g, Cholesterol 25mg,
Sodium 670mg, Carbohydrates 15g, Protein 12g, Fiber 2g.*

Soup 'n' Dumplings

This is probably the dish most people think of when you say "comfort food." It's a great way to create a different meal out of leftover roast beef, pork, or chicken. This is a basic recipe. You may add other vegetables as you choose.

6 cups seasoned stock (beef,
   chicken, or vegetable)
3 cups cubed cooked beef, pork,
   or chicken
Salt and pepper to taste
2 cups baby carrots or larger
   carrots, cut into 1" cubes

1 pound baby onions (small
   boiling onions)
2 cups sliced celery, in 1" pieces
2 cups frozen baby peas
One recipe Dumplings (page 228)

In a large-mouthed kettle, bring the stock to a boil. Add the cubed meat, salt and pepper, carrots, onions, and celery. Bring back to a boil and reduce heat to a simmer. Cook uncovered for 10 minutes. Add the peas and bring back to a gentle boil.

Mix up the dumplings and drop them from a dessert spoon into the gently boiling stock. Cover the kettle and simmer uncovered for 10 minutes. Serve immediately by placing 1 or 2 dumplings in a soup bowl and ladling the vegetables and stock over them. *Makes 6–8 servings.*

Nutrients per serving: Calories 200, Fat 2½ g, Cholesterol 35mg, Sodium 740mg, Carbohydrates 18g, Protein 25g, Fiber 5g.

Turkey 'n' Dressing

350°

If you have leftover cooked turkey or chicken, you can have all the flavor of turkey, gravy, and dressing combined in this casserole with the added zip of broccoli. A real treat and easy to make.

1¼ cups boiling chicken stock
¼ cup (½ stick) margarine or
    butter
4 slices GF bread, cubed
1 teaspoon poultry seasoning
2 cups fresh broccoli, trimmed
    and cut in 1" pieces

2 cups cooked turkey or chicken,
    cubed
One recipe Cream of Chicken
    Soup (page 277)
½ cup milk or nondairy substitute
1 cup grated cheddar cheese,
    divided

Preheat oven to 350°. Lightly butter a 2-quart casserole.

Into the boiling chicken stock, place cut-up margarine, stirring until melted. Remove from the stove and stir in the cubed bread and the poultry seasoning. Spoon into the prepared casserole and top with the broccoli and cubed turkey.

Prepare the soup and blend in the milk and ½ cup of the cheese. Pour the soup mixture over the ingredients in the casserole. Top with the remaining cheese. Bake for 30 minutes or until hot and bubbling. *Makes 6 servings.*

*Nutrients per serving: Calories 410, Fat 27g, Cholesterol 65mg,
Sodium 847mg, Carbohydrates 15g, Protein 25g, Fiber 1g.*

Chicken Casserole with Ham and Cheese 350°

Chicken cordon bleu in a casserole! Add a green salad or fruit to make a complete meal.

1 egg, beaten
1½ cups milk, divided
¾ cup bread crumbs or amaranth
   breading mix
2 pounds boneless, skinless,
   chicken breast, cut into chunks

1 tablespoon oil
8 ounces Swiss cheese, cubed
8 ounces ham, diced
One recipe Cream of Chicken
   Soup (page 277)

Preheat oven to 350°. Lightly grease a 2½-quart casserole.

In a small bowl, combine the egg and ½ cup milk. In another bowl, pour the breading. Dip the chicken chunks into the liquid and then roll in the breading. Heat the oil in a skillet and brown the chicken until golden. Place in the casserole. Add the cheese and ham.

Prepare the soup and blend in the remaining 1 cup milk, stirring well. Pour the soup mixture over the ham and cheese. Bake 30 minutes until bubbly. Let sit 5 minutes before serving. *Makes 8 servings.*

Nutrients per serving: Calories 530, Fat 27g, Cholesterol 185mg,
Sodium 690mg, Carbohydrates 29g, Protein 43g, Fiber 1g.

Apple-Celery Dressing 375°

This is about as close as you can get to Stove-Top Stuffing. I use it for my Thanksgiving turkey and in casseroles, topping the stuffing with chicken pieces, pork chops, or pork tenderloin.

2½ cups GF bread cubes	1 cup diced celery
1–2 teaspoons poultry seasoning	½ cup chopped onion
¼ cup (½ stick) margarine or butter	1 egg, beaten
1 large apple, peeled, cored, and diced	1 cup (more or less) chicken broth
	1 teaspoon salt (or to taste)

Place bread cubes in a large mixing bowl. Stir in the poultry seasoning.

In a large skillet, melt the margarine and sauté the apple, celery, and onion until the apple and onion are translucent. Add this mixture to the bread cubes, along with the egg. Mix in the chicken broth, a little at a time, until the dressing has the texture you desire. (If baked separately, you will probably like a moist mixture. When you stuff a fowl or place the dressing next to a pork roast, the juices from the meat will add to the moisture and you may prefer a drier dressing.) Season with salt.

To bake separately, place the dressing in a 2-quart greased casserole and bake for 1 hour at 375°. *Makes 6–8 servings.*

Nutrients per serving: Calories 110, Fat 7g, Cholesterol 40mg, Sodium 490mg, Carbohydrates 9g, Protein 3g, Fiber 1g.

Fruited Dressing for Pork or Chicken 350°

Oranges and cranberries add zing to this dressing, which I use with low-fat meats such as pork tenderloin and chicken breast. You also save fat by using orange juice in place of margarine or butter.

4 cups GF bread cubes
¾ cup diced celery
½ medium onion, chopped
1 tablespoon vegetable oil
⅓ cup dried cranberries

½ cup orange juice
Salt to taste
One 8-ounce can mandarin
   oranges, drained
Chicken stock or water as needed

Place bread cubes in a large mixing bowl.

In a skillet, place the celery, onion, and oil and cook until celery is translucent. Add the celery and onions to the bread, along with the cranberries and orange juice. Toss gently and taste. Season with salt. Cut the mandarin oranges in ½" segments and fold in gently. If the dressing is too dry, add chicken stock or water.

To bake with meat: Place the dressing in a 1½-quart casserole and top with chicken or pork. Cover and cook at 350° for 40–45 minutes. *Makes 6–8 servings.*

*Nutrients per serving: Calories 150, Fat 2½ g, Cholesterol 0mg,
Sodium 250mg, Carbohydrates 29g, Protein 3g, Fiber 2g.*

Pork and Sweet Potato in Foil   450°

These packets are not exactly casseroles, but since they combine meat, potatoes, and fruit in one dish, I've included them in the casserole chapter. Add a salad to make a complete meal.

Four 14" aluminum foil squares
1 pound pork tenderloin
Salt and pepper to taste
2 medium sweet potatoes, peeled
   and grated

1 apple, peeled, cored, and
   chopped
⅓ cup currant jelly
2 teaspoons hot orange juice
Dash cinnamon

Preheat oven to 450°. Grease each foil square by spraying with vegetable oil spray. Wash pork, cut into slices ½" thick, and season with salt and pepper.

On each square of foil, place one-fourth of the sweet potato and apple in a mound; then arrange one-fourth of the pork in a circle around the edge of the mound. Combine jelly, hot orange juice, and cinnamon in a small bowl and blend. Spoon over the mounds. Fold the packets by bringing up the sides and pinching them together. Seal the side seams. Bake for 20–25 minutes or until the pork is done. *Makes 4 servings.*

Nutrients per serving: Calories 420, Fat 7g, Cholesterol 105mg,
Sodium 120mg, Carbohydrates 59g, Protein 35g, Fiber 8g.

Poor Man's Pie

With a rich and tasty gravy, this easy-to-make shepherd's pie can be served to your family with no apologies.

Note: *This dish can be made with frozen corn and lima beans, peas and carrots, or (my preference) a package of mixed vegetables, which includes all of these.*

1 pound lean ground beef
⅓ cup chopped onions
2 teaspoons Worcestershire sauce
1¾ cups beef broth
  (approximately)
¼ cup GF Mix

Onion salt to taste
1½ cups frozen mixed vegetables,
  slightly thawed (see note)
½ teaspoon pepper (or to taste)
4 servings instant mashed
  potatoes, prepared and seasoned

Preheat oven to 375°.

In a frying pan, cook the ground beef with the onions until the latter are translucent. Stir in the Worcestershire sauce. Drain the drippings into a 2-quart measure and place the meat mix in a 2-quart casserole.

To the pan drippings, add the beef broth to make 2 cups. In the frying pan place flour mix and stir in the broth. Cook over medium heat, stirring, until the gravy is thick. Season with onion salt. Pour about half of the broth over the meat, top with the mixed vegetables, and spoon the mashed potatoes on top. Bake, uncovered, for 30 minutes. Serve with the remaining gravy (reheated). *Makes 4–5 servings.*

*Nutrients per serving: Calories 330, Fat 12g, Cholesterol 40mg,
Sodium 690mg, Carbohydrates 37g, Protein 18g, Fiber 2g.*

Bette's Best Baked Stew   350°

One of the best stews I've tried. With flour-drenched meat and the cream soup, this ends up thickened perfectly. Serve with a light salad and warmed bread or muffins.

1½ pounds sirloin tip steak,
   cubed
¼ cup GF Mix
½ teaspoon salt
¼ teaspoon pepper
One recipe Cream of Chicken
   Soup (page 277)
10–12 pearl onions, peeled
2 tablespoons vegetable oil
1 rounded cup baby carrots
1 cup beef broth
¼ cup sherry

3–4 teaspoons prepared mustard
   (to taste)
¼ cup brown sugar
¼ cup molasses
2 tablespoons Worcestershire
   sauce
1 teaspoon chopped garlic
1 teaspoon Italian seasoning
4 fist-sized potatoes (red or
   Yukon Gold, cut into 1" cubes)
12 mushrooms, quartered

Preheat the oven to 350°. Place cubed steak in a plastic bag and add the flour mix, salt, and pepper. Shake well to coat.

Prepare the soup. Remove from heat and drop in the onions.

Heat the oil in a large ovenproof pot. Brown the beef about 3 minutes. Lower the heat and top with the carrots and cover. Set timer for 4 minutes.

In a small bowl whisk together the broth, sherry, mustard, brown sugar, molasses, Worcestershire sauce, garlic, and Italian seasoning. Add this mixture to the beef when the timer goes off, along with the potatoes, mushrooms, and cream soup with onions. Stir well.

Bake, covered, for 1 hour. *Makes 6–8 servings.*

*Nutrients per serving: Calories 570, Fat 27g, Cholesterol 81mg,
Sodium 954mg, Carbohydrates 52g, Protein 29g, Fiber 5g.*

Cheese and Egg

Cheese and egg dishes are basic in France; here in the States, we think of them mostly for breakfast. I've borrowed the quiche for luncheons, supper, parties, or appetizers. I've used them so much I've become as addicted as the French to this easy and filling dish that can be an anytime comfort. They are so versatile you can add any leftover vegetables, meat, or fish to make the centerpiece for a meal. Don't be afraid to try one of them at any time, whether it be lunch, supper, or breakfast.

Crustless Seafood Quiche 350°

When I had to start watching my cholesterol, I realized that I could no longer eat my favorite easy-to-make seafood quiche. So I revised the recipe, using lower-fat products and sharper cheeses for their flavor. See if you like this version as much as my testers did. The quiche doesn't need a crust because a thin skin forms on the bottom.

Note: This dish can be mixed up early in the day and refrigerated, then pulled out and baked for lunch or dinner. It may take an extra 5–10 minutes' cooking time if it has been refrigerated over 4 hours.

Surimi is the term used for fake crab, lobster, etc., made from bottom fish and starch (some tapioca, some potato, but mostly wheat) and flavored as shellfish.

2 teaspoons olive oil, divided
1 medium onion, chopped
½ green pepper, cored, seeded, and chopped
¾ pound mushrooms, sliced (about 4 cups)
2 eggs plus 2 whites
1½ cups nonfat cottage cheese
½ cup plain yogurt
¼ cup Featherlight Mix

¼ cup grated Parmesan cheese
¼ teaspoon cayenne pepper
¼ teaspoon salt
¼ teaspoon black pepper
½ pound (about 1 cup) cooked crab, shrimp, or surimi
½ cup grated extra-sharp cheddar cheese (2 ounces)
3 green onions, sliced

Preheat oven to 350°. Lightly spray a 10" pie plate or quiche dish with vegetable oil spray.

In a large frying pan, heat 1 teaspoon of the oil on medium-high. Add the onion and green pepper and cook, stirring until softened (about 5 minutes). Transfer them to a large mixing bowl. Add the remaining 1 teaspoon of oil to the pan and cook the mushrooms, stirring, until they have softened and most of their liquid has evaporated (5–7 minutes). Add the mushrooms to the onion mixture.

In a food processor or with an electric mixer, blend the eggs, egg whites, cottage cheese, yogurt, flour mix, Parmesan cheese, cayenne pepper, salt, and black pepper until smooth. Pour into the vegetable mixture and mix well. Fold in the seafood, cheddar cheese, and green onions. Pour into the prepared pan.

Bake for 45–55 minutes or until a knife inserted in the center comes out clean. Remove from oven and let stand 5 minutes before serving. *Makes 6–8 servings.*

Nutrients per serving: Calories 160, Fat 6g, Cholesterol 80mg,
Sodium 380mg, Carbohydrates 10g, Protein 16g, Fiber 1g.

Easy Crab Quiche

The delicate flavor of crab is not hidden by cheese in this light quiche. Make it with real fresh crab or a GF crab surimi; both are excellent.

   Note: *The quiche can be assembled ahead of time and baked just before serving or baked and refrigerated, then reheated and served later.*

1 tablespoon margarine or butter	2 tablespoons dry sherry
2 tablespoons sliced green onions	½ teaspoon seafood seasoning
4 eggs or 1 cup liquid egg substitute	1 cup Swiss cheese, grated
	One (9") unbaked pie crust
2 cups heavy cream or nondairy substitute	½ pound crabmeat or GF surimi

Preheat oven to 425°.

   In a small frypan, melt the margarine and sauté the green onion until tender.

   Beat the eggs with the cream and add the onions, sherry, and seasoning.

   Layer half of the cheese in the pie crust. Top with half the crabmeat. Pour half the cream mixture over the layers. Repeat. Bake for 15 minutes: reduce heat to 325° and bake for 35 minutes longer or until done. Cool slightly before cutting or refrigerate. Cut and reheat before serving. *Makes 6–8 servings.*

Nutrients per serving: Calories 390, Fat 34g, Cholesterol 245mg, Sodium 280mg, Carbohydrates 3g, Protein 17g, Fiber 0g.

Asparagus Quiche

400°

Quiches are easy to prepare for a luncheon or quick supper, and this is one of the easiest for the crust is formed by sprinkling a buttered pie tin with finely ground bread crumbs.

⅓ cup dried GF bread crumbs
¾ pound fresh asparagus
3 tablespoons butter or
   margarine
3 tablespoons GF Mix

½ teaspoon salt
1½ cups milk or nondairy
   substitute
4 eggs, beaten
½ cup grated Swiss cheese

Preheat oven to 400°. Grease a 9" pie pan with butter and shake on the bread crumbs to cover, tilting the pan so that the crumbs cling to the sides as well as bottom.

Cut the asparagus into ½" sections and cook in a small amount of boiling water until tender (5–7 minutes). Drain and set aside.

In a medium saucepan, melt the butter over medium heat; stir in the flour mix and salt. Gradually add the milk, stirring to avoid lumping. Cook until thickened slightly. Spoon a small amount into the eggs and spoon all back into the pan. Stir in the cheese and the asparagus and pour into the prepared pan. Bake for 35 minutes or until a knife inserted near the center comes out clean. Serve warm. *Makes 6–8 servings.*

Nutrients per serving: Calories 160, Fat 11g, Cholesterol 135mg,
Sodium 280mg, Carbohydrates 8g, Protein 8g, Fiber 1g.

Crustless Corn and Shrimp Quiche

Only a few ingredients but a lot of flavor! As with any quiche, the measurements don't have to be exact. You may replace the fresh corn with one package of frozen corn and the shrimp with cooked crab or GF imitation crab or lobster.

1⅓ cups fresh corn (about 2 ears)
½ pound uncooked shrimp,
    peeled, deveined, cut into ½"
    pieces
3 green onions, sliced thin
¾ cup shredded medium cheddar
    cheese
1½ cups nondairy creamer or
    half-and-half

1 cup liquid egg substitute or
    4 eggs
¾ teaspoon salt
Dash of black pepper
¼ teaspoon dried dill weed
    (optional)

Preheat oven to 325°. Grease a deep 10" pie pan.

Husk the corn and cut kernels from the cob. Place in a bowl and mix in the shrimp, green onions, and cheese. Pour into the greased pie pan.

In the same bowl blend the creamer, liquid egg, salt, pepper, and dill weed (if used). Pour over the corn-shrimp mixture in the pie tin. Bake for 45 minutes or until the center is set. Let cool slightly before cutting and serving. *Makes 6 servings.*

Nutrients per serving: Calories 370, Fat 7g, Cholesterol 30mg,
Sodium 810mg, Carbohydrates 57g, Protein 18g, Fiber 1g.

Salmon Quiche

A rich, easy-to-make quiche that serves as a main dish at lunch or dinner or, when cut into small wedges, as an appetizer at the next party. The crust is simply finely ground GF bread crumbs dusted on the pie pan.

⅓ cup fine GF bread crumbs
12 ounces cream cheese
¼ cup milk or nondairy substitute
2 tablespoons butter or
    margarine
1 teaspoon dry mustard
¼ teaspoon dill weed

¼ teaspoon salt
¼ teaspoon celery salt
4 eggs
One 7½-ounce can salmon
1 cup shredded mozzarella cheese
2 green onions, sliced thin

Preheat oven to 325°. Lightly grease a 9" pie pan.

Sprinkle the bread crumbs into the pie pan and shake to make them adhere to the bottom and sides.

With your mixer, beat the cream cheese, milk, butter, mustard, dill weed, salt, and celery salt on medium speed until well blended. Add the eggs, one at a time, beating just until combined.

Remove the skin, bones, and any dark meat from the salmon and stir it into the above mixture, along with the cheese and green onions. Transfer to the prepared pie pan and bake for 45 minutes or until set. Cool slightly before serving or cool and refrigerate if you prefer to serve it at a later time, either reheated or chilled (as an appetizer). *Makes 6 servings as a main dish or 16 servings as an appetizer.*

*Nutrients per serving: Calories 180, Fat 15g, Cholesterol 105mg,
Sodium 270mg, Carbohydrates 2g, Protein 9g, Fiber 0g.*

Hamburger Pie

400°

Very easy to prepare, this filling quiche makes its own crust from the GF Biscuit Mix.

1 pound lean ground beef
1 cup chopped onion
½ teaspoon salt
1 cup cheddar cheese, grated

½ cup Biscuit Mix (page 279)
1 cup milk or nondairy liquid
2 eggs or ½ cup liquid egg
   substitute

Preheat oven to 400°. Grease a 9" pie plate.

In a large frypan, cook the beef and onion until brown. Drain the fat and spread the mixture in the pie plate. Add salt and sprinkle with cheese.

In a small bowl, stir together the Biscuit Mix, milk, and eggs until completely blended. Pour over the cheese. Bake 25 minutes or until a knife inserted in the center comes out clean. Cool slightly before cutting into wedges. *Makes 6 servings.*

*Nutrients per serving: Calories 400, Fat 18g, Cholesterol 165mg,
Sodium 890mg, Carbohydrates 36g, Protein 22g, Fiber 1g.*

Florentine Crepe Cups

When another celiac served these crepe cups, I found them so tasty I asked for permission to include the recipe in the revised version of my first book. They have proved so popular that I am reprinting the recipe here.

Note: *To cut the cholesterol, make the cups with liquid egg substitute and nondairy creamer but use the cheddar cheese and mayonnaise as called for in the recipe.*

CREPES:

3 eggs, slightly beaten, or liquid egg substitute

⅔ cup Four Flour Mix or Featherlight Mix

½ teaspoon salt

1 cup milk or nondairy creamer

FILLING:

3 tablespoons Four Flour Mix or Featherlight Mix

1½ cups sharp cheddar cheese, grated

3 eggs, slightly beaten, or liquid egg substitute

⅔ cup mayonnaise

One 10-ounce package frozen chopped spinach, thawed

¾ cup cooked shrimp

½ teaspoon salt

Combine the ingredients for crepes in a blender or mixer and beat until smooth. Let stand for 30 minutes.

On a hot skillet, drop 2 tablespoons of the crepe batter. Cook one side only and put in 12 muffin tins, uncooked side down.

For the filling, stir together the ingredients and fill the crepes. Bake in a preheated 350° oven for 35–40 minutes or until set. *Makes 6 servings of 2 crepe cups each.*

Nutrients per serving: Calories 420, Fat 25g, Cholesterol 28mg,
Sodium 880mg, Carbohydrates 26g, Protein 21g, Fiber 2g.

Pasta

Any form of pasta, whether it be macaroni and cheese or the noodles in chicken soup, brings back memories of my mother's home cooking and the days when the kitchen was heated by a huge, black woodstove and served as the center of family living. Mother made her noodles by mixing flour and eggs, rolling out the pasta, and cutting it in thin strips to dry. (We never dreamed of salmonella in eggs then!)

Today we can still make our own GF pasta in our shiny, modern kitchens. And many of us still do (see pages 93 and 94). But in the last few years many new gluten-free pastas have come on the market, and today's celiacs can find some in the health food stores and others from suppliers listed in the back of this book. As of this writing, the Tinkyada brand from the health food stores is available in many shapes and works well in a number of casseroles. It is especially good in cold pasta salads. For noodles, I still prefer the pasta I roll out myself and cut on the pastry board. The Bean Flour Pasta (page 94) is especially flavorful.

Homemade Egg Noodles

The result of much experimentation, this pasta is a favorite of mine for baked noodle dishes. The recipe makes a batch just large enough for most of the recipes in this book, but it can be doubled and worked in 2 balls instead of 1 for more servings.

⅓ cup tapioca flour

2 tablespoons potato starch

⅓ cup cornstarch

½ teaspoon salt

1 tablespoon xanthan gum

2 large eggs or ½ cup liquid egg
   substitute

1 tablespoon vegetable oil

In a medium-size bowl, combine the flours, cornstarch, salt, and xanthan gum. In a small bowl, beat the eggs lightly and add the oil. Pour the eggs into the dry ingredients and stir. (The consistency will be much like that of pastry dough.) Work the dough into a firm ball. Knead 1–2 minutes.

Place the ball of dough on a pastry board dusted with cornstarch and roll as thin as possible. One pasta book suggests you should be able to see the board through the dough. The dough is tough and, although almost transparent, will handle well. Slice the noodles into very thin strips, or if using for lasagne, into 1½" × 4" rectangles. The pasta is now ready to be cooked or frozen, uncooked, for later use.

Cook the pasta in salted boiling water to which 1 tablespoon of oil has been added, for 10–20 minutes, depending on the thickness and size of the pieces. You will have to test for doneness. *Makes 3 servings as noodles alone, 5–6 servings in a casserole.*

*Nutrients per serving: Calories 110, Fat 4g, Cholesterol 70mg,
Sodium 210mg, Carbohydrates 16g, Protein 2g, Fiber 1g.*

*F*reeze uncooked homemade pasta to have on hand for quick meals.

Bean Flour Pasta

Since creating this pasta, I have used no other for my homemade noodles and lasagne strips. It is so easy to roll out, cut, and cook. And the faintly nutty flavor is an added bonus. I prefer the liquid egg substitute in this recipe, not only to cut cholesterol but to make easier rolling.

1 cup Light Bean Flour Mix
2 teaspoons xanthan gum
½ teaspoons salt
1 tablespoon vegetable or olive oil

½ cup liquid egg substitute or
   2 eggs
Cornstarch for kneading

In a medium bowl, combine the flour mix, xanthan gum, and salt. In a small bowl, whisk together the oil and egg substitute. Pour into the dry ingredients and stir until a ball forms. Knead 1–2 minutes, adding more cornstarch if necessary. Work it in until the dough will not accept any more and is firm and dry enough to roll.

Place the ball on a cutting board dusted with rice flour and roll as thin as possible. It should be stretchy and elastic but roll out very thin and handle easily. Slice into very narrow strips for spaghetti, wider ones for noodles or fettuccine. If using for lasagne, cut into 1½" × 5" or 6" rectangles. The pasta is ready to cook immediately or to freeze uncooked, for later use.

If you have a hand-crank machine (Atlas or other make), the dough can be flattened and cut with that.

To cook, drop into boiling salted water to which a few drops of vegetable oil have been added. The cooking will take 5–7 minutes, depending on whether it is to be used for a casserole (cooked al dente) or eaten with cheese or sauce. You will have to test for doneness. *Makes 3–4 servings of fettuccine, enough for Quick Lasagne (page 105), or 5–6 servings in a casserole.*

Nutrients per serving: Calories 130, Fat 4g, Cholesterol 70mg, Sodium 200mg, Carbohydrates 20g, Protein 4g, Fiber 0g.

Chicken and Noodles

Nothing spells comfort *more than the words* chicken *and* noodles. *In my prediagnosis days I longed for this dish even though it made me ill. Now I can use rice, potato, or bean flour noodles and eat it whenever I please.*

One batch of noodles (page 93 or 94) or 4 cups dry purchased GF noodles or twists

One recipe Cream of Mushroom Soup (page 277), thinned with ½ cup milk and seasoned with salt if necessary

½ cup plain yogurt

1 cup milk or nondairy substitute

1 cup frozen peas, thawed

¼ cup grated Parmesan cheese, divided

2 cups diced cooked chicken

Preheat oven to 425°. Lightly grease a 9" × 12" baking dish.

Cook the noodles according to directions. Drain well.

While the noodles are cooking, prepare the soup. Stir in the yogurt and milk until smooth. Add the peas and half of the cheese.

Put the drained noodles in the prepared pan; add the chicken. Gently fold in the sauce until all is moist. Top with the other half of the cheese and bake about 15 minutes or until heated through. *Makes 6 servings.*

Nutrients per serving: Calories 640, Fat 14g, Cholesterol 75mg, Sodium 420mg, Carbohydrates 102g, Protein 25g, Fiber 2g.

---

*T*he term *al dente* is used to describe cooked pasta with a slightly chewy texture. It's Italian for "to the tooth," meaning it should be, by the touch of your tooth, not too soft nor too hard, but just right.

Macaroni and Cheese Casserole
375°

Have you missed this old favorite? If so, try my version. It's a tasty, melt-in-your-mouth dish that gives no hint of its gluten-free status. This recipe can be halved to serve 4.

12 ounces GF elbow macaroni
4 tablespoons butter or
  margarine, divided
½ cup chopped onion
4 cups milk or nondairy
  substitute, divided
⅓ cup GF Mix
¼ teaspoon dried thyme

1 teaspoon salt
½ teaspoon ground pepper
1½ cups grated sharp cheddar
  cheese
½ cup grated Parmesan cheese
⅛ teaspoon nutmeg
1 cup GF bread crumbs

Preheat oven to 375°. Butter a 9" × 13" baking dish.

Cook the pasta according to directions.

Meanwhile, melt 3 tablespoons butter in a 2-quart saucepan over medium heat. Add the onion and cook until translucent. Blend ½ cup of the milk with the flour mix and add to the onion. Then whisk in the remaining milk, thyme, salt, and pepper. Cook about 10–12 minutes or until slightly thickened. Stir in the cheeses and nutmeg until the cheeses melt.

Drain pasta and pour into the baking dish. Pour on the hot cheese sauce and mix. Melt the remaining 1 tablespoon butter in a small microwaveable bowl; stir in the crumbs and sprinkle over the top of the casserole. Bake for 35 minutes or until the cheese sauce is bubbly. *Makes 8 servings.*

Nutrients per serving: Calories 510, Fat 18g, Cholesterol 60mg, Sodium 730mg, Carbohydrates 70g, Protein 15g, Fiber 1g.

Microwave Macaroni and Cheese

In this modern version of an old favorite, you need to allow time (from 4 hours to overnight) for the uncooked macaroni to soften and the flavors to blend. Then it's only 15 minutes or so to prepare the dish for serving. If, however, you'd rather make and cook it immediately, see the longer cooking time in the directions.

Note: *Rice pasta does not work in this dish. Use one of the combinations: rice, corn, potato, or soy.*

3 tablespoons margarine or butter	2 cups grated cheddar cheese
2 tablespoons GF mix	(about ½ pound)
1 teaspoon dry mustard	2 cups GF elbow macaroni
1 teaspoon salt	(6 ounces)
½ teaspoon pepper	½ cup dried GF bread crumbs
3 cups milk or nondairy substitute	½ teaspoon paprika

Place 2 tablespoons of the butter in a microwave-safe, 2-quart baking dish. Cook on high for 1 minute until melted. Blend in the flour mix, mustard, salt, and pepper until smooth. Slowly whisk in the milk. Cook on high 7–9 minutes, stirring about every 2½ minutes, until the mixture thickens slightly. Add 1½ cups of the cheese and stir until melted. Stir in the macaroni. Cool slightly. Cover and refrigerate from 4 hours to overnight.

In a small microwave-safe bowl, toss the bread crumbs and paprika. Add the remaining 1 tablespoon butter and cook on high 1½ –2 minutes, stirring once, until lightly toasted.

About 15 minutes before serving, place the covered dish in the microwave. Cook on high 5 minutes; stir. Change power to medium and cook, covered, 8–10 minutes more until the dish is hot and the macaroni is tender (30–35 minutes if not set 4 hours or overnight). Uncover, sprinkle remaining ½ cup of cheese over the macaroni. Top with toasted bread crumbs. Cook on high 2 minutes, until cheese melts. *Makes 4 servings.*

Nutrients per serving: Calories 620, Fat 26g, Cholesterol 60mg, Sodium 140mg, Carbohydrates 74g, Protein 22g, Fiber 1g.

Bean Flour Noodle Bake

350°

A tasty main dish that's so simple and easy, it can replace rice or potatoes as an accompaniment to meats that have no gravy such as ham, meat loaf, fish, or baked chicken.

One recipe Bean Flour Pasta
   noodles (page 94), cooked
6 green onions, sliced thin
6 slices bacon, microwaved crisp
2 cups cottage cheese

1 cup fat-free sour cream
Additional milk to cover noodles
¼ cup Parmesan or Romano
   cheese, shredded

Preheat oven to 350°. Butter a 2½-quart casserole with cover.

Place cooked noodles in the casserole and stir in the green onions, bacon (cut into little bits), cottage cheese, and sour cream. Stir well. If the liquids don't cover the noodles, add enough milk to cover (2–4 tablespoons). Top with the shredded cheese and bake for 35–40 minutes until the liquids bubble. *Makes 6 servings.*

*Nutrients per serving: Calories 290, Fat 10g, Cholesterol 85mg,
Sodium 720mg, Carbohydrates 27g, Protein 21g, Fiber 0g.*

---

*W*hen cooking pasta, always add salt and oil to the water before dropping in the pasta to keep it from sticking together.

Baked Penne with Beef and Red Sauce 350°

This dish resembles the quick and easy Hamburger Helper of prediagnosis days but has a fuller, richer flavor. The preparation time is short and the baking time only about 25 minutes.

2 cups GF penne or macaroni
½ pound lean ground beef
One 28-ounce jar pasta sauce
½ cup water
One 5.5-ounce can V8 juice
One 4.5-ounce can sliced
  mushrooms

1 teaspoon dried basil
½ teaspoon dried oregano
1–2 teaspoons sugar (or to taste)
½ cup shredded fresh Parmesan
  cheese

Preheat oven to 350°. Grease a 2-quart casserole.

Cook the pasta to slightly less than done. Drain and set aside.

In a large skillet, brown the ground beef and cook until browned. Add the pasta sauce, rinsing the jar with the ½ cup of water to add to the sauce. Add the V8 juice and the mushrooms, drained. Stir in the basil, oregano, and sugar. Mix well and bring to a boil. Remove from heat and stir in the pasta.

Spoon into the prepared casserole and bake, covered, for 15 minutes. Uncover; top with the cheese and bake for another 5–10 minutes until the casserole bubbles and the cheese is melted. *Makes 5–6 servings.*

Nutrients per serving: Calories 540, Fat 15g, Cholesterol 60mg, Sodium 1,350mg, Carbohydrates 81g, Protein 19g, Fiber 3g.

Favorite Family Casserole 350°

This noodle dish is easy to make and has the taste that most spaghetti lovers enjoy—lasagne and spaghetti and meat. Best of all, it can be combined up to 24 hours ahead, refrigerated, and baked just 30 minutes before surving. Increase the time 10 minutes if taken directly from the refrigerator.

1 pound ground beef	One package (3 ounces) cream
2 cups spaghetti sauce	cheese
4 cups GF dry noodles	1 cup sour cream
5 green onions sliced thin	¾ cup shredded cheddar cheese

In a skillet, cook the ground beef until browned. Stir in the spaghetti sauce, cover and simmer 15 minutes.

Meanwhile cook the noodles according to package directions. Drain and place them in a 2½ quart baking dish that has been greased. Top with the meat.

Blend together the cream cheese, sour cream, and green onions. Spread over the meat and sprinkle with the cheese. Bake in a preheated 350° oven for 30 minutes. *Makes 8 servings.*

Nutrients per serving: Calories 326, Fat 18g, Cholesterol 73mg, Sodium 599mg, Carbohydrates 25g, Protein 18g, Fiber 2g.

Corn and Noodle Casserole

This creamy and flavorful dish needs only a salad to make a meal—and it's easy to put together. I usually prepare it with spiral noodles and cook them al dente, for they will continue cooking in the casserole.

2 cups GF pasta, cooked
One 15-ounce can creamed corn
¼ cup milk or nondairy liquid
1 egg, beaten
1 cup grated medium cheddar
  cheese

2 green onions, thinly sliced
4 teaspoons bacon bits (or to
  taste)
1 tablespoon butter or margarine

Preheat oven to 350°. Spray a 2-quart casserole with vegetable oil.

Place pasta in the casserole and add the creamed corn, milk, egg, cheese, onions, and bacon bits. Stir gently. Dot the butter on top and bake for 30–40 minutes. *Makes 4–5 servings.*

Nutrients per serving: Calories 320, Fat 17g, Cholesterol 145mg, Sodium 530mg, Carbohydrates 33g, Protein 12g, Fiber 2g.

Ham and Cheese Casserole

A simple, flavorful casserole that can use up leftover ham. I tried some of the lower-cholesterol turkey ham in my test casserole and found it excellent.

2 tablespoons butter or margarine
½ cup chopped onion
½ cup chopped green pepper
One recipe Cream of Mushroom
   Soup (page 277)
½ cup milk or nondairy substitute

1 cup sour cream
One recipe GF noodles (either
   page 93 or 94) or 3½ cups
   purchased noodles
2 cups shredded Swiss cheese
2 cups cubed cooked ham

Preheat oven to 350°. Butter a 2½ -quart casserole.

In a frying pan, melt the butter; sauté the onion and green pepper. Remove from heat. Stir in the prepared soup, milk, and sour cream.

In the casserole layer the ingredients in 3 layers by starting with one-third noodles, one-third cheese, one-third ham, and half of the soup mixture. Repeat, ending with the final layer of noodles, cheese, and ham. Bake 35–40 minutes or until bubbling. *Makes 6 servings.*

Nutrients per serving: Calories 600, Fat 29g, Cholesterol 100mg,
Sodium 1,290mg, Carbohydrates 44g, Protein 42g, Fiber 1g.

Macaroni and Sausage

A quick and filling macaroni bake. The combination of either turkey or pork sausage with cheese and eggs should appeal to almost every taste. I use turkey sausage and liquid egg substitute to lower the cholesterol content. For turkey sausage, see page 289.

1 cup GF macaroni
1 pound turkey or pork sausage
½ cup chopped onion
½ cup sliced celery
One recipe Creamed Soup Base
   (page 277)

⅔ cup milk or nondairy substitute
1½ cups grated sharp cheddar
   cheese
3 eggs, beaten, or ¾ cup liquid
   egg substitute

Preheat oven to 350°. Grease a 2-quart casserole.

Cook the macaroni according to package directions. Drain. Put in a large bowl.

Brown the sausage. Drain. Add to the macaroni. Add the onion and celery.

Prepare the soup base according to directions; blend in the milk. Add the soup mixture to the bowl. Add the cheese and let it melt in. Pour the eggs over the mixture in the bowl. Mix well. Spoon into the prepared casserole and bake for 40–45 minutes. *Makes 4–5 servings.*

Nutrients per serving of the turkey, sausage, and egg substitute: Calories 520, Fat 15g, Cholesterol 45mg, Sodium 900mg, Carbohydrates 35g, Protein 12g, Fiber 1g.

Seafood Casserole 350°

A flavorful main dish from a couple of cups of GF pasta and canned seafood. This is one of my favorite pasta casseroles.

2 cups dry pasta (spirals or noodles) or one recipe Bean Flour Pasta (page 94)
One recipe Shrimp Soup or Sauce (page 278) but don't add shrimp
½ cup dry sherry
½ cup mayonnaise
½ cup milk or nondairy liquid

½ teaspoon dried dill weed (optional)
1 cup diced celery
4–5 green onions, sliced thin
Two 4-ounce cans seafood (shrimp, crab, tuna, or salmon)
1½ cups potato chips, crushed, or ½ cup sliced almonds

Preheat oven to 350°. Grease a 2½-quart casserole.

Cook pasta according to directions and drain.

Make up the shrimp sauce and add the sherry, mayonnaise, milk, and dill weed (if used). Gently toss the celery, green onions, and seafood with the pasta. Blend in the sauce and spoon into the prepared casserole. If the sauce doesn't cover the ingredients, add extra milk or nondairy liquid. Bake 45 minutes. Top with the crushed potato chips before serving. *Makes 6 servings.*

Nutrients per serving: Calories 280, Fat 19g, Cholesterol 75mg, Sodium 220mg, Carbohydrates 8g, Protein 10g, Fiber 1g.

VARIATION:

CHEESE SEAFOOD CASSEROLE: Replace the celery with 1 cup grated Swiss cheese.

Lazy Cook's Lasagne 325°

If you're in too much of a hurry for all that layering, try this fast recipe. It still has all the flavor of the meticulously layered dish.

One recipe Bean Flour Pasta
    (page 94) or 4 cups purchased
    GF noodles
½ cup pasta cooking water
1 pound lean ground beef
1 medium onion, chopped
1 teaspoon chopped garlic
One 15-ounce jar spaghetti sauce

½ teaspoon salt (as needed)
1 cup country-style cottage cheese
½ teaspoon dried basil
½ teaspoon dried oregano
2 tablespoons grated Parmesan
    cheese
2 tablespoons liquid egg substitute
⅔ cup grated mixed pizza cheese

Preheat oven to 325°. Grease a 9" × 13" baking pan.

Cook the noodles according to directions. Drain and save ½ cup of the cooking water.

While the noodles are cooking, sauté the beef, onion, and garlic in a frying pan lightly sprayed with vegetable spray. Be sure the beef shows no pink and the onions are translucent. Add the sauce and cooking water. Simmer 5 minutes. Taste and add the salt as needed.

While the sauce is cooking, combine the cottage cheese, basil, oregano, Parmesan cheese, and egg substitute.

Spread a thin layer of the meat sauce over the bottom of the pan; spoon in all the noodles. Spoon the cottage cheese mixture over the noodles and pour the rest of the sauce over that. Sprinkle the top with the mixed pizza cheese.

Bake 25 minutes. Cool 5 minutes before serving. *Makes 6 servings.*

*Nutrients per serving: Calories 480, Fat 21g, Cholesterol 155mg,
Sodium 970mg, Carbohydrates 38g, Protein 34g, Fiber 2g.*

Quick Lasagne

Not only is this tasty main dish easy to put together, but it can be almost cholesterol-free. With no precooking of the pasta, the recipe can be prepared in minutes. Even if you make your own pasta, it is still easy. Because you use a sausage made from chicken breast, liquid egg, and tofu, the meat can be kept to a minimum. Or see below for the vegetarian version. (To make your own chicken or turkey sausage, see page 289.)

One recipe Bean Flour Pasta (page 94), cut into lasagne strips, or 10 ounces GF lasagne, uncooked

8 ounces chicken sausage, browned, in bits

1 pound firm tofu, drained, or 16 ounces ricotta or cottage cheese

1½ cups shredded mozzarella cheese

¼ cup liquid egg substitute or 1 egg

5 ounces (½ box) frozen chopped spinach, thawed and drained

1 teaspoon salt

¾ teaspoon dried oregano

⅛ teaspoon pepper

One 28-ounce jar spaghetti sauce

1 cup water

Preheat oven to 350°. Spray a 9" × 13" pan with vegetable oil spray.

In a large mixing bowl, combine the cooked sausage, tofu (broken into bits), 1 cup of the mozzarella cheese, egg substitute, spinach, salt, oregano, and pepper.

Begin layering with ¾ cup spaghetti sauce, one-third of the lasagne strips, and half of the mixture in the bowl. Repeat the layers. Top with remaining lasagne strips and remaining sauce. Sprinkle on the remaining mozzarella cheese. Pour the water around the edges.

Bake for 1¾ hours or until bubbly. Let stand for 15 minutes before serving. *Makes 12 servings.*

Nutrients per serving: Calories 330, Fat 18g, Cholesterol 85mg, Sodium 910mg, Carbohydrates 25g, Protein 19g, Fiber 2g.

VARIATION:

VEGETARIAN LASAGNE: Eliminate the chicken sausage and use one 10-ounce box of spinach.

Salads

SEE ALSO

At delis and when eating out, the basic ingredients for most of the salads are safe for celiacs but we find trouble with the dressings. Either the server or attendant at the counter doesn't know (or care) or somewhere in the list of ingredients is one of the toxic glutens. It's different with pasta salads; just say the word pasta and we know we can't have those.

Although salad bars can be carefully navigated while out, the dressings still have to be questioned. Thus, most complicated mixed salads for celiacs must be made at home, and so far, all pasta ones.

In the following pages, I've given a wide variety of salads and dressings. Here, any cook can find salads to please her crowd. I've included pastas now that we can buy many good ones made from rice or corn mixes. Not all hold up well but pastas are getting better every year and a celiac should find one in the nearest health food store or by mail order that will satisfy her taste. And, although we may think we are tired of rice, I've included several salads here with wonderful ingredients and tasty dressings that give the rice new flavor.

Macaroni Salad with Ham and Peas

A full-meal salad with pasta, meat, and vegetables. This has a light and bright flavor due to the simple oil-and-vinegar dressing.

SALAD:
- 3–4 cups GF elbow macaroni
- ¾ cup cooked ham, cut into ⅓" cubes
- ¾ cup chopped celery
- 4–5 green onions, sliced thin
- ¾ cup frozen peas, thawed
- 1 red bell pepper, chopped

DRESSING:
- 2½ tablespoons garlic-flavored wine vinegar
- 1½ tablespoons lemon juice
- 1½ tablespoons honey mustard
- ⅓ cup olive oil
- ½ teaspoon sugar (optional)

Cook the macaroni according to package directions but test before the cooking time is up so it can be drained while still al dente. Rinse with cold water to stop the cooking.

Place the cooked pasta in a large bowl. Add the ham, celery, onions, peas, and bell pepper.

Place vinegar, lemon juice, mustard, and oil in a small jar. Screw on the cover and shake well. Taste and add sugar if desired. Shake again. Pour the dressing over the salad and toss well. Refrigerate for 1 hour or more before serving. *Makes 8–10 servings.*

Nutrients per serving: Calories 310, Fat 8g, Cholesterol 5mg, Sodium 200mg, Carbohydrates 56g, Protein 4g, Fiber 1g.

Shrimp Pasta Salad

This is a favorite hot-weather salad from my childhood. I used to eat the shrimp and celery and leave the pasta, never realizing I was unconsciously avoiding the pasta that would cause stomach distress. Now, with a variety of GF pastas on the market, I eat the whole thing.

SALAD:
2 cups cooked GF elbow or
   short-cut macaroni
½ pound (1½ cups) cooked
   shrimp
1 cup diced celery

¼ cup chopped onion
Salt or celery salt to taste

DRESSING:
⅓ cup mayonnaise
⅓ cup ketchup

Gently blend the salad ingredients, trying not to break the fragile pasta. Mix the mayonnaise and ketchup and blend into the salad. To reduce the fat, thin the dressing with nonfat milk or a milk substitute. Chill for several hours or overnight to allow the flavors to meld. *Makes 4 servings.*

Nutrients per serving: Calories 400, Fat 16g, Cholesterol 90mg, Sodium 660mg, Carbohydrates 54g, Protein 12g, Fiber 1g.

Crab Salad

This quick and tasty salad makes a whole luncheon meal. Double the ingredients to serve it as a buffet salad. When it's used as a plate salad, place it on chopped lettuce; for the buffet table, put it into a bowl lined with lettuce leaves.

1 cup chopped imitation
    crabmeat (or fresh crab,
    cooked)
¼ cup finely sliced green onions
¼ cup sliced celery
⅛ teaspoon garlic salt
Pepper to taste
½ cup country cottage cheese
    (low-fat okay)

½ cup low-fat sour cream
1 teaspoon prepared mustard
Lettuce (chopped for base or
    leaves for bowl)
Olives, pickles, or tomato
    sections for garnish as
    desired

In a medium bowl, combine the crabmeat, onions, celery, garlic salt, and pepper. In a small bowl, stir together the cottage cheese, sour cream, and mustard. Blend them carefully into the salad.

On each plate, place a handful of lettuce and spoon the salad onto it. Garnish with olives, pickles, or tomato sections. *Makes 2–3 servings.*

Nutrients per serving: Calories 180, Fat 2g, Cholesterol 20mg, Sodium 1,040mg, Carbohydrates 20g, Protein 21g, Fiber 1g.

Hawaiian Salad

A filling salad for hot days. This can be a luncheon salad, but I often serve it as a main dish on those days when it's too hot to cook. Add a muffin or slices of toast on the side.

One 5½-ounce can pineapple
  tidbits
One 12.5-ounce can chunk
  chicken or 1½ cups cooked
  chicken or turkey
2 ribs celery, sliced thin

½ cup coconut
½–⅔ cup seedless red grapes,
  halved
½ cup mayonnaise
Chopped lettuce

Drain the pineapple and reserve the juice. In a bowl, blend the pineapple, chicken, celery, coconut, and grapes. Thin the mayonnaise to the consistency of cream with some of the reserved juice. Mix into the salad. Chill. Serve on a bed of chopped lettuce. *Makes 4 servings.*

*Nutrients per serving: Calories 255, Fat 10g, Cholesterol 5mg,
Sodium 107mg, Carbohydrates 24g, Protein 2g, Fiber 2g.*

VARIATION:

In place of the mayonnaise mixed with pineapple juice, use ⅓ cup yogurt plus a dash of lemon or pineapple juice.

Chicken Salad with Curry Dressing

A tasty treat for lunch or dinner on those days when you don't want to heat up the kitchen.

SALAD:

1½ cups cooked chicken, cut into
   bite-sized pieces
1 orange, peeled and cut into
   ½" squares, or 1 can mandarin
   oranges, cut into sections
½ cup coarsely chopped
   walnuts
1 cup sliced celery
2 tablespoons minced onions
1 cup chopped lettuce

DRESSING:

¼ cup mayonnaise
¼ cup plain yogurt
2 tablespoons orange juice
1 teaspoon sugar
½ teaspoon curry powder
   (or to taste)

In a large mixing bowl, combine the chicken, orange, walnuts, celery, and onion.

In a small bowl, combine the dressing ingredients. Pour over the salad in the large bowl and gently combine. Serve on a plate covered with about 1 cup of the chopped lettuce. *Makes 4 servings.*

Nutrients per serving: Calories 310, Fat 23g, Cholesterol 55mg, Sodium 170mg, Carbohydrates 10g, Protein 1g, Fiber 4g.

Chicken Rice Salad

A filling luncheon or supper main dish served cold for those hot days. It's also a good choice for a picnic or potluck dinner.

SALAD:
4 cups chicken stock
1 cup uncooked wild rice
1 cup uncooked brown rice
4 cups cooked chicken, cubed
3 green onions, thinly sliced
½ cup celery, sliced
1 cup coarsely chopped pecans
1 cup golden raisins

VINAIGRETTE:
¼ cup orange juice
¼ cup vinegar (apple cider or wine)
¼ cup vegetable oil
2 teaspoons prepared mustard
1 tablespoon sugar

In a large kettle or saucepan, bring the chicken stock to a boil. Add the wild rice; bring back to a boil, lower heat, and simmer for 15 minutes. Put in the brown rice and bring back to a boil; stir, lower heat, and simmer 45 minutes longer. The liquid should be absorbed and the rice tender. Cool to room temperature.

In a large bowl, combine the cooked rice, chicken, green onions, celery, pecans, and raisins.

In a glass jar, combine the orange juice, vinegar, and oil; stir in the mustard and sugar. Shake thoroughly to blend before stirring gently into the salad. Refrigerate for at least 4 hours; overnight is better. *Makes 8–10 servings.*

Nutrients per serving: Calories 380, Fat 19g, Cholesterol 50mg, Sodium 105mg, Carbohydrates 32g, Protein 21g, Fiber 2g.

VARIATION:

Use 4 cups of one of the "exotic" grains (pages 21–27), cooked according to package directions.

Chicken Pasta Salad

With the new GF pastas on the market, we can now find just the right shape for our pasta salads. You can use the small shells, short elbow macaroni, or even the rice orzo for this one.

1½ cups uncooked pasta
1½ cups cooked chicken, diced
5 green onions, sliced thin

½ cup diced celery
2 tablespoons black olives, sliced

Cook the pasta according to package directions and cool.

Gently mix the chicken, onions, celery, and olives into the cold pasta and add the Hint-of-Orange dressing found on page 288 until you feel the salad is moist enough. (You may not need the full recipe of dressing.) *Makes 4–5 servings.*

Nutrients per serving: Calories 200, Fat 9g, Cholesterol 110mg, Sodium 290mg, Carbohydrates 17g, Protein 14g, Fiber 1g.

VARIATION:

As a substitute for the orange-flavored dressing, thin ⅓ cup mayonnaise with milk or milk substitute.

> *T*o cool cooked food such as boiled potatoes for salad, spread them out on a clean dish towel.

Chicken Waldorf Salad

A salad that's sure to please with its wonderful mix of textures. Use it as a main meal for lunch, with muffins or toast and a dish of fruit for dessert.

SALAD:

2 cups cooked chicken, diced

2 apples, cored and diced

1 cup sliced celery

⅔ cup chopped walnuts

½ head of lettuce, chopped

DRESSING:

⅓ cup mayonnaise

⅓ cup plain yogurt

1 tablespoon honey (or to taste)

In a large bowl, mix the chicken, apples, celery, and walnuts. Combine the dressing ingredients and tumble with the ingredients in the bowl.* Gently toss with the lettuce. Serve from a large salad bowl or divide among 4 plates. *Makes 4 servings.*

Nutrients per serving: Calories 610, Fat 31g, Cholesterol 65mg, Sodium 270mg, Carbohydrates 66g, Protein 27g, Fiber 14g.

VARIATION:

VEGETARIAN WALDORF SALAD: Omit the chicken but follow the directions above.

*If you don't want to serve the salad immediately, you can refrigerate it at this point and finish it later.

Simple Summer Aspic

We don't have many hot days in a western Washington summer, but when the temperature soars, this is the salad I crave. I keep one in the refrigerator whenever we have our so-called hot spells.

Two 6-ounce cans V8 juice
 (spicy or plain)
One 3-ounce package lemon
 gelatin
4–5 ice cubes

1 cup finely chopped celery
1–2 tablespoons grated or finely
 chopped onion
Dab of mayonnaise for topping
 (optional)

Spray a 1-quart salad mold with vegetable-oil spray.

In a small saucepan, heat the V8 juice to simmering.

Place the gelatin in a medium bowl and slowly stir the hot juice into it until the gelatin is completely dissolved. Add the ice cubes and stir until they are dissolved. Place in the refrigerator and chill until partially set. Fold in the celery and onion and pour into the prepared mold. To serve, either unmold or cut into bars in the pan and serve on a lettuce leaf; top with a dab of mayonnaise (if used). *Makes 4–5 servings.*

Nutrients per serving: Calories 35, Fat 0g, Cholesterol 0mg, Sodium 310mg, Carbohydrates 7g, Protein 1g, Fiber 1g.

Country Apple Coleslaw

This is a wonderfully crisp salad recipe to go with the pasta dishes in this book. The recipe was sent to me by one of my testers. It has an unusual reversal of preparation by making the dressing in the microwave and then tossing in the salad ingredients and chilling before serving.

DRESSING:

¼ cup vinegar (red wine or apple cider)

3 tablespoons brown sugar

¼ teaspoon salt

SALAD:

One 10-ounce package coleslaw

2 cups chopped apples, unpeeled

½ cup raisins

In a microwaveable salad bowl, combine the dressing ingredients and microwave on High for 1 minute.

Add the salad ingredients and toss well to coat. Chill or serve at room temperature. *Makes 6–8 servings.*

Nutrients per serving: Calories 100, Fat 1g, Cholesterol 5mg,
Sodium 80mg, Carbohydrates 23g, Protein 1g, Fiber 3g.

Vegetarian Rice Salad

Make this salad with half wild rice and half brown or any kind of grain you prefer. It's good all ways with its sharp, orangey vinaigrette dressing.

SALAD:
2 cups uncooked rice (brown and
    wild or all brown), cooked as
    package suggests and cooled
⅔ cup golden raisins
⅔ cup seedless grapes, halved
⅔ cup diced celery
3 green onions, thinly sliced
⅔ cup chopped walnuts (toasted)
Salt and pepper to taste

VINAIGRETTE:
¼ cup orange juice
¼ cup rice vinegar
2 teaspoons prepared mustard
¼ cup vegetable oil
1 tablespoon sugar

Place cooked and cooled rice in large mixing bowl. Add the raisins, grapes, celery, green onions, and walnuts. Tumble gently to mix. Season with salt and pepper.

Combine the orange juice, vinegar, mustard, oil, and sugar. Mix well and blend into the salad. Refrigerate for at least 4 hours; overnight is better. *Makes 5 servings.*

Nutrients per serving: Calories 440, Fat 8g, Cholesterol 0mg, Sodium 60mg, Carbohydrates 78g, Protein 10g, Fiber 6g.

Reunion Salad

There was a time when every reunion table held several molded salads. Sadly, they lost favor since few cooks varied their fruit-and-Jell-O contents. This one has enough crunch and chew to regain that old appeal. Try it for your next family reunion.

One 20-ounce can crushed
  pineapple
2 tablespoons sugar
One 3-ounce package apricot
  gelatin
One 8-ounce package cream
  cheese, softened and cut into
  cubes

1 medium apple, peeled, cored,
  and chopped
½ cup chopped walnuts
1¼ cups nondairy whipped
  topping

Pour the pineapple, including the juice, into a medium saucepan and add the sugar. Heat to boiling. Stir in the gelatin until dissolved; add the cream cheese. Stir until melted. Remove from heat and pour into a large bowl. Chill until mixture is slightly thickened (about 1 hour).

Stir in the chopped apple and nuts. Fold in the topping. Pour into a ring mold and chill for at least 4 hours to overnight. Unmold but keep chilled until serving. *Makes 9–12 servings.*

Nutrients per serving: Calories 232, Fat 14g, Cholesterol 25mg, Sodium 93mg, Carbohydrates 24g, Protein 3g, Fiber 1g.

Crunchy Broccoli Salad

A wonderfully crisp and crunchy salad to take to that potluck or family dinner. This pairs well with any meat, whether barbecued or baked. Make the large recipe as given here or cut down on ingredients to serve fewer people. The salad ingredients may be tossed the night before the party and the dressing added 1–2 hours before serving. This salad keeps well; it's just as tasty the second day.

SALAD:
2½ cups broccoli florets
½ pound bacon, microwaved
  crisp and crumbled
⅔ cup golden raisins
½ cup roasted sunflower seeds
¼ cup chopped red onion
½ cup coarsely chopped walnuts

DRESSING:
¾ cup mayonnaise
3–4 tablespoons nondairy
  creamer
3 tablespoons sugar
2 tablespoons white wine vinegar

In a large salad bowl, combine the salad ingredients, breaking up any large florets. Thin the mayonnaise with the nondairy creamer. Add the sugar and vinegar. If serving within several hours, toss the dressing with the salad. Allow to chill for 2 hours before serving. *Makes 10–12 servings if this is the only salad. Serves 16 at potlucks.*

Nutrients per serving: Calories 310, Fat 26g, Cholesterol 20mg, Sodium 420mg, Carbohydrates 14g, Protein 8g, Fiber 1g.

Cranberry Crunch Salad

A colorful and tasty molded salad for your holiday table. The cranberries add tang, while the apples and pecans furnish crunch.

1 envelope unflavored gelatin
1 cup cold water
¼ teaspoon salt
2 tablespoons sugar
½ cup mayonnaise
2 tablespoons lemon juice
1 teaspoon grated lemon peel

One 16-ounce can whole berry
  cranberry sauce
One 8-ounce can pineapple
  tidbits, drained
1 apple, peeled and diced
⅓ cup chopped pecans

Place the gelatin and water in a small saucepan and let stand for 1 minute until softened. Add the salt and sugar and stir over low heat until fully dissolved. Remove from heat and stir in the mayonnaise, lemon juice, and peel. Pour into a mixing bowl and chill until partially set (about 1 hour).

Meanwhile, combine the cranberry sauce, pineapple, apple, and pecans.

When the gelatin has partially set, beat it until fluffy and fold in the cranberry-fruit mixture. Pour into a 6-cup mold that has been coated with vegetable oil spray. Chill until firm (4 hours to overnight). *Makes 10–12 servings.*

Nutrients per serving: Calories 170, Fat 10g, Cholesterol 5mg, Sodium 105mg, Carbohydrates 21g, Protein 1g, Fiber 1g.

Christmas Jell-O Salad

This colorful and tasty salad pairs perfectly with that holiday bird or ham. And best of all, it can be made ahead to save time and energy on the holiday.

One 6-ounce package raspberry
  gelatin
1¾ cups boiling water
One 16-ounce can whole berry
  cranberry sauce

One 20-ounce can crushed
  pineapple
1–1½ cups Mock Crème Fraiche
  (see page 282)

Spray a large gelatin mold with vegetable oil spray.

Dissolve the gelatin in the hot water. Add the cranberry sauce and pineapple with juice. Spoon half of the mixture into the prepared mold. Refrigerate until firm, leaving the remaining mixture out.

Spoon on the Mock Crème Fraiche in a layer and add the rest of the gelatin mixture. Refrigerate until solid. Unmold onto lettuce leaves or a flat plate and decorate with sprigs of parsley or holly. *Makes 10 servings.*

*Nutrients per serving: Calories 100, Fat 0g, Cholesterol 0mg,
Sodium 30mg, Carbohydrates 25g, Protein 3g, Fiber 1g.*

Breakfast

SEE ALSO

When I was told about this gluten-free diet for life, my very first thought was "What will I eat for breakfast?"

At the time, almost every cold cereal in the grocery store contained gluten either in the base of wheat or in the flavoring of barley malt. And besides, I didn't really like cold cereal. My taste went to toast, pancakes, or French toast, but every GF bread felt and tasted like cardboard. Now we can have any of these made from bread that no one would guess is gluten-free, plus new coffee cakes and hot cereal made of flakes or grains of buckwheat or quinoa, and breakfast bars of millet. We can even have toast from wonderful breads made of rice or bean mixes with the addition of new flours like teff, millet, or quinoa. Now breakfast can be as varied as you desire and you may never have to want again.

Creamy Kasha (Buckwheat) Cereal

Many of us remember that steaming bowl of hot cereal that our mothers forced us to eat when the weather turned cold. No one will have to be forced to eat this wonderfully tasty cereal, which smells like chocolate while it's cooking.

⅔ cup water
⅓ cup milk or nondairy
   creamer
2 tablespoons kasha (buckwheat
   groats)
Dash of salt

1½ teaspoons brown sugar
   (more if desired)
1 tablespoon butter
¼ teaspoon cinnamon
2 tablespoons dried cranberries
   or raisins

In a small pan, bring the water and milk to a boil. Add the buckwheat, salt, sugar, butter, cinnamon, and dried fruit of choice. Keep the cereal at a gentle boil and stir frequently for 8–11 minutes or until desired consistency is achieved. Serve immediately with added cream. *Makes 1–2 servings.*

Nutrients per serving: Calories 120, Fat 7g, Cholesterol 20mg, Sodium 85mg, Carbohydrates 13g, Protein 3g, Fiber 1g.

Buckwheat Pancakes

A taste from my childhood! These pancakes made with part buckwheat flour with its slightly astringent flavor take me back to summer camping in the mountains and our annual vacations at a cottage at the beach.

¾ cup Featherlight Mix
½ cup buckwheat flour
2 tablespoons sugar
½ teaspoon baking soda
½ teaspoon salt
1½ teaspoons baking powder

2 cups buttermilk
3 tablespoons vegetable oil
2 eggs, separated
½ cup chopped slivered almonds
  (optional)
Oil for griddle

In a mixing bowl, whisk together the Featherlight mix, buckwheat flour, sugar, baking soda, salt, and baking powder. In another bowl, combine the buttermilk, vegetable oil, and egg yolks. Stir into the dry ingredients.

Beat the egg whites in a bowl until medium-firm peaks form. Fold the whites gently into the batter.

Preheat a griddle or skillet over medium-high heat. Lightly brush with oil for the first pancakes. Drop the batter from a spoon to form 4" circles. Sprinkle each top with about ½ tablespoon almonds (if used). Cook until the tops form small bubbles, then turn and cook until the other sides are golden. Repeat with the remaining batter and nuts (if used). If necessary, brush the griddle with oil for each batch. Maple syrup is a great topping for these pancakes. *Makes about eighteen 4˝ pancakes.*

*Nutrients per serving: Calories 80, Fat 3g, Cholesterol 25mg,
Sodium 700mg, Carbohydrates 10g, Protein 2g, Fiber 1g.*

Fake Swedish Pancakes

For a special morning treat on a holiday, bake these rich, light, silver-dollar-sized pancakes and don't count the calories. They taste more like crepes than pancakes for they use little flour.

4 eggs
2 cups sour cream (low-fat is okay)
¼ cup Four Flour Mix
3 tablespoons sugar

1 teaspoon vanilla
½ teaspoon baking soda
½ teaspoon salt
¼ cup oil
Oil or vegetable spray for griddle

In the bowl of your mixer, beat the eggs lightly. Add the sour cream, flour mix, sugar, vanilla, baking soda, salt, and oil. Beat until thoroughly combined.

Preheat a griddle or frying pan on medium-high heat, lightly greasing it if needed. Drop the batter by small spoonfuls to make 2½" pancakes. (The pancakes are soft and difficult to turn if made any larger.) When bubbles appear, turn them and cook until browned. Serve hot with syrup or jam. These freeze well, and any leftovers can be microwaved for another meal. *Makes 5–6 servings.*

Nutrients per serving: Calories 340, Fat 29g, Cholesterol 175mg, Sodium 370mg, Carbohydrates 14g, Protein 7g, Fiber 0g.

VARIATION:

BANANA-MACADAMIA PANCAKES: Add 1 mashed ripe banana and ½ cup chopped macadamia nuts to the batter before dropping on the griddle.

Amaranth or Quinoa Waffles

The addition of one of the "exotic" flours gives a new and improved flavor to my original crispy waffle.

1¾ cups Featherlight Mix	3 egg whites
¼ cup amaranth or quinoa flour	¼ cup vegetable oil
½ teaspoon salt	1½ cups milk or nondairy
4 teaspoons baking powder	substitute
1 tablespoon sugar	1 teaspoon vanilla
1 egg	

In a medium bowl, whisk together the flour mix, amaranth (or quinoa), flour, salt, baking powder, and sugar.

Break the eggs, placing the whites in a bowl suitable for beating. Place the egg yolk in a mixing bowl. Beat yolk together with the oil, milk, and vanilla. Stir in the dry ingredients until blended. Beat the egg whites until soft peaks form. Fold them gently into the batter. Don't overbeat.

Bake on a heated waffle iron. Serve hot, topped with syrup or fruit preserves. *Makes 6–8 six-inch waffles.*

Nutrients per serving: Calories 240, Fat 9g, Cholesterol 30mg, Sodium 410mg, Carbohydrates 34g, Protein 5g, Fiber 1g.

---

*B*ake things like waffles ahead of time and freeze them for everything from breakfast to dessert to a main dish at supper.

Gingerbread Waffles with Teff

The faint hint of ginger and the bran flavor of teff make these waffles superior. Serve them for breakfast with butter and syrup or use them as a dessert at lunch with whipped cream.

1½ cups Featherlight Mix
½ cup teff flour
1 teaspoon ginger
1 teaspoon baking soda
2 teaspoons baking powder
½ teaspoon salt

2 eggs
¼ cup sugar
1 cup buttermilk
⅓ cup molasses
⅓ cup oil

In a medium bowl, whisk together the flour mix, teff, ginger, baking soda, baking powder, and salt.

In the bowl of your mixer, beat the eggs until blended. Add the sugar, beating until creamy. Add the buttermilk, molasses, and oil. Beat until blended. Stir in the dry ingredients until smooth.

Cook in a waffle iron according to the manufacturer's directions. Serve hot. *Makes 8 waffles.*

*Nutrients per serving: Calories 300, Fat 11g, Cholesterol 55mg,
Sodium 440mg, Carbohydrates 46g, Protein 5g, Fiber 2g.*

Biscuits and Gravy

A high-calorie, high-fat comfort breakfast that is still irresistible to many southerners who grew up on it. Save this for a late-morning brunch that will fill the family and guests until dinner. Serve with fruit to complete the meal.

½ pound sliced bacon, diced
1 pound pork sausage
½ teaspoon oregano (or to taste)
Pinch of thyme

2 cups milk or nondairy substitute
3 tablespoons GF Mix
One recipe biscuits from Biscuit
  Mix (page 279)

In a large skillet, cook the bacon and sausage until well done. Drain some of the fat but leave enough to make good gravy. Add the spices and stir in 1½ cups milk. In a pint jar, shake the rest of it with the flour mix until smooth. Add to the pan and stir until the gravy is thickened and cooked. If too thick for your taste, thin with more milk, stirring constantly.

Cut the biscuits in half and pour the gravy over each half-biscuit. *Makes 4 servings.*

Nutrients per serving: Calories 560, Fat 45g, Cholesterol 105mg,
Sodium 1,620mg, Carbohydrates 8g, Protein 29g, Fiber 0g.

Biscuits and Gravy (Low-Fat)

Down South, this may be called Red Gravy but for those in other parts of the country, biscuits and gravy on a menu can mean meat-based rather than bacon. This adaptation, created by my son-in-law, will satisfy many heart patients who don't want to give up all of their old favorites when they go on a low-fat diet. Fruit makes a great addition to this breakfast.

4 slices bacon, diced
1 pound ground chicken
½ teaspoon oregano (or to taste)
Pinch of thyme

2 cups 1% milk (or more to taste)
3 tablespoons GF Mix
12 slices GF french bread, toasted

In a large skillet, cook the bacon and chicken until well done. Add the spices. Stir in 1½ cups of the milk. In a pint jar, shake the flour mix with the rest of the milk until smooth and add to the pan. Stir until the gravy is thickened and cooked. If too thick for your taste, thin with more milk, stirring constantly.

Serve the gravy over the toasted bread. *Makes 6 servings.*

*Nutrients per serving: Calories 290, Fat 7g, Cholesterol 45mg,
Sodium 330mg, Carbohydrates 34g, Protein 21g, Fiber 1g.*

Baked French Toast

This is an easy way to make just enough French toast for the celiac while others are feasting on their egg-bread dish with gluten.

4 slices GF bread, buttered
3 eggs or ¾ cup liquid egg
   substitute
2 teaspoons sugar

¼ teaspoon cinnamon
½ cup milk or nondairy
   substitute

Preheat oven to 375°. Butter an 8½" × 4½" loaf pan.

   Place the buttered bread, butter side up, in piles of two in the pan.

   Combine the eggs, sugar, cinnamon, and milk. Pour this mixture over the bread in the pan. Bake for 35–40 minutes. Serve hot with jam or syrup. *Makes 2 servings.*

*Nutrients per serving: Calories 290, Fat 13g, Cholesterol 250mg,
Sodium 300mg, Carbohydrates 24g, Protein 12g, Fiber 1g.*

Hot Cross Buns

No matter what the weather, the sure sign of Easter is the appearance of hot cross buns at the local bakery.

DRY INGREDIENTS:
1½ cups Featherlight Mix
½ cup teff flour
2 scant teaspoons xanthan gum
½ teaspoon salt
2 tablespoons Egg Replacer
¼ cup brown sugar
1 teaspoon cinnamon
½ teaspoon nutmeg
3 tablespoons almond meal or
   buttermilk powder

WET INGREDIENTS:
¾ cup (scant) warm water
1 teaspoon sugar
1 tablespoon dry yeast
2 eggs
2 tablespoons honey
¾ tablespoon dough enhancer
3 tablespoons margarine or
   butter, melted
½ cup raisins, dried cranberries,
   or citron (or a combination)

Grease an 8" or 9" square cake pan. Dust with rice flour.

In a medium bowl, whisk together the dry ingredients.

In the warm water, dissolve the sugar and add the yeast, stir, and let sit until the top foams about ½ inch (proofing).

In the bowl of your mixer, place the eggs, honey, dough enhancer, and melted margarine. Blend well. Add most of the yeast-water. Blend. With the mixer on low, spoon in the dry ingredients. The dough should be just thick enough to fall from the mixer in a smooth waterfall. If more water is needed, add only 1 tablespoon of the remaining yeast-water at a time until the desired texture is reached. Add the raisins.

Drop the dough in rounded spoonfuls in rows of three across and three down in the prepared pan. Cover and let rise about 25 minutes. Bake at 380° for approximately 22 minutes. If desired, for a finishing touch, combine ¼ cup powdered sugar with enough milk to make an icing that can be piped in the form of a cross on each bun when cooled. *Makes 9 buns.*

*Nutrients per bun: Calories 250, Fat 7g, Cholesterol 45mg,
Sodium 190mg, Carbohydrates 43g, Protein 5g, Fiber 3g.*

Swedish Coffee Cake

350°

This recipe will please those who prefer a cakelike coffee cake. It comes from a fellow celiac, who told me, "This was given to my mom by a neighbor when I was a little girl, and she frequently would make it as she was preparing dinner so we could enjoy it warm out of the oven after dinner. The original, of course, was made with wheat flour."

1½ cups Four Flour Mix	1 egg
1 teaspoon xanthan gum	3 tablespoons vegetable oil
1 cup sugar	2 teaspoons melted butter
2 teaspoons baking powder	Cinnamon and sugar sprinkled as
½ teaspoon salt	topping
1 cup milk or nondairy substitute	

Preheat oven to 350°. Grease a 9" × 9" pan.

In a mixing bowl, whisk together the flour mix, xanthan gum, sugar, baking powder, and salt.

In a 2-cup measuring cup, measure the 1 cup of milk, then break in the egg and oil. Stir well. Add to the dry ingredients and stir until well mixed. Spoon into the prepared pan and drizzle with melted butter. Sprinkle on cinnamon and sugar. Bake for 30 minutes. *Makes 8–9 servings.*

Nutrients per serving: Calories 240, Fat 7g, Cholesterol 30mg, Sodium 240mg, Carbohydrates 42g, Protein 3g, Fiber 1g.

Fruit Coffee Cake with Streusel 350°

Start the day with this fruit-flavored coffee cake with the chewy taste of yeast bread, topped with a streusel of almonds and brown sugar. To crush the almonds, place them in a plastic Ziploc bag and flatten with a rolling pin.

CAKE:

¾ cup finely cut dried fruit (cherries, apricots, prunes, raisins, etc.)

¾ cup water

⅔ cup fruit nectar (5½-ounce can)

⅓ cup vegetable oil

2 cups Featherlight Mix

1 teaspoon xanthan gum

½ cup granulated sugar

1 tablespoon yeast

1½ teaspoons baking powder

½ teaspoon cinnamon

¼ teaspoon salt

2 egg whites, beaten with a fork

STREUSEL:

¼ cup sliced almonds, crushed

¼ cup brown sugar

2 tablespoons butter or margarine, melted

Preheat oven to 350°. Grease an 8" × 10" oblong pan.

In a small saucepan, combine the cut fruit and water. Bring to a boil and remove from heat; add the nectar and oil. Let cool to lukewarm.

In a large mixing bowl, whisk together the flour mix, xanthan gum, sugar, yeast, baking powder, cinnamon, and salt. Add the cooled fruit mixture and the egg whites and stir until just combined. Spoon into the prepared pan and spread evenly.

In a small bowl, combine the crushed almond and brown sugar; add the butter and mix well. Sprinkle over the cake. Bake for 30–35 minutes. Serve warm. *Makes 12 servings.*

Nutrients per serving: Calories 231, Fat 8g, Cholesterol 5mg, Sodium 122mg, Carbohydrates 36g, Protein 4g, Fiber 1g.

Sour Cream Coffee Cake   350°

Make a simple cake that starts with a mix for a special breakfast treat. Baked in a fluted pan, this can be a beautiful centerpiece on the table. Be sure to grease the pan well or the cake will break, with only the top half coming out of the pan easily. Since cake mixes come in a couple of sizes, I have given 2 sets of measurements.

	FOR 12-OUNCE PACKAGE	FOR 18-OUNCE PACKAGE
Eggs	3	4
Sugar	⅓ cup	½ cup
Oil	½ cup	¾ cup
Sour cream	⅔ cup	1 cup
Chopped nuts	½ cup	¾ cup
Brown sugar	3 tablespoons	¼ cup
Cinnamon	2 teaspoons	1 tablespoon

Preheat oven to 350°. Grease a bundt pan well.

Beat the eggs until thick and fluffy. Add the sugar and oil. Beat again. Blend in the cake mix, sour cream, and nuts.

Spoon half the batter into the prepared pan. Combine the brown sugar and cinnamon. Sprinkle over the batter in the pan. Swirl lightly with a knife. Spoon on the remaining batter. Bake for 45–60 minutes or until done. Let stand 5 minutes.

Reverse onto a serving plate and serve warm or cold. *Makes 12–16 servings.*

Nutrients per serving: Calories 180, Fat 15g, Cholesterol 60mg,
Sodium 25mg, Carbohydrates 9g, Protein 3g, Fiber 0g.

Chicken and Meat

Of course we can have chicken and red meats grilled, roasted, or fried as long as we don't add anything but salt and pepper and approved seasonings. Pretty boring, aren't they? We may have to order this way when we eat out but never at home. Comfort foods have sauces, gravies, breadings—all those wonderful additions that make the meat more interesting, more palatable, and much more likely to have some gluten added.

In this chapter I've included recipes for meat dishes as good as those we remember from our prediagnosis days: meat loaves, pot roasts, and sirloin tips with gravy. Try any of them and think of home and Mother and cooking that titillated the palate and comforted the stomach.

Microwave Chicken and Dumplings

This old-fashioned favorite now cooks in less than an hour for a meal that once took half a day.

1 chicken, cut up
   (2½–3½ pounds)
2 cups hot water
½ cup chopped onion
½ cup chopped celery
4 medium carrots, sliced
2 teaspoons salt
½ teaspoon pepper
¼ cup cornstarch
½ cup cold water

PARSLEY DUMPLINGS:
1 cup Featherlight Mix
½ teaspoon xanthan gum
2 teaspoons Egg Replacer
2 teaspoons baking powder
1 teaspoon sugar
¼ teaspoon salt
2 teaspoons dried parsley flakes
1 rounded tablespoon buttermilk
   powder
1 egg, beaten
⅔ cup water

In a 3-quart microwaveable casserole, place the chicken, water, vegetables, and seasonings. Cover and microwave on medium for 15 minutes, rearranging chicken pieces after 8 minutes.

Stir the cornstarch and cold water together in a small bowl and stir into the casserole, blending well. Microwave on medium for 15–25 minutes until the chicken is tender.

Meanwhile, mix the dumpling batter in a small bowl by whisking together the flour mix, xanthan gum, Egg Replacer, baking powder, sugar, salt, parsley, and buttermilk powder. Beat the egg; add water and stir the liquid into the dry ingredients.

When the chicken is tender, spoon the dumplings around the edge of the casserole and microwave on medium for 5–6 minutes uncovered, rotating the dish ¼ turn after cooking 3 minutes. Cook until the dumplings are puffed and no longer doughy. *Makes 4–6 servings.*

Nutrients per serving: Calories 650, Fat 13g, Cholesterol 250mg, Sodium 1,370mg, Carbohydrates 47g, Protein 83g, Fiber 4g.

Turkey Loaf

350°

Usually, turkey or chicken tastes bland, but this loaf, spiced with ground ham and containing GF graham crackers, comes out moist and tasty. Use leftover ham or buy a small amount and grind it in a food processor if you don't have a meat grinder.

½ pound ground ham
1½ pounds ground turkey or
   chicken
⅔ cup crushed graham crackers
   (page 227)
⅓ cup milk or nondairy
   substitute
¼ cup minced onion
⅛ teaspoon pepper
2 eggs, lightly beaten

TOPPING:
½ cup ketchup
¼ cup brown sugar
2 tablespoons vinegar
⅓ teaspoon onion salt

Preheat oven to 350°.

In a large bowl, put in the ham, ground turkey, graham crackers, milk, onion, and pepper. Mix well. Add the eggs and mix again. Shape into one large 9" × 5" loaf pan or 2 smaller loaves in a 9" × 9" pan. Bake either for 1 hour. Drain off fat.

Meanwhile, combine the topping ingredients in a small bowl. Spoon over the hot meat when the 1 hour is up and return the loaf (or loaves) to the oven for 30 minutes (1 loaf) or 15 minutes (2 loaves). Let set for 5 minutes before cutting to serve. *Makes 8 servings.*

Nutrients per serving: Calories 260, Fat 9g, Cholesterol 104mg, Sodium 1,002mg, Carbohydrates 19g, Protein 31g, Fiber 1g.

Heavenly Chicken

A well-seasoned creamy chicken breast in gravy that's great with noodles, rice, or mashed potatoes. Put it in your electric hot pot and forget about it until it's time to serve.

6 boneless chicken breast
  halves
¼ cup butter or margarine
One 7-ounce package Italian
  salad dressing

One recipe mushroom soup from
  cream soup base (page 277)
½ cup dry white wine
4 ounces cream cheese (can use
  tub with chives and onion)

Wash the chicken and place it in an electric hot pot.

In a medium saucepan, melt the butter and stir in the rest of the ingredients until combined. Pour over the chicken. Turn electric cooker to low and cook for 4–5 hours.

Serve hot chicken and sauce over noodles, rice, or mashed potatoes. *Makes 6 servings.*

Nutrients per serving: Calories 405, Fat 17g, Cholesterol 110mg, Sodium 1,043mg, Carbohydrates 26g, Protein 32g, Fiber 1g.

Chicken in Sherry Sauce

This top-of-the-stove casserole is one of my favorite ways of preparing chicken breast for it makes it moist and flavorful—and the leftovers taste even better the next day. I usually serve mashed potatoes with this dish for the gravy is wonderful. To make it even better, I sometimes sauté extra mushrooms if I have any in my refrigerator and add them to the sauce.

6 chicken breast halves or thighs
Oil for frying

SAUCE:
One recipe Cream Soup Base,
   cooked (page 277)
One 4-ounce can mushrooms,
   undrained
½ cup golden sherry

In a large skillet, brown the chicken in a small amount of oil.

While the chicken is cooking, prepare the soup base. Add the undrained mushrooms and the sherry. Pour over the browned chicken to cover. Reduce heat and cook until the chicken is tender. *Makes 6 servings.*

*Nutrients per serving: Calories 215, Fat 18g, Cholesterol 72mg,
Sodium 59mg, Carbohydrates 2g, Protein 15g, Fiber 0g.*

Kona Chicken

Coconut, curry, and orange juice combine to give this baked chicken a crust you can't ignore. It smells fabulous when cooking and tastes as good as it smells.

One 6-ounce container frozen
    orange juice concentrate,
    thawed
1 beaten egg
1 cup dried GF bread crumbs
1 cup grated coconut

1 tablespoon curry powder
¼ teaspoon salt
1 cut-up fryer or 3 chicken
    breasts, halved
½ cup margarine or butter,
    melted

Preheat oven to 375°. Spray a shallow baking dish with vegetable oil cooking spray.

In a small bowl, combine the orange juice concentrate and egg. In a plastic bag, mix the bread crumbs, coconut, curry powder, and salt.

Dip the chicken into the orange juice mixture, then into the bread crumb mixture. Place in prepared baking dish. Drizzle the melted margarine over the top and bake for 45 minutes. Serve either with a rice dish or with the Easy Candied Sweet Potatoes (page 174). *Makes 6 servings.*

*Nutrients per serving: Calories 440, Fat 24g, Cholesterol 110mg,
Sodium 480mg, Carbohydrates 26g, Protein 30g, Fiber 2g.*

Maple-Flavored Chicken 325°

Chicken is one of America's favorite foods, and the breast is especially esteemed for its low fat content. But with most ways of cooking it, the breast ends up tasting like cardboard. Finally, we have a chicken breast that is moist and flavorful with a sauce to pour on the rice it's served with.

6 boneless chicken breast halves
Salt to taste
Pepper to taste
1 cup syrup, maple flavored
   (try Log Cabin)

½ cup fruit or white vinegar
½ cup ketchup
¼ cup brown sugar

Cooked rice, to serve

Preheat oven to 325°. Line a 9" × 13" pan with foil and grease.

Season the chicken with the salt and pepper. Place skin side down in the prepared pan. In a small bowl, combine the syrup, vinegar, catsup, and brown sugar and pour over the chicken. Cover with foil and bake for 1½ hours.

Turn chicken and bake, uncovered, for 30 minutes, basting every 10 minutes to moisten. Pour off the sauce but save it as a gravy to serve over the chicken and rice. *Makes 6 servings.*

Nutrients per serving: Calories 390, Fat 6g, Cholesterol 145mg,
Sodium 500mg, Carbohydrates 29g, Protein 54g, Fiber 1g.

Creamy Curry Sauce with Chicken, Pork, or Shrimp

This recipe, reprinted from The Gluten-free Gourmet Cooks Fast and Healthy, *is a cozy comfort meal that uses leftover cooked chicken or pork or fresh-cooked or canned shrimp. It has a rich flavor which can be adjusted to anyone's curry taste. You may buy chutney or try one of the recipes (page 284 or 285) with this dish.*

2 tablespoons butter or margarine
1 cup chopped onion
1 apple, pared, cored, and diced
½ cup thinly diced celery
3 tablespoons GF Mix
1–2 tablespoons curry powder
  (to taste)
4 teaspoons sugar
1 tablespoon fresh grated
  gingerroot

2 cups broth (chicken or
  vegetable)
1 cup milk or nondairy liquid
⅓ cup coconut flakes or ¼ cup
  coconut milk (optional)
1 teaspoon salt (or to taste)
2 cups cooked chicken, pork,
  or shrimp
Chopped peanuts, raisins, or
  chutney (optional)

In a large heavy kettle or Dutch oven, melt the butter. Add the onion, apple, and celery. Turn heat to low, cover, and cook for 10 minutes, stirring occasionally.

In a small bowl, blend the flour mix, curry powder, sugar, and gingerroot. Add to the pan and stir until smooth. Add the broth and cook until thickening starts. Add the milk, coconut (if used), and salt. Turn heat to low and cook uncovered 20 minutes.

Add the chicken, pork, or shrimp and allow to stay on the burner until the meat is heated through. Serve over white rice. This can be topped with chopped peanuts, raisins, or chutney of your choice. *Makes 6 servings.*

Nutrients per serving: Calories 280, Fat 13g, Cholesterol 60mg,
Sodium 380mg, Carbohydrates 23g, Protein 18g, Fiber 2g.

Chicken Fried Steak

An old favorite takes on a wonderful new taste with the Four Flour Mix. One of my testers served this to me, and I had to agree it was the best I'd ever had. This is perfect if you have an electric frypan but it can be made in any large skillet.

1½ cups milk or nondairy
    substitute
⅔ cup Four Flour Mix
1½ teaspoons salt
½ teaspoon pepper
Dash of paprika

¼ teaspoon oregano, crushed
4 cubed beef steaks
2 tablespoons vegetable oil
2 tablespoons margarine or
    butter

Pour ½ cup of the milk into a low shallow dish (pie plate). On a piece of foil, combine the flour mix, salt, pepper, paprika, and oregano. Reserve 1 tablespoon of the seasoned flour for gravy. Coat the cubed steaks first with the flour, then dip into milk and again coat with the flour.

Heat the oil plus 1 tablespoon of the margarine in a heavy skillet until the margarine browns. Add the steaks and cook 2 minutes on each side. Transfer the steaks to a plate.

Add the remaining margarine to the skillet. Stir in the remaining milk except for ¼ cup, which is now mixed in a small bowl with the reserved tablespoon of flour. When the milk is hot, add this mixture to the skillet to form gravy. Cook until thickened. Scrape the browned bits from the skillet as the gravy comes to a boil. To serve, pour the gravy over the steaks or return the steaks to the gravy. *Makes 4 servings.*

*Nutrients per serving: Calories 160, Fat 7g, Cholesterol 50mg,
Sodium 220mg, Carbohydrates 6g, Protein 18g, Fiber 0g.*

Mama's Pot Roast

No book of comfort foods would be complete without at least one recipe for beef pot roast. The original version of this recipe was handed down in my family from Mother's English ancestors. Over the years I've converted it to incorporate all the new and modern ingredients as they came along. Now I've converted again to our GF ingredients.

2 tablespoons oil or shortening
3½–4 pounds boneless beef roast
One recipe Cream of Mushroom
 Soup (page 227)
One pouch onion soup mix
1¼ cups water, divided

6 fist-sized potatoes, peeled and
 cut into chunks
6 large carrots, peeled and cut
 into 2" pieces
2 tablespoons GF Mix

In a Dutch oven or large pan with a cover, heat the oil and brown the roast on all sides. Remove and set aside. Pour off excess oil.

In the same pan, combine the cooked mushroom soup, onion soup mix, and 1 cup of the water. Heat to boiling. Return the roast to the pan and reduce heat to low. Cover and cook for 2 hours, turning the roast several times.

Add the potatoes and carrots. Cover and cook for 40 minutes more or until the vegetables are done. Transfer the roast and vegetables to a serving platter.

In a small bowl, stir together the flour mix and the remaining ¼ cup of water. Gradually stir this into the sauce in the pan, stirring until it thickens. Serve over the meat and vegetables. *Makes 10–12 servings.*

*Nutrients per serving: Calories 700, Fat 48g, Cholesterol 130mg,
Sodium 115mg, Carbohydrates 30g, Protein 35g, Fiber 3g.*

*A*t high altitudes, roasting times will be longer. Ignore the time listed in the recipe and roast to the desired internal temperature.

Sirloin Tips with Cream Gravy 300°

This is another of the beef-and-gravy sauces to go over noodles. It takes twice as long to prepare as the Beef Bourguignon (page 152) but doesn't contain wine. Both recipes use sirloin tips in cubes. For the noodles, you may make your own pasta (pages 93 and 94) or purchase your favorite GF noodles.

1¼ pounds sirloin tips, cut into
    1" cubes
2 tablespoons butter or
    margarine
1 tablespoon cooking oil
3 cups fresh mushrooms, sliced
1 teaspoon minced garlic
½ cup beef broth

¼ cup rice vinegar (apple cider
    is okay)
1½ teaspoons soy sauce
2 teaspoons prepared mustard
2 teaspoons cornstarch
½ cup whipping cream
Hot cooked noodles

Preheat oven to 300°. Have handy a 2-quart, ovenproof baking dish with a cover.

In a large skillet, brown the meat in the butter and oil. Place in the baking dish. Sauté the mushrooms and garlic in the same skillet about 3 minutes. Pour the mushrooms and liquid over the meat. Cover the baking dish and bake for 2 hours or until the meat is tender.

In the same skillet, combine the broth, vinegar, and soy sauce. Bring to a boil and boil 2 minutes. In a small bowl, combine the mustard, cornstarch, and cream. Add to the mixture in the skillet, stirring, and boil 2 minutes. Add the juices from the casserole and cook over medium heat until the gravy is thickened and bubbly. Stir in the meat and mushrooms. Serve over noodles. *Makes 4–5 servings.*

*Nutrients per serving: Calories 450, Fat 26g, Cholesterol 105mg,
Sodium 1,150mg, Carbohydrates 14g, Protein 42g, Fiber 1g.*

Stove-Top Barbecued Ribs

My nephew in Alaska introduced me to these delicious barbecued ribs. His meat was moose, not beef, but the recipe is the same. These are especially good served over noodles. Make your own noodles from Bean Flour Pasta (page 94) or buy a favorite GF brand.

1 tablespoon vegetable oil
3–4 pounds beef short ribs
2 cups water

SAUCE:
One 6-ounce can tomato paste
1 cup ketchup
½ teaspoon minced garlic
¾ cup brown sugar
1 small onion, chopped
½ cup cider vinegar
2 tablespoons prepared mustard
1½ teaspoons salt
½ cup water

Heat the oil in a Dutch oven. Add the ribs and brown them before adding the water. Bring to a boil and simmer for 1½ hours. Drain.

In a small bowl, combine the tomato paste, ketchup, garlic, brown sugar, onion, vinegar, mustard, and salt. Add the water and mix well. Pour over the ribs and bring to a boil. Reduce heat and simmer covered for 1 hour. Serve over cooked noodles or rice. *Makes 6 servings.*

Nutrients per serving: Calories 550, Fat 26g, Cholesterol 110mg, Sodium 1,410mg, Carbohydrates 35g, Protein 47g, Fiber 2g.

Beef Bourguignon

Try this easy beef-and-gravy dish over white rice or noodles. It takes 1 hour to simmer and turns out tender and tasty. For best results, use sirloin tips rather than stew meat.

2 tablespoons butter
1½ pounds sirloin tips, cut into
   1" cubes
1 medium onion, chopped
1 tablespoon ketchup
1 tablespoon GF Mix

2 cups beef broth
½ cup dry red wine
Two 4-ounce cans sliced
   mushrooms, drained
Salt and pepper to taste

In a deep, heavy frying pan with a lid, melt the butter. Add the meat and onion; brown the meat on all sides. Reduce heat and add the ketchup and flour mix, stirring as the mixture thickens. Add the beef broth and return to a boil; pour in the wine. Cover and simmer for 50 minutes.

To the beef, add the mushrooms and seasonings and continue simmering for 10 minutes longer. To serve for a crowd, pile the rice or noodles on a platter and top with the meat and gravy. For individual servings, top 1 serving of rice or noodles with 1 serving of beef. *Makes 4–5 servings.*

Nutrients per serving: Calories 290, Fat 13g, Cholesterol 95mg, Sodium 690mg, Carbohydrates 8g, Protein 31g, Fiber 2g.

To cut meat more easily and get uniform sizes, try cutting it while partially frozen.

Meat Loaf with Wine and Cheese

375°

This homey old favorite takes on a sophisticated taste with the addition of red wine and Romano cheese. This is especially good in cold sandwiches.

1½ pounds ground beef
¼ cup red wine
1 tablespoon lemon juice
1 tablespoon dried parsley
2 tablespoons minced onion

⅓ cup GF bread crumbs
¼ cup grated Romano cheese
1 teaspoon grated lemon peel
1 teaspoon salt
¼ teaspoon lemon pepper

Preheat oven to 375°.

Combine all the ingredients, mixing with your hands or a spoon until well blended. Pat into an oblong shape and place in a 9" × 5" loaf pan. Bake for 50 minutes or until done. Let sit 5 minutes in the pan before turning out to slice. *Makes 6 servings.*

Nutrients per serving: Calories 340, Fat 25g, Cholesterol 90mg, Sodium 550mg, Carbohydrates 4g, Protein 22g, Fiber 0g.

---

*U*se the microwave to precook meat and poultry for faster, moister grilling. Figure 3 minutes per pound on high.

Country-Style Pork Chops

A very old quickie that makes gravy with the meat. This recipe is another calling for that "can of mushroom soup" that we can make with our powdered soup base and a can of sliced mushrooms.

1 tablespoon oil
6 pork chops
1 tablespoon chopped onion
½ teaspoon dried thyme,
   powdered

One recipe Mushroom Soup
   using powdered soup base
   (page 277)
¼ cup milk (or to desired gravy
   thickness)

In a large skillet, heat the oil and brown the pork chops; transfer them to a platter. In the same skillet, sauté the onions and thyme. Add the prepared soup and milk and bring to a boil. Place the chops in the gravy and cover. Cook until the chops are done. *Makes 6 servings.*

Nutrients per serving: Calories 190, Fat 12g, Cholesterol 65mg, Sodium 50mg, Carbohydrates 0g, Protein 19g, Fiber 0g.

---

*I*n sautéing, the thicker the piece of meat, the lower the heat—this gives heat time to reach the food's center before the outside burns.

Seafood

Now that seafood can be found in all markets—even in heartland cities—people eat it for "brain" food, for their health, and for a change. It is naturally gluten free, but we can get bored with it simply grilled and we know we can't have the popular "fish and chips" with its wheat-laden coating. Try the following recipes for casseroles, GF breading, and several ways of baking fish for more eating pleasure.

A number of these recipes call for surimi, the imitation crab or lobster. It can be a challenge to find surimi that is gluten free. But I do find it by carefully reading ingredients.

At the end of the chapter, there is a recipe for baking a whole salmon (head included). This isn't difficult, but it's very impressive to have the fish on a parsley-covered tray look as if it's alive and swimming. Try one sometime for a party, potluck dinner, or special-occasion buffet.

Crab and Shrimp Casserole

When I was young, this old favorite of the family was only available when my mother threw the simple ingredients together during our summer vacation spent at an Oregon beach cabin. Now, with refrigeration and rapid transportation, the seafood can be found all year, even in the heartland.

½ pound cooked shrimp
½ pound cooked crab or GF
   surimi
1½ cups chopped celery
½ cup diced onion

1 cup mayonnaise
½ cup diced green pepper
1 teaspoon Worcestershire sauce
½ teaspoon salt
¾ cup crushed potato chips

Preheat oven to 350°. Butter a 2-quart casserole.

In a large mixing bowl, gently mix all the ingredients except the potato chips and spoon them into the casserole. Top with the chips.

Bake 35–40 minutes or until a knife inserted in the center comes out clean. *Makes 6 servings.*

Nutrients per serving: Calories 280, Fat 19g, Cholesterol 75mg, Sodium 220mg, Carbohydrates 8g, Protein 10g, Fiber 1g.

Crab Cakes

Most coast dwellers will salivate at the thought of these tasty treats. Made with fresh crab, canned crab, or GF surimi, these crab cakes will remind you of trips to the seaside, where they are on every menu.

½ pound cooked crabmeat,
   imitation crab, or one 6-ounce
   can crabmeat
1 egg
¾ cup crushed potato chips
2 tablespoons shredded coconut

3 green onions, finely chopped
2 tablespoons mayonnaise
1 tablespoon parsley, chopped
1 teaspoon lemon juice
2 tablespoons cooking oil for
   frying

Pick over the crabmeat to remove any shell fragments or cartilage. Break into bite-sized pieces.

In a medium mixing bowl, beat the egg. Add ½ cup of the potato chips, the coconut, green onions, mayonnaise, parsley, and lemon juice and stir well. Gently mix in the crabmeat. Shape into 6 patties about ½" thick. Coat the cakes with the remaining crushed chips.

In a large skillet, heat the oil and add the crab cakes. Turn heat to medium and cook 2–3 minutes on each side or until golden brown. Serve immediately. *Makes 6 cakes.*

Nutrients per crabcake: Calories 140, Fat 11g, Cholesterol 65mg,
Sodium 150mg, Carbohydrates 2g, Protein 7g, Fiber 0g.

Easy Deviled Crab 450°

Here is a great way to serve some of that GF surimi whether it be fake crab or lobster. Of course the dish is wonderful with fresh crab when it's in season. I have used both large clam shells (fresh from our own beach) and purchased ramekins.

3 tablespoons butter or
   margarine
2 teaspoons GF Flour Mix
1 cup milk, heated
1 teaspoon salt
Dash of cayenne pepper
1 teaspoon Worcestershire sauce

2 egg yolks, slightly beaten
2 cups crabmeat (fresh or
   imitation)
½ teaspoon lemon juice
¼ cup sherry (optional)
⅔ cup dried GF bread crumbs,
   buttered

Preheat oven to 450°.

In a medium saucepan, melt the butter and stir in the flour mix and milk. Add the salt, pepper, and Worcestershire sauce. Add the egg yolks and cook over medium-high heat, stirring constantly until the mixture starts to thicken. Add the crab and cook until the sauce is thickened and the crab is hot. Remove from heat and stir in the lemon and sherry (if used).

Spoon the mixture into 4 individual baking shells or ramekins and cover with the buttered bread crumbs. Bake about 20–25 minutes until brown. *Makes 4 servings.*

Nutrients per serving: Calories 260, Fat 14g, Cholesterol 175mg, Sodium 1,450mg, Carbohydrates 12g, Protein 20g, Fiber 0g.

Coconut Rice and White Fish Packets 450°

A tasty meal in a pouch! This is one of my most flavorful ways of cooking many fish, from deepwater bass to halibut. The pineapple chunks can be changed to papaya or mango. If desired, add a dash of red pepper with the other seasonings.

½ cup canned coconut milk
½ cup water
2 cups instant rice
2 green onions, sliced thin
4 white fish fillets (no bones or
    skin)

Salt and pepper to taste
½ cup marmalade
1 cup pineapple chunks, fresh or
    canned

Heat oven to 450°. Prepare 4 sheets of aluminum foil, 12" × 18" each, and spray with vegetable oil.

Soak the rice in the mixture of coconut milk and water for 7 minutes. Add the sliced green onions.

Divide the soaked rice between the 4 pieces of foil; top with the fish fillet. Salt and pepper them and add 2 tablespoons marmalade. Surround with the pineapple chunks and seal, leaving room for expansion.

Place packets on cookie sheet in hot oven and bake 15–20 minutes or until the fish flakes easily. Serve in the packets, warning guests to open them carefully to avoid steam. *Makes 4 servings.*

Nutrients per serving: Calories 460, Fat 13g, Cholesterol 165mg,
Sodium 610mg, Carbohydrates 57g, Protein 30g, Fiber 4g.

Salmon and Rice in Foil Packets

450°

A full meal in a packet with no fuss or bother. The directions are for oven baking, but you can put the packets on the grill if you want to keep the heat and smell out of the house.

2 cups instant rice
1 cup chicken broth
2 green onions, sliced
4 salmon fillets (no bones or skin)

1 teaspoon salt
½ cup mango chutney
1 cup pineapple chunks
   (fresh or canned)

Preheat oven to 450°.

In a medium bowl, place rice and chicken broth. Add the green onion. Let soak while preparing 4 sheets of aluminum foil, 12" × 18" each, by spraying with vegetable oil.

On each piece of foil, place one-fourth of the rice and top with a fillet; sprinkle with ¼ teaspoon salt and top with 2 tablespoons chutney and ¼ cup pineapple chunks.

Seal the packets, leaving room for expansion during baking, and place on a cookie sheet in the oven. Bake 15–20 minutes or until the salmon flakes easily. Serve in the packets, warning guests to open carefully to avoid steam. *Makes 4 servings.*

*Nutrients per serving: Calories 390, Fat 12g, Cholesterol 0mg,
Sodium 780mg, Carbohydrates 51g, Protein 20g, Fiber 3g.*

Oven-Fried Fish 1

500°

Save calories and have great-tasting fish by baking fillets—of catfish, sole, halibut, or cod—that are approximately ⅓″ to ½″ thick. You may have to slice across the thicker halibut or cod pieces to cut them down to this thickness.

1 cup cornmeal
1 teaspoon seafood seasoning
1 tablespoon dried parsley
¼ teaspoon salt
½ cup buttermilk

2 pounds fish fillets, cut into 4″
   pieces
1 tablespoon melted butter,
   margarine, or vegetable oil

Preheat oven to 500°. Oil a 9″ × 13″ baking pan.

Blend the cornmeal, seafood seasoning, parsley, and salt and place the mix in a shallow bowl or dish. Pour the buttermilk into another shallow bowl.

Wash the pieces of fish and dip them into the buttermilk, then roll in the cornmeal mix, coating all sides. Arrange in the prepared pan in a single layer. Drizzle on the melted butter. Bake for 10–15 minutes or until the fish is golden and flakes easily with a fork. Serve immediately. *Makes 6–8 servings.*

Nutrients per serving: Calories 300, Fat 19g, Cholesterol 115mg,
Sodium 260mg, Carbohydrates 28g, Protein 32g, Fiber 5g.

Oven-Fried Fish 2

400°–350°

Here is another way to have your fried fish without all the fat. This recipe, which uses different seasonings from the one on the preceding page, produces fillets that are juicy and tender with all the flavor intact.

2 pounds catfish fillets
2 tablespoons lemon juice
1 cup milk or nondairy
    liquid
1½ cups cornmeal
1 teaspoon celery salt

¾ teaspoon cayenne pepper (to
    taste)
1 teaspoon dried lemon peel
½ teaspoon dried thyme
1 teaspoon paprika
Salt and pepper to taste

Preheat oven to 400°. Grease a baking sheet.

Wash the fillets and cut into serving-size pieces. Stir the lemon juice into the milk in a shallow bowl. Let stand until thickened.

Mix the cornmeal with the celery salt, cayenne pepper, dried lemon peel, thyme, and paprika. Spread on a large plate or in a pie tin.

Season the pieces of fish with salt and pepper. Dip them into the milk, then coat them with the cornmeal mixture. Place on the baking sheet and bake for 20 minutes at 400°; reduce heat to 350° and bake 5 minutes more or until the crust is golden and the fish flakes easily. *Makes 6 servings.*

*Nutrients per serving: Calories 260, Fat 19g, Cholesterol 115mg,
Sodium 260mg, Carbohydrates 28g, Protein 32g, Fiber 5g.*

Grilled Oysters

A recipe for those lucky enough to be able to purchase oysters in the shell. It is the easiest way not only to open them but also to cook and serve them. And it just might be the tastiest.

3–4 dozen oysters in their shells
1 cup (2 sticks) butter, melted
Salt and pepper to taste (optional)

2 tablespoons lemon or lime juice
2 teaspoons grated lemon or lime
  peel

Wash any sand or seaweed from the oysters. Fire up the barbecue to medium-high heat.

In a small saucepan, combine the butter, salt and pepper (if used), lemon juice, and grated lemon peel. Keep warm.

Place the oysters on the barbecue, with the deeper (or concave) half down. The tops should open at least ¼" in about 5 minutes. Remove from the barbecue with a waterproof mitt, pry off the top shell with an oyster knife, and drizzle with the lemon butter.

The best way to enjoy these oysters is to stand around the barbecue and eat them while they're still hot. The other option is to place the oysters, still in the bottom shell, on a large platter and then drizzle on the lemon butter. *Makes 9–16 appetizer servings of 3–4 oysters each. Makes 3–6 main-dish servings of 8–10 oysters each.*

*Nutrients per serving: Calories 300, Fat 20g, Cholesterol 40mg,
Sodium 370mg, Carbohydrates 10g, Protein 19g, Fiber 0g.*

Baked Salmon: An Edible Centerpiece 400°

Both attractive and delicious, this fish centerpiece will make any hostess look like a gourmet cook, yet it's really quite easy to prepare the day before the party, reception, or potluck dinner. Serve the fish cold from the refrigerator on the same foil-covered sheet used for baking and surround it with parsley to cover any drippings. It's that easy.

1 whole fresh salmon, head
   attached (3–6 pounds)
Salt or fish seasoning
1½ cups vegetable broth
One envelope Knox plain gelatin
   (2 teaspoons)

Parsley for decoration
Olive slices or grape halves for
   eyes
Lemon for decoration (optional)
Mayonnaise or tartar sauce for
   serving (optional)

Preheat oven to 400°. Prepare a cookie sheet or large flat pan by lining with foil.

Wash the salmon well. (The fish market should have cleaned it and left the head attached.) If the fish hasn't been scaled, do so now and sprinkle the stomach cavity with salt or your favorite seafood seasoning.

To plan baking time: Measure the fish depth at the widest point from the stomach slit to the top of the back. This should be from 3½" to 6" or so. Allow 10 minutes for each inch plus an extra 10 minutes. (For example, a 4"-depth fish would bake for 50 minutes.)

To mount the fish as if it is swimming: Form a 2½"–3" triangular stand with stiff cardboard to fit into the cavity of the fish. Place the fish upright on the stand on the tin or pan and bend gently to a swimming position. Wrap the whole (fish and tray) with more aluminum foil and seal, but don't let the foil touch the fish (or the skin so touched will peel off as if scarred when you remove the foil after baking). Bake at 400° for the time planned for the fish size.

Remove from the oven and carefully remove the wrapping foil. Cool completely and then refrigerate until cold. (This fish will still be on the cooking sheet or baking tray.)

To glaze: Heat the vegetable broth to boiling and dissolve the gelatin in it. Spoon the warm glaze over the cold fish several times at intervals of 20 minutes or so. The fish will now appear shiny.

To serve: Arrange the parsley to cover the tray around the fish. Place the olive slices over the cooked eyes, using a toothpick to hold them in place. Thinly slice the lemon (if used) and tuck it around the fish in the parsley; place the mayonnaise (if used) in a bowl nestled in the parsley on the tray. Let people serve themselves after you cut the skin at the top of the backbone and start peeling it away to show the flesh of the fish. *Makes 20–30 servings depending on whether this is an appetizer or the dinner entrée.*

Nutrients per serving: Calories 170, Fat 10g, Cholesterol 55mg, Sodium 95mg, Carbohydrates 1g, Protein 18g, Fiber 0g.

Vegetables

POTATOES

OTHER VEGETABLES

The vegetable recipes in this chapter all carry a hint of the past—a time when vegetables were creamed, baked, or fried in oil. Whether these were tricks to make us eat our vegetables or to give us comfort when we did, our parents didn't say. But they were tasty as well as memorable.

Today's fat-free, steamed substitutes may contain fewer calories, but they also contain fewer memories. So live a little. Try your vegetables and savor the past.

Twice-Baked Potatoes   400°

I can't remember when these potatoes became popular, but I keep them made up and in the freezer as a handy comfort food.

Note: *Nowadays a microwave can substitute for the first baking with excellent results if the potatoes are prepared a day ahead and refrigerated. Using an electric mixer rather than a masher produces a fluffier potato.*

4 large baking potatoes (russet)

¼ cup (½ stick) butter or
   margarine

½ cup sour cream or cottage
   cheese (low-fat okay)

¼ cup sliced green onions
   (optional)

½ teaspoon salt

Pepper to taste

½ teaspoon onion salt

½ cup milk or nondairy
   substitute

¼ cup grated cheddar
   cheese

Preheat oven to 400°.

Scrub the potatoes and pierce them with a knife so they won't explode. Arrange them on oven rack and bake for 45–55 minutes or until tender when gently squeezed using a hot pad.

When cool enough to handle, split the potatoes in half lengthwise. Working over a medium bowl, scoop out the insides, leaving a shell about ¼" thick. Spread the butter on the insides of the 8 shells.

Add the remaining ingredients (except cheese) to the potato pulp and mash or mix with a mixer until smooth. Spoon the potato into the shells, topping with the grated cheese. Arrange in a baking pan and return to the oven for 15 minutes or until the filling is hot and the cheese is melted. *Makes 4 servings.*

*Nutrients per serving: Calories 230, Fat 9g, Cholesterol 25mg,
Sodium 390mg, Carbohydrates 29g, Protein 9g, Fiber 3g.*

Potatoes with Crab Stuffing

Use these baked potatoes, full of flavor with green onions, cream cheese, and fresh or canned crab, as the main dish at lunch or supper. To complete the meal, add some fruit or top lettuce with Thousand Island Dressing (page 287).

4 baking size russet potatoes
¼ cup mayonnaise
½ cup whipped cream cheese
   (chive and onion, etc.)
⅓ cup green onions, thinly
   sliced
2 tablespoons light cream or
   nondairy substitute, if
   necessary

¾ cup shredded cheddar cheese
1 cup crabmeat (canned okay)
Extra Parmesan or cheddar
   cheese for sprinkling top
   (optional)

Preheat oven to 400°.

Clean and prick the potatoes and bake for 55 minutes or until very tender and soft when squeezed. Remove from oven and let cool enough to handle.

Cut the potatoes in half lengthwise and scoop out the insides, leaving a ¼" shell. Place the pulp in a mixing bowl and beat with a mixer until soft and fluffy. Stir in the mayonnaise, cream cheese, onions, and as much of the light cream as needed to make the potato mixture soft for filling. Using a spoon, gently blend in the cheddar cheese and crabmeat.

Scoop the mixture into the shells, dividing evenly. (The tops will be rounded.) If desired, top with a bit of extra cheese. Place the stuffed potatoes on a baking sheet and return to the oven for 20–25 minutes or until heated through and the cheese on top is well melted. *Makes 4 servings.*

Nutrients per serving: Calories 440, Fat 29g, Cholesterol 95mg,
Sodium 540mg, Carbohydrates 30g, Protein 16g, Fiber 3g

Jo Jo Potatoes

350°

Baked, buttered, and seasoned. A new way to serve a favorite food.

4 baking potatoes
⅓ cup butter or margarine
¼ cup GF Mix or Featherlight
   Mix

¼ cup grated Parmesan cheese
Dash of pepper
½ teaspoon salt

Preheat oven to 350°. Scrub the potatoes and cut lengthwise into 8 or 10 wedges.

Place the butter in a shallow baking pan large enough to hold the potatoes in a single layer. Put the pan in the oven to melt the butter.

In a plastic bag, place the flour mix, cheese, pepper, and salt; shake the bag to combine these ingredients. Moisten the potatoes with water and add them to the bag; shake to coat them completely. Arrange the potatoes in a single layer in the melted butter in the pan and bake for 45–60 minutes or until tender. If desired, turn once. *Makes 4–5 servings.*

Nutrients per serving: Calories 270, Fat 14g, Cholesterol 35mg,
Sodium 440mg, Carbohydrates 31g, Protein 5g, Fiber 3g.

VARIATION:

Add a sprinkling of garlic salt and onion salt to the bag for more flavorful potatoes.

Easy Scalloped Potatoes   375°

This recipe makes creamy scalloped potatoes with little fuss and bother. Shove the casserole in the oven and take time out to relax before dinner, or if you know you're going to be late, stir this up before work and have one of the kids put it into the oven when they get home from school.

5 fist-sized potatoes
5–7 green onions, sliced thin
Salt and pepper to taste
½ cup leftover or deli ham or
   corned beef, diced (optional)

SAUCE:
2 tablespoons butter or margarine
4 tablespoons Creamed Soup
   Base (page 277)
¼ cup cold water
1¼ cups chicken stock
1 cup milk or nondairy substitute

Preheat oven to 375°. Grease a 2½-quart casserole with cooking spray.

Peel and thinly slice the potatoes and place them in the casserole. Add the onions and tumble to mix. Season with salt and pepper. If using meat, mix it in with the seasonings.

Sauce: In a medium saucepan, place the butter and the soup base blended with the cold water. Add the chicken stock and bring to a boil over medium-high heat, stirring occasionally. This mixture will be as thick as canned cream soup. Add the milk and pour over the potatoes. Bake for 1 hour or until the potatoes are tender. *Makes 4–5 servings.*

Nutrients per serving (without ham): Calories 230, Fat 4g, Cholesterol 25mg, Sodium 440mg, Carbohydrates 37g, Protein 11g, Fiber 1g.

VARIATIONS:

POTATOES AU GRATIN: Eliminate the meat but add 1 cup grated sharp cheddar cheese to the sauce before pouring it onto the potatoes. If desired, top with ½ cup buttered GF bread crumbs.

MUSHROOM-FLAVORED POTATOES: In place of the green onions, use the recipe for Cream of Mushroom Soup (page 277) and thin it with the cup of milk before pouring over the potatoes.

Potato Patties with Apple

One of the quick-fix potato dishes from the past that takes just seconds to grate in the food processor and minutes to cook in the skillet. The apple gives these potato patties both moisture and flavor. Serve with meats that have no gravy such as meat loaf or baked ham. The patties are also tasty with fried chicken.

Note: *If you don't have a food processor, grate the potatoes, apple, and onion.*

3 large russet potatoes, peeled
1 large apple, peeled and cored
½ medium onion (½ cup)
3 tablespoons sorghum flour
2 eggs

1 tablespoon lemon juice
Salt and pepper to taste
¼ teaspoon cinnamon
Pinch of nutmeg
Oil for frying

In a food processor, place the potatoes, apple, and onion (cut into chunks). Process until coarsely ground. Add the flour, eggs, lemon juice, salt, pepper, cinnamon, and nutmeg. Process until the texture is fine. Shape into patties and fry in a thin layer of hot oil over medium heat until golden brown on both sides. *Makes 4 servings.*

Nutrients per serving: Calories 290, Fat 4g, Cholesterol 105mg, Sodium 75mg, Carbohydrates 60g, Protein 7g, Fiber 10g.

Easy Candied Sweet Potatoes

When I was growing up, sweet potatoes were only on the menu for a holiday treat. Now they are popular anytime. They used to take my mother half the morning to prepare and a longer time baking but this sweet potato dish may be made in minutes as your meat and vegetables are cooking, so dinner can be on the table in half an hour.

1 pound (2 medium) sweet potatoes	2 tablespoons brown sugar
Boiling water	1 tablespoon butter or margarine
1 teaspoon orange zest	½ teaspoon pumpkin pie spice
½ cup orange juice	¼ teaspoon salt

Peel and slice the potatoes into ⅓"–½" slices. Place them in a large skillet and cover with boiling water. Cover and cook for 10 minutes or until the potatoes are tender. Drain.

Sauce: In a small bowl, combine the orange zest, orange juice, brown sugar, butter, pumpkin pie spice and salt. Pour over the drained potatoes. Bring to a boil and cook, uncovered, for 5 minutes or until the potatoes are glazed, spooning the sauce over them occasionally. *Makes 4 servings.*

Nutrients per serving: Calories 220, Fat 3g, Cholesterol 10mg, Sodium 210mg, Carbohydrates 44g, Protein 3g, Fiber 1g.

Sweet Potato Fritters

Eggs and spice turn the familiar sweet potato into an entirely different dish. These may be fried with very little oil in a frying pan on the stove top (see directions below) or may be deep-fried at 365° in oil to cover (4–6 cups) for 5–8 minutes.

4½ cups grated sweet potatoes
   (3–4 potatoes)
½ cup GF Mix
1 tablespoon brown sugar
1 teaspoon salt

½ teaspoon pepper
1 scant teaspoon apple pie spice
2 eggs, slightly beaten
Oil for frying

Chop about 2 cups of the grated potatoes into smaller pieces and place them in a large bowl. Add the flour mix, brown sugar, salt, pepper, and spice and tumble to cover. Pour in the eggs and stir to combine.

Heat 2–3 tablespoons oil in a frying pan and form 3" patties, using about ¼ cup of the potato mix each. Place as many patties in the pan as possible and brown both sides. Lower heat, cover, and cook about 6 minutes or until cooked through. Remove from pan and cook next batch, keeping the first ones warm in the oven until all are finished. *Makes 15–16 patties, or 5–6 servings.*

Nutrients per serving: Calories 139, Fat 1g, Cholesterol 27mg, Sodium 136mg, Carbohydrates 16g, Protein 2g, Fiber 2g.

Sweet Potatoes with Orange Pecan Sauce 350°

A favorite dish for that holiday buffet. These potatoes may be prepared in advance and refrigerated (up to a day ahead) until just 35 minutes or so before serving. Use potatoes you've boiled and peeled or canned ones.

Note: *The glaze may be doubled and the extra used as a sauce for ham.*

6 medium sweet potatoes (boiled and peeled) or 30 ounces canned

⅓–½ cup brown sugar (to taste)

1 tablespoon cornstarch

½ teaspoon ground cinnamon

¼ teaspoon ground nutmeg

1 cup orange juice

2 tablespoons margarine or butter

Salt to taste

¼ cup finely chopped pecans

Preheat oven to 350°.

Cut the cooked potatoes into ⅓"-thick slices and place them in a buttered 3-quart casserole.

In a small saucepan, combine brown sugar, cornstarch, cinnamon, and nutmeg. Gradually stir in the orange juice. Bring to a boil and cook, stirring frequently, until slightly thickened. Add the margarine in small chunks. Season the potatoes with salt and pepper and pour the sauce over them. Sprinkle on the pecans.

Bake for 35 minutes or until the sauce bubbles and the potatoes are heated through. *Makes 6–8 servings.*

Nutrients per serving: Calories 210, Fat 5g, Cholesterol 0mg, Sodium 50mg, Carbohydrates 41g, Protein 2g, Fiber 3g.

Green Beans Almondine

Sometimes I yearn for those quick-and-easy casseroles from my prediagnosis days so much that I just have to create a substitute for them. The traditional recipe for Green Beans Almondine, an old family favorite, includes canned mushroom soup, canned onion rings, and canned chow mein noodles—all forbidden foods. My version is tasty, packed with protein, and satisfies the craving.

4 cups cooked green beans (fresh,
    fresh frozen or canned),
    drained
One recipe Cream of Mushroom
    Soup (page 277)
½ cup milk or nondairy liquid

1 teaspoon soy sauce
    (optional)
½ cup slivered almonds
Dash of garlic powder
Salt to taste
¾ cup crushed potato chips

Preheat oven to 350°.

In a 2½-quart casserole, place the beans.

Prepare the soup and, while it's still hot, stir in the milk, soy sauce (if used), slivered almonds, garlic powder, and salt. Pour over the beans in the casserole and stir. Add the crushed potato chips on top.

Bake, covered, for 30 minutes or until the sauce is bubbling. *Makes 8–10 servings.*

Nutrients per serving: Calories 360, Fat 15g, Cholesterol 30mg, Sodium 510mg, Carbohydrates 44g, Protein 14g, Fiber 3g.

Spinach with Shrimp 375°

It was evident to me that spinach had moved from an "Ugh!" vegetable to one high on the party list when I noticed several spinach casseroles at the last family gathering. Even those who ordinarily won't touch spinach will enjoy this light delicate souffle.

One 10-ounce package frozen,
    chopped spinach, thawed
½ cup chopped onion
¾ pound raw shrimp, shelled and
    cut into thirds

¾ cup mayonnaise
¼ cup grated Parmesan cheese
1 tablespoon lemon juice
½ teaspoon salt
4 egg whites

Preheat oven to 375°. Butter a 2½-quart casserole.

In a mixing bowl, combine the spinach, onion, shrimp, mayonnaise, cheese, and lemon juice. Add the salt to the egg whites and beat to form stiff peaks. Fold this into the spinach mixture. Spoon into the prepared casserole and bake for 25 minutes or until firm. Serve immediately. *Makes 4–5 servings.*

Nutrients per serving: Calories 419, Fat 36g, Cholesterol 150mg, Sodium 864mg, Carbohydrates 6g, Protein 20g, Fiber 2g.

Creamed Broccoli

An old-fashioned favorite that will fool anyone into eating broccoli. Just try it!

3 cups fresh broccoli florets or
    one 10-ounce package frozen
    broccoli
One recipe Cream of Mushroom
    Soup (page 277)

½ cup grated cheddar cheese
¼ cup milk
¼ cup mayonnaise (light okay)
1 egg, beaten

Preheat oven to 350°. Butter or grease an 8" square casserole.

Steam the fresh broccoli 5–7 minutes or cook the frozen vegetable according to package directions. Pour into bottom of the prepared casserole.

Cook soup until thickened. Remove from heat. Stir in the cheese until melted; gradually add the milk, mayonnaise, and beaten egg, stirring until well blended. Pour over the broccoli in the casserole. Bake for 45 minutes. Serve hot. *Makes 6 servings.*

*Nutrients per serving: Calories 300, Fat 13g, Cholesterol 50mg,
Sodium 440mg, Carbohydrates 34g, Protein 13g, Fiber 2g.*

---

*D*o salt water for things that have a short boiling time, for example, vegetables.

Spiced Cabbage with Apple

Cabbage was a favorite winter vegetable before the days of supermarkets and world shipping. It lost favor for a while but has now come back into style. You can use either red or white cabbage in this recipe, but it is especially appealing in red.

Note: *This can be served immediately or prepared and refrigerated to be reheated and served later.*

1 small head red or green cabbage	1 teaspoon salt
¼ cup margarine or butter, divided	2 apples, peeled, cored, and sliced
⅔ cup water	2 tablespoons sugar
4 whole cloves	2 tablespoons lemon juice

Shred the cabbage (about 6 cups).

In a large skillet, heat 2 tablespoons of the margarine and the water to boiling. Stir in the cabbage, cloves, salt, and apples. Cover and simmer until the cabbage is crisp-tender (5–8 minutes).

Stir in the remaining 2 tablespoons margarine, sugar, and lemon juice. Cover and simmer 3–5 minutes more. Remove the cloves and serve immediately. Or, if prepared ahead, cover and refrigerate for up to 24 hours. *Makes 6–8 servings.*

Nutrients per serving: Calories 123, Fat 8g, Cholesterol 20mg, Sodium 435mg, Carbohydrates 14g, Protein 1g, Fiber 2g.

Corn and Shrimp Fritters

A marvelous medley of flavors. For an easy meal, pair the fritters with a fruit salad and muffins or thick slices of GF bread.
    Note: *If using canned corn, increase the GF Mix to 3 tablespoons.*

One large ear of cooked corn or
    one 8.75-ounce can whole
    kernel corn, drained
½ pound uncooked shrimp,
    peeled, deveined, and chopped
½ cup bean sprouts, chopped
    to ½" thick
½ cup grated carrot
2 tablespoons minced onion

½ teaspoon salt
Dash of pepper (to taste)
2 tablespoons GF Mix (see note)
1 large egg or ¼ cup liquid egg
    substitute
3 tablespoons coconut flakes
2 tablespoons vegetable oil for
    frying

If using fresh corn, cut the kernels from cob. Place them in a medium bowl with the shrimp, bean sprouts, carrot, onion, salt, pepper, and the flour mix. Tumble together.
    Beat the egg slightly and add to the bowl, along with the coconut flakes. Mix well.
    Heat oil in a large skillet. With wet hands form 6–8 patties. Cook over medium-high heat about 5 minutes per side or until browned. Serve hot. *Makes 3–4 servings of 2 patties each.*

*Nutrients per serving: Calories 260, Fat 12g, Cholesterol 140mg,
Sodium 710mg, Carbohydrates 25g, Protein 16g, Fiber 2g.*

*D*on't salt water for corn, as it toughens it.

Stir-Fry Vegetables with Meat

Using a package of frozen vegetables and cut-up chicken or beef, you can put this dish on the table in minutes. Serve alone with bread or muffins or over hot white rice.

½ pound beef or chicken, cut into
   thin strips
1 tablespoon oil
1 tablespoon water
One 16-ounce package frozen
   stir-fry vegetables (Sugar Snap
   Stir-Fry)

SAUCE:
1¼ cups chicken broth
2 rounded tablespoons cornstarch
2 tablespoons GF soy sauce
3 tablespoons vinegar
3 tablespoons sugar

In a large wok or deep skillet, fry the meat in the hot oil until cooked. Add water and vegetables. Cover and cook 5–7 minutes on medium high.

Combine the sauce ingredients and add to the pan. Cook until heated through. Serve over hot cooked white rice. *Makes 3–4 servings.*

*Nutrients per serving: Calories 270, Fat 10g, Cholesterol 35mg,
Sodium 320mg, Carbohydrates 30g, Protein 16g, Fiber 1g.*

Sandwiches

Sandwiches were something celiacs only dreamed about when I was diagnosed in the 1970s. Today, with all the great breads we can make or sometimes buy, we can enjoy great fillings, toppings, and wraps.

Here you'll find everything from appetizer-like toppings to pizza to be made in your own kitchen or pizza crusts to be taken to that neighborhood parlor to be filled and baked. I've given a short list of fillings for wraps, but you can add your own, whether it be Greek olives or chili peppers.

Crab-Cheese Melt

This open-faced sandwich is a popular item served in many of our local seafood restaurants. I take my own bread or English muffin and have the chef put his version on my bread. But I still make it at home when crab is in season or I can find GF crab or lobster surimi. Either fresh or canned crab works well.

12 ounces crabmeat or GF
  imitation crab or lobster
¾ cup country-style cottage
  cheese, blended smooth
⅓ cup mayonnaise
½ cup grated cheddar cheese

3 green onions, sliced thin
5 drops Tabasco sauce
2 teaspoons Worcestershire sauce
  or 1 teaspoon GF soy sauce
6 crumpets or English muffins, or
  12 slices GF bread

Preheat oven to 400°.

Break the crabmeat into bite-sized pieces. Set aside.

In a medium bowl, blend the cottage cheese and mayonnaise. Stir in the grated cheddar, onions, Tabasco sauce, and Worcestershire sauce. Gently fold in the crab pieces.

Split the crumpets and divide the crab mixture on the 12 pieces. Place on 2 large baking sheets and bake for 10–12 minutes. Serve hot from the oven. *Makes 12 open-faced sandwiches.*

Nutrients per serving: Calories 815, Fat 13g, Cholesterol 35mg,
Sodium 280mg, Carbohydrates 125g, Protein 24g, Fiber 7g.

VARIATIONS:

PALISADES CRAB-CHEESE MELT: Slice canned artichoke hearts and place them on the crumpets before spreading with the seafood mixture.

CHARLIE'S OPEN-FACED CRAB SANDWICH: Top the seafood mixture with a large slice of ripe tomato before baking.

Shrimp-Cheese Open-Faced Sandwiches

This easy-to-make sandwich tastes like a mini-pizza and is very popular with guests either as a summer deck snack or to serve to that gang huddled around the television on football days. The topping can be stirred up ahead of time (by a day or two) and refrigerated, so all the hostess has to do is spread it on a bread of choice and broil the sandwiches before serving. See below for a variation to serve as hors d'oeuvres.

8 ounces sharp cheddar cheese
One 4-ounce can shrimp,
    drained
3 green onions
One 8-ounce can ripe olives,
    drained

¼ green pepper, washed and
    seeded
½ cup (1 stick) margarine, melted
One 8-ounce can tomato sauce
6 crumpets or English muffins,
    sliced, or 12 slices GF bread

Grind together or blend in a food processor the cheese, shrimp, onions, pitted olives, and green pepper. Stir in the melted margarine and tomato sauce.

Spread the mixture on the sliced buns or slices of bread. Put them on cookie sheets and place under the broiler until the spread melts and bubbles. The mixture will keep several days in the refrigerator and the buns or bread can be spread shortly ahead of time. *Makes approximately 1 ½ pints, or 12 open-faced sandwiches.*

Nutrients per serving: Calories 220, Fat 13g, Cholesterol 45mg,
Sodium 875mg, Carbohydrates 19g, Protein 4g, Fiber 2g.

VARIATION:

To serve as hors d'oeuvres, the bread may be cut into circles with a biscuit cutter or (as I prefer) into triangles, 2 or 4 to a slice, depending on how fancy your party.

The Ultimate Tuna Melt

This grilled tuna-cheese sandwich is packed with flavor. Serve it with corn chips for lunch or as a light supper on hot days.

Note: If you prefer open-faced sandwiches, just pile the filling on the 8 pieces of bread and bake following the direction below.

8 slices GF bread

Butter or margarine

One 12-ounce can tuna, drained

6 tablespoons mayonnaise

6 tablespoons sweet relish

¼ cup finely chopped celery

3 tablespoons minced onion

1 teaspoon lemon juice

2 green onions, thinly sliced

Salt and pepper

¾ cup grated sharp cheddar cheese

Preheat oven to 475°. Lightly butter each bread slice on 1 side and place on a cookie sheet, four with the butter side down. Set aside.

In a large bowl, combine tuna and mayonnaise. Stir in the relish, celery, onion, lemon juice, and green onions. Mix until well combined. Salt and pepper to taste. Gently fold in the cheese.

Divide the tuna mixture onto four of the bread slices, spreading on the unbuttered side. Close with the remaining slices (with the butter side up). Bake for 4–6 minutes or until toasty brown. *Makes 4 sandwiches.*

Nutrients per serving: Calories 510, Fat 27g, Cholesterol 55mg, Sodium 1,030mg, Carbohydrates 40g, Protein 31g, Fiber 2g.

Fish Salad Sandwich

This delicious sandwich is filling enough to serve as a complete lunch. Add a bit of fruit and you have a light supper.

1 pound boned, skinned
    white-fleshed fish (mahimahi,
    halibut, cod, etc.)
½ cup crushed pineapple, drained
¼ cup thinly sliced celery
¼ cup chopped macadamia nuts
    or cashews
¼ cup shredded dried coconut

4 green onions, sliced thin
¼ cup mayonnaise (or more as
    needed)
2 tablespoons milk or nondairy
    substitute (as needed for
    thinning)
4 hamburger buns or 8 slices GF
    bread

Poach washed fish in boiling water for 5–7 minutes or until it flakes open and is opaque throughout. Cool to room temperature in refrigerator while preparing the rest of the salad.

Shred fish. Add the pineapple, celery, nuts, coconut, and onions. Thin the mayonnaise with the milk and stir into the fish. Tumble well.

Divide the fish salad evenly over the cut buns or the bread. Serve open-faced. *Makes 4 servings.*

Nutrients per serving: Calories 330, Fat 23g, Cholesterol 40mg,
Sodium 160mg, Carbohydrates 8g, Protein 25g, Fiber 1g.

VARIATION:

FOR SALAD: Eliminate the bread and tumble the makings of the sandwich with 2 cups chopped lettuce. Serve on plates.

Reuben Sandwiches

These sandwiches are one of my favorite uses for any of the rye or dark breads. They are very tasty when made with the Sesame Bean Bread (page 51) of The Gluten-free Gourmet Bakes Bread.

Note: If your bread slices are from a small (8½″ × 4½″) 1-pound loaf, use 2 slices for each slice in the recipe; if from a large or bread-machine loaf, follow the recipe.

One 14½-ounce can sauerkraut

3 tablespoons prepared mustard

2 tablespoons honey

⅓ cup Thousand Island Dressing
  (page 287)

8 slices rye or other dark bread

12 slices deli corned beef

8 thin slices Swiss cheese

Margarine for spreading

Drain the sauerkraut and combine with the mustard and honey.

Spread the dressing on 4 bread slices. Place on them the meat, sauerkraut, and then cheese. Top with the remaining bread. Spread the top with margarine and place, buttered side down, in a warmed skillet over medium heat. Spread margarine on top side. Brown the sandwiches on both sides until golden and the cheese is melted. *Makes 4 sandwiches.*

*Nutrients per serving: Calories 460, Fat 18g, Cholesterol 80mg,
Sodium 2,250mg, Carbohydrates 49g, Protein 26g, Fiber 2g.*

TO MAKE A SINGLE SANDWICH: Mix one-fourth of the sauerkraut with a scant tablespoon mustard and 1½ teaspoon honey. Use 1⅓ tablespoon of dressing, 3 slices of corned beef, and 2 slices of cheese.

Wraps (Choux)

450°–350°

At a national celiac conference we were served our sandwich fillings in wet and wilted lettuce leaves wrapped in a soggy napkin. I decided there had to be a better way to serve today's sandwich wrap. This wonderful choux pastry bun works perfectly; and they are much easier to make than bread. And definitely superior to wilted lettuce.

1 cup water	½ teaspoon salt
½ cup shortening	1 tablespoon sugar
1 cup Featherlight Mix	4 eggs

Preheat oven to 450°. Grease a cookie sheet.

Combine the water and shortening in a medium saucepan. Bring to a rapid boil. In a medium bowl, combine the flour mix, salt, and sugar. Stir the dry ingredients into the hot liquid. Keep stirring until the mixture forms a ball that separates from the sides of the pan. It will be very thick. Remove from heat and transfer to the bowl of your mixer.

Using the cake paddle (not the bread hook), beat the mixture until smooth. Add the eggs, one at a time, beating well after each egg is added. After the 4th egg, continue beating for 3½ minutes.

Drop the dough onto the prepared cookie sheet (crosswise), fashioning 5 buns that resemble hot dog buns (7" long × 1½" wide × 1" high). Smooth the buns with a rubber spatula.

Bake for 20 minutes, then reduce heat to 350° and bake for 20 minutes more. Remove from oven and prick with a knife to let steam escape. Serve cold, with any of the wrap fillings you choose. *Makes 5 buns.*

Nutrients per bun: Calories 180, Fat 12g, Cholesterol 85mg,
Sodium 135mg, Carbohydrates 15g, Protein 4g, Fiber 0g.

Fillings for Wraps

The burrito of Mexican ancestry has turned into one of today's eating fashions. Both the Rice Tortillas (page 192) and the Choux Pastry Wraps (page 190) can contain a variety of ingredients. Almost any combination of crisp vegetables, meat, and dressings can be used together in the popular wrapped sandwiches. Use your imagination to combine several of the following:

Spreadable cream cheese

Mayonnaise

Sliced turkey, chicken, or ham

Canned tuna, chicken, or corned beef

Deviled ham

Flaked crab, fresh, canned, or frozen

Chopped cooked bacon

Small cooked shrimp

Cheese, grated or sliced

Shredded lettuce

Alfalfa sprouts

Bean sprouts

Finely diced onion

Finely diced celery

Chopped cucumbers

Sliced or diced fresh tomatoes

Pickle relish

Chopped black olives

Rice Tortillas

These top-of-the-stove wraps are made in the traditional way by flattening and rolling the dough and then cooking on a hot griddle. They are more trouble to prepare than the Choux Wraps (page 190), but they can be made and kept flat in the freezer for use anytime.

2 cups GF Mix or Featherlight
  Mix
1½ teaspoons xanthan gum
2 teaspoons sugar

1 teaspoon salt
2 teaspoons milk powder or
  nondairy substitute
1 cup warm water

In the bowl of your electric mixer, whisk together the flour mix, xanthan gum, sugar, salt, and milk powder. Add the water and beat on medium for 1 minute.

Remove the dough from the mixer and shape into a ball; divide into 6–8 pieces and, working on plastic wrap dusted with cornstarch, roll each piece into a thin 10"–12" round. Roll all the pieces, separating them with plastic wrap before cooking.

Cook each tortilla on a medium-hot griddle about 1 minute per side. *Makes 6 large or 8 smaller tortilla wraps.*

Nutrients per serving: Calories 180, Fat 1g, Cholesterol 0mg, Sodium 370mg, Carbohydrates 38g, Protein 4g, Fiber 2g.

Seasoned Pizza Crust 400°

Several generations of Americans have embraced the open-faced sandwich we call pizza as our own. We cover it with meat, seafood, vegetables, and even fruit. And we eat it for lunch, dinner, and on dates.

Note: *These crusts can be filled and cooked at home immediately or partly baked (for 10 minutes) and frozen for later use. Or take them to your local pizzeria, which will add toppings, bake the pies, and serve them to you on the premises.*

DRY INGREDIENTS:

1¾ cups rice flour

1¼ cups tapioca flour

1 tablespoon xanthan gum

2 teaspoons gelatin

1 tablespoon Egg Replacer

⅓ cup sugar

3 tablespoons dry milk powder or nondairy substitute

1½ teaspoons Italian Pizza seasoning

1 teaspoon salt

1 tablespoon yeast

WET INGREDIENTS:

4 egg whites

3 tablespoons vegetable oil

1 teaspoon dough enhancer

1½ cups lukewarm water

Preheat oven to 400°. Lightly grease 2 cookie sheets or round, solid-bottom pizza pans.

In a medium bowl, whisk together the dry ingredients.

Place the wet ingredients in the bowl of your heavy duty mixer and blend. (Reserve some of the water.) Turn the mixer to low and add the flour mix. Add more water if needed to get a firm dough that can still be spread. Beat on high for 3½ minutes.

Divide the dough in half onto the prepared sheets and spread in circles about 12" in diameter, making sure the edges are raised to contain the sauce. (I do this with a thin spatula, turning the pan and forcing the dough to thin out except at the edges.)

Let rise about 10 minutes and then bake for 10 minutes while preparing your toppings. Spread on your choice of pizza sauces, cheeses, and meats. Bake again about 22–25 minutes. *Makes two 12-inch thick pizza crusts or 14-inch thin ones. Each pizza serves 6–8.*

Nutrients per serving: Calories 200, Fat 5g, Cholesterol 5mg, Sodium 220mg, Carbohydrates 35g, Protein 4g, Fiber 1g.

Breads

Why more breads when I wrote a whole book on them earlier? Because these breads have additions of our new flours making them both more tasty as well as more nutritious. The revised recipes may sound familiar since they are often based on the ones we've been using for years, but notice the addition of teff, Montina, or another of the new exotic flours. Not everyone is expected to like all of them, since some celiacs may be sensitive to some of the added flours; but, within the chapter, I'm sure you will find at least one of the breads you like well enough to prepare as a staple.

If you keep the bread's dry ingredients mixed up and bagged in your refrigerator, it takes only 5 minutes to make up the wet ingredients and blend them all into dough in your heavy-duty mixer. Let it rise only 35 minutes and then put in the oven to bake. All this can be done while you're preparing dinner, and your fresh bread will be baked, cooled, sliced, and bagged in plastic in a short evening with almost no extra work. Of course, bread should not be sliced when hot, but who can resist cutting off a thick heel before it cools? All of these breads freeze well.

Unfortunately, not everyone has tried yeast baking. This is too bad for there is nothing more comforting than bread fresh from the oven. And since these are really as easy to make as a cake (since they are "batter" breads), I beg you who haven't tried to make them to get out your mixer and whip one up. An easy way to start is to turn to the Honey Graham Crumpets (page 214) and stir them up with a hand held mixer. Or, if using yeast seems too difficult, mix up a batch of the cakelike muffins, using baking powder and/or baking soda.

Sorghum Bread

400°

A springy, white sourdough bread with a rich flavor. The Featherlight Mix plus sorghum flour gives this bread the taste and texture of a white bread made with wheat. More nutrition for those who can't use bean flour.

DRY INGREDIENTS:
3 cups Featherlight Mix
1 cup sorghum flour
4 teaspoons xanthan gum
1 teaspoon salt
2 teaspoons Egg Replacer
2 teaspoons unflavored gelatin
⅓ cup buttermilk powder or
   almond meal
⅓ cup sugar

WET INGREDIENTS:
2 cups lukewarm (110°) water
   (more or less)
½ teaspoon sugar
1 tablespoon yeast
1 egg plus 3 egg whites
1 teaspoon dough enhancer or
   vinegar
⅔ cup sourdough starter
6 tablespoons vegetable oil

Grease two 8½" × 4½" loaf pans and dust with rice flour.

In a medium bowl, whisk together the dry ingredients.

Measure the water and stir in the sugar and yeast to proof. Foam should rise about ½".

In the bowl of your heavy-duty mixer, whisk the egg, egg whites, dough enhancer, sourdough starter, and oil. Add most of the yeast-water.

With the mixer turned to low, add the flour mix a little at a time. Check to be sure the dough is thin enough (should be like a thick cake batter). Add more of the suggested yeast-water as necessary. Turn the mixer to high and beat for 3½ minutes.

Spoon the dough into the prepared pans, cover, and let rise about 35–45 minutes for rapid-rising yeast; 60 or more minutes for regular yeast (or until the bread has risen about one-half more than its original size). Bake in a preheated 400° oven for 60–65 minutes, covering with aluminum foil after the first 10 minutes.

Nutrients per slice: Calories 140, Fat 3g, Cholesterol 10mg,
Sodium 85mg, Carbohydrates 26g, Protein 2g, Fiber 1g.

Light Graham Bread 400°

With teff flour, you can make a delicate-tasting graham-like bread that's every bit as light and tasty as one using wheat flour.

DRY INGREDIENTS:
⅔ cup teff flour (dark preferred)
1⅓ cups Featherlight Mix
1½ teaspoons xanthan gum
½ teaspoon salt
1 teaspoon gelatin
1 teaspoon Egg Replacer
2 tablespoons brown sugar

WET INGREDIENTS:
1 cup lukewarm water (more or less)
Pinch of sugar
1 tablespoon yeast
1 egg plus 1 egg white
1 teaspoon dough enhancer or
  vinegar
3 tablespoons oil
2 tablespoons honey

Grease an 8½" × 4½" loaf pan.

In a medium bowl, whisk together the dry ingredients.

To the cup of lukewarm water, add a pinch of sugar and the yeast. Set aside to proof until the foam is approximately ½".

In the bowl of your mixer, break the eggs; add the dough enhancer, oil, and honey. Blend on low. Add the yeast-water and blend. Slowly spoon in the dry ingredients. If the dough doesn't fall from the paddle in a thick waterfall, add more lukewarm water by the tablespoon until the dough has the right consistency (like thick cake batter). Beat 3½ minutes on high.

Spoon into the prepared pan, cover, and let rise for about 35 minutes for quick-rising yeast and 1 hour for regular. Bake at 400° for 1 hour, covering with aluminum foil after the first 10 minutes. Remove from the pan immediately. Cool before slicing.

*Nutrients per slice: Calories 110, Fat 3g, Cholesterol 15mg,
Sodium 80mg, Carbohydrates 19g, Protein 2g, Fiber 1g.*

VARIATIONS:

SESAME GRAHAM BREAD: Add 2 tablespoons sesame seeds to the dry ingredients.

NUTTY GRAHAM BREAD: Add 3 tablespoons almond meal to the dry ingredients and 2 tablespoons chopped nuts after mixing and before spooning into the pan.

Nut and Raisin Bread

400°

The slightly branlike taste of the teff gives a wonderful flavor to this new raisin bread. This recipe can be doubled for 2 loaves.

DRY INGREDIENTS:

⅔ cup teff (ivory preferred)

¼ cup sorghum flour

1 cup plus 2 tablespoons
  Featherlight Mix

1½ teaspoons xanthan gum

2 tablespoons almond meal or
  buttermilk powder

½ teaspoon salt

1 teaspoon unflavored gelatin

2 tablespoons brown sugar

1 teaspoon Egg Replacer

WET INGREDIENTS:

1 cup lukewarm water
  (more or less)

½ teaspoon sugar

1 tablespoon yeast

1 egg plus 1 egg white

½ teaspoon dough enhancer

3 tablespoons oil

2 tablespoons honey

Additional lukewarm water
  (up to ¼ cup)

2 tablespoons chopped walnuts
  or pecans

3 tablespoons raisins

Grease an 8½" by 4½" loaf pan.

In a medium bowl, whisk together the dry ingredients.

To the cup of water, add the sugar and yeast. Set aside to proof until the foam is approximately ½".

In the bowl of your mixer, break the eggs; add the dough enhancer, oil, and honey. Blend on low. Add the yeast-water and blend. Slowly spoon in the dry ingredients. Turn the mixer to high and beat. If the dough doesn't fall from the paddle in a thick waterfall, add more lukewarm water by the tablespoon until the dough has the right consistency (like thick cake batter). Beat 3½ minutes on high.

Spoon the dough into the prepared pan, cover, and let rise about 35 minutes for quick-rising yeast and 1 hour for regular yeast. Bake in a 400° preheated oven for about 65 minutes, covering with aluminum foil after the first 10 minutes. Remove from the pan immediately. Cool before slicing.

Nutrients per slice: Calories 211, Fat 6g, Cholesterol 22mg, Sodium 135mg, Carbohydrates 36g, Protein 4g, Fiber 2g.

VARIATION:

CINNAMON-NUT BREAD: Add 1 teaspoon cinnamon to the dry ingredients. Omit the raisins and increase the nuts to ¼ cup.

---

*N*ot all xanthan gums are the same; if you find your bread dough always comes out too thin, try increasing the xanthan gum amount by one-third. Example: If 3 teaspoons are called for, use 4.

Touch-of-Honey Millet Bread 400°

The slightly sweet taste of millet gives this bread its distinctive flavor. A great sandwich loaf for it slices well and keeps its fresh soft texture.

DRY INGREDIENTS:

1 cup millet flour
1 cup Featherlight Mix
2 teaspoons xanthan gum
½ teaspoon salt
½ teaspoon unflavored gelatin
1 teaspoon Egg Replacer
1 tablespoon sugar
3 tablespoons almond meal

WET INGREDIENTS:

1 cup lukewarm water
   (more or less)
½ teaspoon sugar
2¼ teaspoons yeast
1 egg plus 1 egg white
½ teaspoon dough enhancer
3 tablespoons oil
1 tablespoon honey

Grease an 8½" by 4½" loaf pan.

In a medium bowl, whisk together the dry ingredients.

To the cup of water, add the sugar and yeast. Set aside to proof until the foam is approximately ½".

In the bowl of your mixer, break the eggs; add the dough enhancer, oil, and honey. Blend on low. Add the yeast-water and blend. Slowly spoon in the dry ingredients. Turn to high and beat. If the dough doesn't fall from the paddle in a thick waterfall, add more water by the tablespoon until the dough has the right consistency (like thick cake batter). Beat 3½ minutes on high.

Spoon the dough into the prepared pan; cover and let rise for about 35 minutes for quick-rising yeast and about 1 hour for regular. Bake in a 400° preheated oven for 1 hour, covering with aluminum foil after the first 10 minutes. Remove from the pan immediately. Cool before slicing.

Nutrients per slice: Calories 130, Fat 4g, Cholesterol 15mg,
Sodium 80mg, Carbohydrates 19g, Protein 3g, Fiber 2g.

Seattle Coffee Bread

The mild taste of Montina flour blends well with the bean flour in this bread. Its color and flavor are enhanced with coffee crystals. Use it for toast, sandwiches, or just plain eating.

DRY INGREDIENTS:
1½ cups Four Flour Mix
½ cup Montina flour
1½ teaspoons xanthan gum
1 teaspoon Egg Replacer
1 teaspoon unflavored gelatin
½ teaspoon salt
3 tablespoons sugar
3 tablespoons almond meal or
    buttermilk
1 teaspoon dried orange (or
    lemon) peel

2 tablespoons sunflower seeds
    (optional)
1 tablespoon instant coffee
    crystals or cocoa powder

WET INGREDIENTS:
1 cup lukewarm water (more or less)
1 teaspoon sugar
1 tablespoon yeast
1 egg plus 1 egg white
½ teaspoon dough enhancer
3 tablespoons vegetable oil

Grease an 8½" × 4½" loaf pan and dust with rice flour.

In a medium bowl, whisk together the dry ingredients.

To the cup of water, add the sugar and yeast. Set aside to proof until the foam is approximately ½".

In the bowl of your mixer, break the eggs; add the oil and dough enhancer. Beat on low until foamy. Add most of the yeast-water, reserving 2 tablespoons to adjust the thickness of dough. With the mixer on low, slowly spoon in the dry ingredients. The dough should have the consistency of thick cake batter. Use the remaining yeast-water if necessary and add more water if needed to achieve the right consistency. Beat 3½ minutes on high.

Spoon the dough into the prepared pan and let it rise until the dough reaches the top of the pan (about 35 minutes for fast-acting yeast and about 60 minutes for regular). Bake in a 400° preheated oven for about 50–55 minutes, covering with aluminum foil after the first 10 minutes. Remove from the pan and rub the top and sides with butter or margarine for a softer crust. Cool before slicing.

Nutrients per slice: Calories 120, Fat 4g, Cholesterol 15mg,
Sodium 80mg, Carbohydrates 17g, Protein 3g, Fiber 2g.

Potato Bread 400°

This bread, made from the special mix for corn-intolerant people, turned out to be so good that I often make it for my white bread. The combination of the large amount of potato starch in the mix and the addition of sorghum give it an excellent texture plus the wonderful flavor. For those who don't already have the mix made up, change the figures given on page 36 as "parts" to "cups" for this recipe.

DRY INGREDIENTS:

3 cups Potato Flour Mix

1 cup sorghum flour

3 teaspoons xanthan gum

2 teaspoons Egg Replacer

2 teaspoons unflavored gelatin

⅓ cup almond meal or buttermilk
   powder

WET INGREDIENTS:

2 cups warm water (more or less)

1 teaspoon sugar

1 tablespoon yeast

1 egg plus 3 egg whites

1 teaspoon dough enhancer

6 tablespoons vegetable oil

Grease two 8½" × 4½" loaf pan and dust with rice flour.

In a medium bowl, combine the dry ingredients.

In a glass measure, stir the water with the sugar and yeast. Set aside to proof until the foam is approximately ½".

In the bowl of your heavy-duty mixer, gently beat the eggs, dough enhancer, and vegetable oil. Add most of the yeast-water. With the mixer on low, slowly spoon in the dry ingredients. The remaining yeast-water should be added, as needed, after the bread has started mixing. Check to be sure the dough is like a thick cake batter. Add more of the reserved water as necessary. Turn the mixer to high and beat for 3½ minutes.

Spoon the dough into the prepared pans, cover, and let rise about 35–45 minutes for rapid-rising yeast, 60 or more minutes for regular yeast. Bake in a preheated 400° oven for 1 hour, covering with aluminum foil after 10 minutes.

*Nutrients per slice: Calories 230, Fat 7g, Cholesterol 15mg,
Sodium 25mg, Carbohydrates 39g, Protein 4g, Fiber 1g.*

Montina Bread with Seeds and Nuts 400°

Montina flour is mild, so this bread, with its rice base, has a wonderful texture but is a mild tasting, dark rice bread. The seeds and nuts give it more flavor. Excellent for tasty meat sandwiches or breakfast toast with flavorful jam.

DRY INGREDIENTS:

1½ cups Featherlight Mix
½ cup Montina flour
2 teaspoons xanthan gum
½ teaspoon salt
1 teaspoon Egg Replacer
1 teaspoon unflavored gelatin
3 tablespoons almond meal or
   buttermilk powder
⅓ cup sugar

WET INGREDIENTS:

1 cup lukewarm water (more or
   less)
½ teaspoon sugar
1 tablespoon yeast
1 egg plus 1 egg white
½ teaspoon dough enhancer
¼ cup vegetable oil
1 tablespoon honey (optional)
2 tablespoons chopped nuts
   (walnuts, pecans, other nuts)
2 tablespoons sunflower seeds

Grease an 8½" × 4½" loaf pan.

In a medium bowl, whisk together the dry ingredients.

To the cup of water, add the sugar and yeast; stir. Set aside to proof until the foam is approximately ½".

In the bowl of your mixer, place the eggs; add the dough enhancer, oil, and honey (if used). Blend on low. Add the yeast-water and blend. Slowly spoon in the dry ingredients. Turn the mixer to high and beat. If the dough doesn't fall from the paddle in a thick waterfall, add more water by the tablespoon until the dough has the right consistency (like thick cake batter). Beat for 3½ minutes on high.

Spoon into the prepared pan, cover, and let rise for about 35 minutes for quick-rising yeast and 1 hour for regular. Bake in a preheated 400° oven for 1 hour, covering with aluminum foil after the first 10 minutes. Remove from the pan immediately. Cool before slicing.

Nutrients per slice: Calories 140, Fat 6g, Cholesterol 15mg,
Sodium 80mg, Carbohydrates 20g, Protein 3g, Fiber 2g.

VARIATIONS:

RAISIN BREAD: Instead of seeds and nuts, use ¼ cup of raisins.

RAISIN-NUT BREAD: Replace the seeds and nuts with 2 tablespoons each of raisins and chopped nuts.

*T*o bring bread back to "just baked" freshness, microwave on high for 25 seconds.

Sourdough Bread Starter

Sourdough breads are well worth making the starter, keeping it, and baking our bread either from a bean flour or rice flour mix. This is made, fermented, and then replenished each time it's used. The older the starter, the tastier the bread.

If you are making new starter, prepare it at least the day before you plan to bake. Three days is better. Store it in its crock or glass jar (never metal or plastic) on the kitchen counter or in the refrigerator. If refrigerated, pull it out at least 10 hours before baking or the night before.

Rice flour works well for a starter for both rice- and bean-based breads.

2¼ teaspoons dry yeast granules

1 cup lukewarm potato water or water with 1 teaspoon instant potato flakes

1 teaspoon sugar

1 cup white rice flour

In a 1- or 1½-quart glass jar or pottery crock, dissolve the yeast in the potato water. Stir in the sugar and rice flour. Cover and let the jar sit out until fermented (1–3 days), stirring every few hours at first. The mixture will bubble up and ferment and then die down with a skim of liquid on the top. Be sure to stir well before using. The consistency should be about that of pancake batter.

Replenish after use by feeding the remaining starter with ½ cup (or 1 cup) lukewarm water and ¾ cup (or 1½ cups) rice flour, as needed, each time you bake.

---

*I*f a bread recipe calls for 2¼ teaspoons of yeast and you plan to bake in the oven, you can decrease the proofing time by increasing the yeast to 1 tablespoon. (Do not do this if using a bread machine.)

Mile-High Sourdough

400°

This is a light, springy loaf that rises and rises. I give the recipe for 2 mile-high loaves, but the measurements can be halved to make just one. The Featherlight Mix can be used, but the loaf will be smaller and heavier.

Note: *The amount of yeast is less than usual when sourdough starter is used. This can be increased for faster rising. I use 1 tablespoon and get really mile-high buns (see variation).*

DRY INGREDIENTS:

4 cups Four Flour Mix

3 teaspoons xanthan gum

1 teaspoon salt

2 teaspoons Egg Replacer

2 teaspoons unflavored gelatin

⅓ cup almond meal or buttermilk powder

⅓ cup sugar

2 teaspoons dry yeast granules

WET INGREDIENTS:

1 egg plus 3 egg whites

1 teaspoon dough enhancer or vinegar

1 cup sourdough starter (page 206)

6 tablespoons vegetable oil

2 cups lukewarm water (more or less)

Grease two 8½" × 4½" loaf pans and dust with rice flour.

In a medium bowl, combine the flour mix, xanthan gum, salt, Egg Replacer, gelatin, almond meal, sugar, and yeast. Set aside.

In another bowl (or the bowl of your heavy-duty mixer), whisk the egg, egg whites, dough enhancer, sourdough starter, oil, and most of the water. The remaining water should be added as needed, after the bread has started mixing.

With the mixer turned to low, slowly add the dry ingredients. Check to be sure the dough is thin enough (like thick cake batter for the rice flour and a little thinner for the bean flour). Add more of the reserved water as necessary. Turn the mixer to high and beat for 3½ minutes.

Spoon the dough into the prepared pans, cover, and let rise about 35–45 minutes for rapid-rising yeast; 60 or more minutes for regular yeast (or until the bread has risen about one-half more than its original size). Bake in a preheated 400° oven for 50–60 minutes, covering with aluminum foil after the first 10 minutes.

Nutrients per slice: Calories 140, Fat 4g, Cholesterol 5mg,
Sodium 80mg, Carbohydrates 22g, Protein 3g, Fiber 1g.

VARIATIONS:

MILE-HIGH SOURDOUGH BUNS: Place 12 English muffin rings on cookie sheets and spray with vegetable oil spray. Divide the dough evenly among the 12 rings. Let rise about 25–35 minutes. Bake in a preheated 400° oven for 20–22 minutes.

MILE-HIGH SESAME BREAD OR BUNS: Add 2½ tablespoons sesame seeds to the dry ingredients; add 2 teaspoons molasses to the wet ingredients; change the sugar to brown sugar.

MILE-HIGH GRANOLA BREAD OR BUNS: Add ½ cup chopped granola to the dry ingredients.

MILE-HIGH CINNAMON-RAISIN BREAD OR BUNS: Add 2 teaspoons cinnamon to the dry ingredients and stir in ½ cup golden raisins after beating and before spooning the dough into the prepared pans.

MILE-HIGH CINNAMON-RAISIN-NUT BREAD OR BUNS: Stir in ¼ cup raisins and ¼ cup nuts after beating and before spooning the dough into the prepared pans.

---

*W*hen doubling a bread recipe, do not double the amount of yeast.

Sesame Teff Bread

400°

A real winner. This tastes like a heavy dark wheat bread.

DRY INGREDIENTS:

2½ cups teff flour

1½ cups tapioca flour

3 teaspoons xanthan gum

1 teaspoon salt

2 teaspoons Egg Replacer

2 teaspoons unflavored gelatin

⅓ cup almond meal or NutQuik
   (or powdered Ensure)

⅓ cup brown sugar

3 tablespoons sesame seeds

2¼ teaspoons dry yeast granules

WET INGREDIENTS:

1 egg plus 3 egg whites

1 teaspoon dough enhancer

⅔ cup sourdough starter (page
   206)

6 tablespoons vegetable oil

2¼ cups lukewarm water
   (more or less)

Grease two 8½" × 4½" loaf pans and dust with rice flour.

In a medium bowl, combine the teff flour, tapioca flour, xanthan gum, salt, Egg Replacer, gelatin, almond meal, brown sugar, sesame seeds, and yeast.

In the bowl of a heavy-duty mixer, whisk the egg, egg whites, dough enhancer, sourdough starter, oil, and most of the water. The remaining water should be added as needed, after the bread has started mixing.

With the mixer turned to low, add the flour mix a little at a time. Check to be sure the dough is thin enough (like thick cake batter). Add more of the reserved water as needed. Turn the mixer to high and beat 3½ minutes.

Spoon the dough into the prepared pans, cover, and let rise about 35 minutes for rapid-rising yeast; 60 or more minutes for regular yeast (or until the bread has risen about one-half more than its original size). Bake in a preheated 400° oven for 50–60 minutes, covering with aluminum foil after the first 10 minutes.

*Nutrients per slice: Calories 140, Fat 4g, Cholesterol 5mg,
Sodium 80mg, Carbohydrates 22g, Protein 3g, Fiber 2g.*

Sweet "Rye" Sourdough

400°

Using teff flour, this rye bread tastes much like the real rye breads. The loaf is tender and springy, the flavor rich and slightly sweet, while the loaf rises and rises.

Note: *The amount of yeast can be cut when sourdough starter is used. This can be increased for faster rising when baking the bread in the oven but not if using an automatic bread machine.*

DRY INGREDIENTS:
3 cups Four Flour Mix or
    Featherlight Mix
1 cup brown teff flour
3 teaspoons xanthan gum
1 teaspoon salt
2 teaspoons Egg Replacer
2 teaspoons unflavored gelatin
½ teaspoon rye flavor powder
4 teaspoons caraway seeds
1 teaspoon espresso powder
⅓ cup buttermilk powder

2–3 teaspoons dry yeast granules
⅓ cup sugar

WET INGREDIENTS:
1 egg plus 3 egg whites
1 teaspoon dough enhancer or
    vinegar
1 cup sourdough starter (page 206)
1 tablespoon molasses
6 tablespoons vegetable oil
2 cups plus 2 tablespoons
    lukewarm water (more or less)

Grease two 8½" × 4½" loaf pans and dust with rice flour.

In a medium bowl, combine the dry ingredients (including the yeast). Set aside.

In the bowl of your heavy-duty mixer, whisk the egg, egg whites, dough enhancer, sourdough starter, molasses, oil, and most of the water. The remaining water should be added as needed, after the bread has started mixing.

With the mixer turned to low, add the dry ingredients, a little at a time. Check to be sure the dough is thin enough (like thick cake batter for the rice flour and a little thinner for the bean flour). Add more of the reserved water as necessary. Turn the mixer to high and beat for 3½ minutes.

Spoon the dough into the prepared pans, cover, and let rise about 35–45 minutes for rapid-rising yeast; 60 or more minutes for regular yeast (or until the bread has risen about one-half more than its original size). Bake in a preheated 400° oven for 50–60 minutes, covering with aluminum foil after the first 10 minutes.

Nutrients per slice: Calories 140, Fat 3g, Cholesterol 10mg, Sodium 90mg, Carbohydrates 24g, Protein 3g, Fiber 2g.

VARIATION:

RYE BUNS: Grease 2 sets (6 buns each) of hamburger bun pans or place 12 English muffin rings on cookie sheets and spray with vegetable oil spray. Divide the dough evenly among the 12 rings. Cover and let rise about 25–35 minutes. Bake 21–22 minutes.

Yeast is a living organism and loses life as it ages, so always check the date on your yeast package. Make sure it is fresh.

Canned Bread

350°

This could be called "Traveling Bread," for with GF canned bread in the suitcase, a celiac can travel for weeks and still have "fresh" bread by opening a jar. It's as simple to seal the jar of bread fresh from the oven as it was in years past to can fruit "open kettle" style. All that's needed are widemouthed canning jars, boiling water to sterilize the lids, and a little bit of practice.

DIRECTIONS: Grease the bottom half of clean, widemouthed pint jars and dust with rice flour. Fill half full (1 cup) with prepared dough. Wipe all grease and batter from the mouth of each jar. Place the jars on a cookie sheet. Bake open jars at 350° for about 40 minutes. About 10 minutes before the bread is finished, put water on to boil to scald the inner lids and heat the rings, keeping them in the water at least 3 minutes (and until used). Remove one jar from the oven and quickly place the scalded lid (shaken dry) on the clean hot top. Screw the ring down tightly. If the bread has risen above the top, press it back into the jar. Repeat the process until all jars are sealed. Do not move the jars until the vacuum seals them. Check to be certain each jar has sealed.*

Canned bread may be stored on the shelf for approximately 6 months.

SUGGESTIONS:

A recipe for a single loaf (2 cups flour) will fill 3 pint jars. Beginners are advised to start with this number. The jars and lids will be hot, and you have to handle them carefully and quickly.

Any yeast-free loaf bread recipe will can successfully. We have tested Banana-Nut Bread, Pineapple-Walnut Bread, plain loaf breads, and cakes. Large pieces of fruit should be avoided. Purees and fine nuts work well.

Yeast breads should be treated like any yeast loaf, with the rising preceding the baking. Baking time will be the same (40 minutes at 350°). If, after baking, a yeast bread has risen above the top of the jar, cut the top of the loaf off, rather than pressing it down. If it needs to be cut, do so and then return the jar to the oven to sterilize it again.

Jars and rings are reusable. Always purchase new lids.

*This process was developed and tested in the Department of Food Science, Penn State University, under the direction of Dr. Gerald Kuhn. Additional information was obtained from Connie Moyers, home economist, Roosevelt County Cooperative Extension Service, Portales, New Mexico. The first testing of GF breads was done by Virginia Schmuck and Genevieve Potts in that city.

Bette's Best Hamburger Buns

400°

These buns have the flavor and texture of breads using the sourdough starter. Even if you don't have the sourdough flavoring, these are still excellent buns.

Note: *Hamburger bun pans may be ordered from King Arthur Flour (see list of suppliers in back of book).*

DRY INGREDIENTS:	WET INGREDIENTS:
1½ cups Featherlight Mix	1¼ cups lukewarm water
½ cup sorghum flour	(more or less)
2 teaspoons baking powder	1 tablespoon yeast
2 scant teaspoons xanthan gum	½ teaspoon sugar
1 teaspoon gelatin	1 egg plus 1 egg white
½ teaspoon salt	½ teaspoon dough enhancer
2 tablespoons sugar	2 tablespoons sourdough flavor
2 tablespoons buttermilk powder	(optional)
or almond meal	¼ cup oil

Grease one hamburger bun pan (6 buns) or place 8 muffin rings on a cookie sheet and spray with vegetable oil spray.

In a medium bowl, combine the dry ingredients.

Measure 1 cup of the water. Stir in the yeast and sugar. Set aside to proof until the foam is about ½".

In the bowl of your mixer, beat the egg, egg white, dough enhancer, sourdough flavor (if used), and oil. With the mixer on low, blend in the yeast-water. With the mixer still on low, add the flour mix. The batter should have the consistency of thick cake batter. Add the remaining yeast-water by tablespoon if needed. Turn the mixer to high and beat for 3½ minutes.

Spoon the dough into the prepared pans, cover, and let rise 20–25 minutes. Bake in a preheated 400° oven 22 minutes. *Makes 6–8 buns.*

*Nutrients per serving: Calories 230, Fat 8g, Cholesterol 25mg,
Sodium 260mg, Carbohydrates 36g, Protein 4g, Fiber 3g.*

Honey Graham Crumpets

375°

An old favorite takes on a whole new flavor with the use of teff flour. These crumpets require only a handheld mixer and can be baked in either English muffin rings or a hamburger bun pan.

Note: *Hamburger bun pans may be ordered from King Arthur Flour (see list of suppliers in back of book) if you can't find them at your local kitchen store.*

DRY INGREDIENTS:

⅔ cup teff flour

1⅓ cups Featherlight Mix

1½ teaspoons xanthan gum

2 teaspoons baking powder

1 teaspoon Egg Replacer

1 teaspoon unflavored gelatin
  (optional)

2 tablespoons brown sugar

1 tablespoon buttermilk powder
  or almond meal

1 teaspoon salt

WET INGREDIENTS:

½ teaspoon sugar

1¼ cups lukewarm water
  (more or less)

2¼ teaspoons yeast

⅓ cup liquid egg substitute or 1
  egg plus 1 egg white

½ teaspoon dough enhancer or
  vinegar

3 tablespoons oil

2 tablespoons honey

Place 8 English muffin rings on a cookie sheet and spray with vegetable oil or grease a 6-bun hamburger pan.

In a medium bowl, whisk together the dry ingredients.

Add the sugar to the water and stir in the yeast. Set aside to proof until the foam is approximately ⅓"–½".

In a large mixing bowl, place the egg substitute, dough enhancer, oil, and honey. Blend with a handheld mixer. Add the yeast-water and beat until incorporated.

Add half the dry ingredients and beat until smooth. Stir in the remaining dry ingredients and beat with a spoon until smooth. Add more water, 1 tablespoon at a time, if needed, until the dough has the consistency of heavy cake batter.

Spoon into the prepared rings (or pan), cover, and let rise in a warm place for about 20–25 minutes for rapid-rising yeast and 40–50 minutes for the regular. Bake in a preheated 375° oven for 20–23 minutes until the crumpets are lightly browned and pulled slightly from the ring edges. Remove the rings while still warm.

Nutrients per bun: Calories 210, Fat 8g, Cholesterol 25mg,
Sodium 160mg, Carbohydrates 34g, Protein 5g, Fiber 3g.

Dough enhancer may be ordered from several suppliers listed in the back of this book or found locally at some stores that sell bread baking supplies. Be sure to check if theirs is gluten free.

Crumpets Plus

375°

These easy-to-make buns are probably my favorite bread alternative. They can be used at breakfast, lunch, dinner, or snack time. As you can see, I've increased my original recipe and made a few variations.

DRY INGREDIENTS:

2 cups GF Mix or Featherlight
   Mix or Four Flour Mix

1 rounded teaspoon xanthan gum

2 teaspoons baking powder

1 teaspoon unflavored gelatin

1½ teaspoons Egg Replacer

½ teaspoon salt

2 tablespoons dry milk powder,
   almond meal, or NutQuik
   (optional)

WET INGREDIENTS:

2 tablespoons sugar, divided

1¼ cups lukewarm water
   (more or less)

1 tablespoon dry yeast granules

1 egg plus 1 egg white

½ teaspoon dough enhancer

4 tablespoons margarine or
   butter, melted, or oil

Place 8 English muffin rings on a cookie sheet and spray with cooking oil.

In a medium bowl, whisk together your choice of flour mix plus the remaining dry ingredients.

Place 1 teaspoon of the sugar in a 2-cup measure; add the water and yeast. Set aside to proof until the foam is ½".

In the bowl of your mixer, place the remaining sugar, the egg, and extra whites, dough enhancer, and margarine. Beat slightly. Add the yeast-water; beat to mix. Add half of the flour mix and beat until smooth. Add the remaining flour mix and beat about 3 minutes.

Spoon the dough into the prepared rings, cover, and let rise until doubled in bulk (about 25–35 minutes for rapid-rising yeast, 45–60 minutes for regular yeast). Bake in a preheated 375° oven for 20–22 minutes. Cool slightly before removing rings. *Makes 8 crumpets.*

Nutrients per serving: Calories 225, Fat 6g, Cholesterol 35mg, Sodium 310mg, Carbohydrates 33g, Protein 3g, Fiber 1g.

VARIATIONS:

CINNAMON-RAISIN CRUMPETS: Add 1 teaspoon cinnamon to the dry ingredients and just before spooning into rings, stir in ⅓ cup raisins.

MULTIGRAIN CRUMPETS: Add sesame, poppy, and/or chopped sunflower seeds, chopped soy or other nuts.

SESAME SEED CRUMPETS: Add 2 teaspoons sesame seeds to the dry ingredients.

ORANGE CRUMPETS: Use warmed orange juice for the liquid and add 1 teaspoon orange zest or dried orange peel to the dry ingredients.

---

*I*ngredient temperatures: Everything should be **cold** for pastry; **warm** (room temperature) for bread.

Walnut Bread

350°

This great-tasting bread is heavy and thickly studded with walnuts. The zucchini adds moisture, so it keeps well for days. Use it in place of cookies for dessert or serve it to guests with coffee or wine.

DRY INGREDIENTS:

1 cup teff flour
1 cup Featherlight Mix
2 teaspoons xanthan gum
1 teaspoon cinnamon
½ teaspoon cloves
1 teaspoon baking soda
2 teaspoons baking powder
1 teaspoon unflavored gelatin
½ teaspoon salt
1 teaspoon dried lemon peel
1 teaspoon Egg Replacer

WET INGREDIENTS:

2 eggs
½ cup sugar
⅓ cup oil
⅓ cup orange juice (more if needed)
1½ cups grated zucchini
1 cup chopped walnuts

Preheat oven to 350°. Grease an 8½" × 4½" loaf pan and dust with rice flour.

In a medium bowl, whisk together the dry ingredients.

In the bowl of your mixer, cream the eggs, sugar, and oil. Add the orange juice and with the mixer on low, spoon in the dry ingredients. Beat until blended. The dough should be about as thick as cake batter. If too thick, add more orange juice by the tablespoon until the desired consistency is reached. Fold in the zucchini and walnuts.

Spoon the dough into the prepared pan and bake 1 hour. Turn out of pan to cool. Slice when cold.

Nutrients per slice: Calories 180, Fat 8g, Cholesterol 25mg, Sodium 200mg, Carbohydrates 24g, Protein 4g, Fiber 2g.

Banana Bread Deluxe

This very special banana bread owes its light texture to the cream cheese and its delicate flavor to teff flour. The flavor is richer the second day if the bread is kept well wrapped.

DRY INGREDIENTS:

1 cup teff flour (ivory preferred)

1¼ cups Featherlight Mix

2 teaspoons xanthan gum

2 teaspoons baking powder

1 teaspoon baking soda

1 teaspoon Egg Replacer

1 teaspoon unflavored gelatin

WET INGREDIENTS:

One 8-ounce package cream cheese

1 cup sugar

¼ cup margarine or butter (½ stick)

2 eggs

1 cup mashed bananas blended with ½ cup buttermilk

½ cup chopped pecans

Preheat oven to 350°. Grease two 8½" × 4½" loaf pans and dust with rice flour.

In a medium bowl, whisk together the dry ingredients.

In the bowl of your mixer, cream the cream cheese with the sugar and margarine. Add the eggs, beating after each addition. Blend in the banana-buttermilk mixture. With the mixer on low, add the dry ingredients and beat only until blended. Stir in the nuts.

Spoon the dough into the prepared pans and bake for 40–45 minutes or until a tester comes out clean. Cool before slicing.

Nutrients per slice: Calories 250, Fat 11g, Cholesterol 40mg, Sodium 220mg, Carbohydrates 34g, Protein 4g, Fiber 2g.

Sweet Potato and Cranberry Loaf 350°

Teff, sweet potato, and cranberry sauce combine to make a flavorful tea bread that's tasty enough for dessert but filling enough for breakfast.

DRY INGREDIENTS:
1 cup Featherlight Mix
1 cup teff flour (dark is excellent)
2 scant teaspoons xanthan gum
¾ cup sugar
1 rounded teaspoon baking soda
2 teaspoons baking powder
1 teaspoon pumpkin pie spice
½ teaspoon salt

WET INGREDIENTS:
1 cup cooked sweet potatoes,
   mashed
1 cup whole cranberry sauce
3 slightly beaten eggs
⅓ cup vegetable oil
½ cup buttermilk

½ cup chopped pecans (optional)

Preheat oven to 350°. Grease a 9" × 5" loaf pan and dust with rice flour.

In a large mixing bowl, whisk together the dry ingredients. Set aside.

In a medium bowl, combine the sweet potatoes and cranberry sauce. Add the beaten eggs and oil. Blend well, beating in the buttermilk. Stir this mixture into the dry ingredients, beating just until blended. Fold in the pecans (if used).

Spoon the dough into the prepared pan and bake for 1 hour, then test for doneness. If the tester does not come out clean, bake for an additional 8 minutes or so. Cool in the pan for 10 minutes before turning out onto a rack to cool completely. Cool before slicing. The flavor is best if the loaf is allowed to cool for several hours or overnight. *Makes 18 servings.*

*Nutrients per slice: Calories 190, Fat 5g, Cholesterol 35mg,
Sodium 200mg, Carbohydrates 33g, Protein 3g, Fiber 2g.*

Pineapple-Zucchini Bread with Teff 350°

No book of comfort foods would be complete without this old favorite that's been revised and updated with teff flour to increase the flavor. If you don't have teff and wish to try the bread, substitute 1 extra cup of your chosen flour mix.

DRY INGREDIENTS:
1 cup teff flour
2 cups Four Flour Mix or
　Featherlight Mix
3 teaspoons xanthan gum
1 teaspoon baking powder
2 teaspoons baking soda
1 teaspoon salt
1½ teaspoons cinnamon
¾ teaspoon nutmeg

WET INGREDIENTS:
3 eggs
1⅓ cups sugar
1 cup vegetable oil
1 teaspoon dried lemon peel
2 cups zucchini, coarsely
　shredded
One 8-ounce can crushed
　pineapple, drained

1 cup chopped walnuts
1 cup raisins

Preheat oven to 350°. Grease two 4½" × 8½" pans.

In a large mixing bowl, whisk together the dry ingredients.

In the bowl of your mixer, beat the eggs on medium speed until foamy. Add the sugar, oil, and lemon peel. Beat for 2 minutes. Stir in the zucchini and pineapple.

Stir the flour mix into the wet ingredients in the mixer. Blend well. Add the walnuts and the raisins.

Spoon the dough into the prepared pans. Bake 50–55 minutes or until a tester comes out clean. Cool in the pans for 10 minutes before removing to finish cooling. *Makes 15 slices.*

*Nutrients per slice: Calories 390, Fat 19g, Cholesterol 40mg,
Sodium 370mg, Carbohydrates 52g, Protein 6g, Fiber 4g.*

Teff Muffins

350°

With the flavor of dark teff flour so much like bran, these muffins taste like old-fashioned bran muffins. They're delicious whether you use nuts or raisins or both.

⅔ cup dark teff flour
⅓ cup tapioca flour
½ teaspoon xanthan gum
¼ teaspoon salt
1 teaspoon baking powder
½ teaspoon baking soda
¼ cup sugar

½ cup chopped nuts or ½ cup
   raisins (or both at ¼ cup each)
2 eggs
2 tablespoons oil or melted butter
½ cup buttermilk, orange juice,
   or soy milk

Preheat oven to 350°. Grease ten 2" muffin cups or six 2½" cups or line with paper liner and spray with vegetable oil spray.

In a medium mixing bowl, combine the teff flour, tapioca flour, xanthan gum, salt, baking powder, baking soda, and sugar. Add the nuts and/or raisins.

In a small bowl, beat the eggs; add the oil and buttermilk. Add to the dry ingredients and mix only until all the flour is damp. (The batter may be slightly lumpy.)

Spoon the batter into the muffin cups and bake about 20 minutes. *Makes ten 2˝ muffins.*

*Nutrients per muffin: Calories 120, Fat 4g, Cholesterol 50mg,
Sodium 209mg, Carbohydrates 18g, Protein 3g, Fiber 2g.*

Coffee Muffins

Stir up these muffins, with their delicate coffee flavor, for breakfast, lunch, or dinner. For increased flavor, add more coffee crystals. For a mocha taste, use the chocolate chips.

1½ cups Four Flour Mix	3 tablespoons butter or
½ cup sugar	margarine, melted
2 teaspoons baking powder	2 eggs
½ teaspoon baking soda	2 teaspoons instant coffee crystals
¼ teaspoon salt	¾ cup buttermilk
¼ teaspoon cinnamon	¾ cup chocolate chips (optional)

Preheat oven to 375°. Grease 12 muffin cups.

In a medium bowl, whisk together flour mix, sugar, baking powder, baking soda, salt, and cinnamon.

In a mixing bowl, whisk the butter, eggs, and coffee crystals until smooth. Stir in half the flour mixture until just moistened. Add half the buttermilk and half the remaining flour and stir. Finish with the other half of each. Do not beat!

Divide the batter between the muffin cups and bake 22–25 minutes. *Makes 12 muffins.*

Nutrients per muffin: Calories 290, Fat 9g, Cholesterol 57mg, Sodium 396mg, Carbohydrates 47g, Protein 6g, Fiber 1g.

Bette's Bran Muffins

400°

A favorite at family gatherings, these really do taste like those bran muffins that are a popular item at many bakeries. I never mention that mine are gluten free and the bran comes from rice or corn cereal—and everyone eats them.

1¾ cups Four Flour or Bean Mix
1½ cups crushed rice-corn cereal
1 teaspoon xanthan gum
⅓ cup sugar
2 teaspoons baking powder
1 teaspoon baking soda
½ teaspoon salt
1 teaspoon Egg Replacer

One 6-ounce jar baby squash
½ cup orange juice
⅓ cup corn syrup
3 tablespoons vegetable oil
2 eggs slightly beaten or ½ cup
   liquid egg substitute
½ cup raisins

Preheat oven to 400°. Line 18 muffin cups with paper liners and spray with vegetable oil spray.

In a large mixing bowl, whisk together the flour mix, cereal, xanthan gum, sugar, baking powder, baking soda, salt, and Egg Replacer.

In a medium bowl, combine the squash, orange juice, corn syrup, oil, and beaten eggs. Pour this mixture into the dry ingredients and stir until well mixed. Stir in the raisins.

Divide into the prepared paper cups and bake at 400° for 20 minutes. Cool slightly before removing from the pan or removing the paper shells. *Makes 18 muffins.*

Nutrients per serving: Calories 140, Fat 3g, Cholesterol 25mg,
Sodium 200mg, Carbohydrates 25g, Protein 3g, Fiber 1g.

Banana-Nut Montina Muffins 375°

The triple flavor of spice, banana, and walnuts goes well with the bland mixture of Montina flour and Featherlight Mix. These light and tender muffins can serve as breakfast bread or beside a luncheon salad.

⅔ cup Montina flour
⅔ cup Featherlight Mix
⅓ teaspoon salt
½ teaspoon baking soda
1 rounded teaspoon baking
    powder
⅓ cup sugar
½ teaspoon pumpkin pie spice

3 tablespoons chopped nuts
    (walnuts, pecans, etc.)
2 ripe bananas, mashed
1 tablespoon lemon juice
⅓ cup butter or margarine,
    melted
2 eggs, slightly beaten with fork
⅓ cup buttermilk

Preheat oven to 375°. Line 12 muffin cups with paper liners and spray with vegetable oil spray.

In a mixing bowl, whisk together Montina flour, flour mix, salt, baking soda, baking powder, sugar, and spice. Mix in the nuts.

In a medium bowl, stir together the bananas, lemon juice, melted butter, eggs, and buttermilk. Add to the dry ingredients and beat until just mixed.

Spoon the batter into the muffin tins. Bake for 18–20 minutes. Serve while warm. *Makes 12 muffins.*

*Nutrients per muffin: Calories 140, Fat 3g, Cholesterol 25mg,
Sodium 200mg, Carbohydrates 25g, Protein 3g, Fiber 1g.*

Featherlight Biscuits

450°

Finally, a plain biscuit that flakes and tastes delicious. All my other biscuit recipes call for egg, but these don't. Use these for biscuits and gravy, for shortcake, or for eating with butter.

⅞ cup Featherlight Mix	1 teaspoon sugar
½ teaspoon xanthan gum	½ teaspoon salt
1½ teaspoons baking powder	3 tablespoons shortening
½ teaspoon baking soda	½ cup buttermilk

Preheat oven to 450°.

In a mixing bowl, combine the flour mix, xanthan gum, baking powder, baking soda, sugar, and salt. Using a pastry blender or two knives, cut in the shortening until the mixture resembles coarse crumbs. Stir in the buttermilk and work gently until the dough forms a ball.

Turn out onto a surface dusted with sweet rice flour and pat or lightly roll to ¾" thickness. Cut the dough into 2½" squares or form round biscuits using a 2½" round cutter. Place 1" apart on ungreased baking sheets. Bake for 10–12 minutes. *Makes 8 biscuits.*

Nutrients per biscuit: Calories 130, Fat 6g, Cholesterol 25mg, Sodium 320mg, Carbohydrates 18g, Protein 0g, Fiber 0g.

Nutty Graham Crackers

325°

These crackers taste so much like the wheat-based ones that you will think you are eating wheat. The secret is the teff-sorghum combination of flours.

½ cup teff flour (dark or ivory)
½ cup sorghum flour
½ cup tapioca flour
½ cup cornstarch
½ cup almond (or pecan) meal
½ teaspoon xanthan gum
1½ teaspoons salt
1½ tablespoons baking powder

1 teaspoon cinnamon
¾ cup (1½ sticks) butter or
  margarine
¼ cup honey
1 cup brown sugar
1 teaspoon vanilla
1–2 tablespoons water (if needed)

Preheat oven to 325°. Grease two 12" × 15½" baking sheets.

In a medium bowl, whisk together the teff, sorghum, tapioca and cornstarch flours, almond meal, xanthan gum, salt, baking powder, and cinnamon.

In the bowl of your mixer, beat together the butter, honey, brown sugar, and vanilla. Add the dry ingredients. This should form a soft dough ball that will handle easily. (You probably will not need the water, but add if necessary.) Divide the dough into 2 balls.

Place each ball on a cookie sheet and cover with plastic wrap; roll it out until it covers the sheet and is about ⅛" thick, like pastry dough. Cut with a pastry wheel into 3" squares. Prick each square with a fork 5 times.

Bake for about 25 minutes, reversing the position of the pans at the halfway point in baking. *Makes about 5 dozen crackers.*

*Nutrients per cracker: Calories 60, Fat 2½ g, Cholesterol 5mg,
Sodium 90mg, Carbohydrates 10g, Protein 1g, Fiber 1g.*

Dumplings

The one food that most people thought of when I said I was writing a book on comfort food was "Dumplings!" Some dreamed of them with chicken and others with soup. My mother even dropped them into boiling berry sauce for a "comfort" dessert.

My first attempts with rice flour were heavy and doughy, but this new one is light and fluffy as a dumpling should be. Use them with chicken (page 141), with sweetened berries swimming in juice, as on page 268, or drop them on any boiling soup you can cover.

1 cup Featherlight Mix
½ teaspoon xanthan gum
2 teaspoons Egg Replacer
2 teaspoons baking powder
½ teaspoon baking soda
1 teaspoon sugar for soup,
   1 tablespoon for dessert fruits

¼ teaspoon salt
1 rounded tablespoon buttermilk
   powder
1 egg, beaten
⅔ cup water

In a mixing bowl, whisk together the flour mix, xanthan gum, Egg Replacer, baking powder, baking soda, sugar, salt, and buttermilk powder.

In a small bowl, beat the egg with a fork and add the water. Stir the liquid into the dry mix, holding back a bit of the water to be sure the batter isn't too thin. It should hold its shape when spooned out to drop into the boiling soup or berry sauce.

Have your liquid boiling and spoon out the batter with a dessert-sized spoon, dropping in 10 separate balls. Let the liquid return to a boil, reduce heat to simmer, cover, and cook for 10–12 minutes. (No peeking!) Remove from the stove and serve immediately for soups. Serve warm for desserts. *Makes 10 dumplings.*

Nutrients per dumpling: Calories 70, Fat ½ g, Cholesterol 20mg,
Sodium 200mg, Carbohydrates 13g, Protein 1g, Fiber 0g.

Desserts

Do desserts belong in a book of comfort foods? I certainly think they do. I cannot ever remember considering a meal finished without that "something sweet" at the end. True, when I was sickly but didn't know I was a celiac, that "something" was usually canned fruit from our outdoor, underground cellar for, even then, cakes and cookies gave me stomach distress. And I usually just ate the filling out of a pie and discarded the crust.

Now, with recipes for cakes, cookies, and pie crusts from GF flours, we can have our choice at home. We can make the cakes and pies that we remember from our youth and that take us back to times that stand out in our memories.

I know there are more and more of these sweets showing up at the GF suppliers and realize that not everyone has memories that go back to home cooking. But for the best-tasting desserts (as well as the least expensive), there is nothing like baking at home. I hope you try some of this very varied list.

Prize Carrot Cake

350°

Almost everyone loves carrot cake, and this version is especially good. Extra flavor and moistness come from the unusual addition of green tomato puree. If you don't have green tomatoes, the hard, unripe ones from the grocery work fine in this recipe.

2¾ cups Featherlight Mix
1¼ teaspoons xanthan gum
2 teaspoons Egg Replacer
2½ teaspoons baking soda
1 teaspoon salt
2 teaspoons cinnamon
½ teaspoon ginger
1¾ cups sugar

4 eggs
1½ cups vegetable oil
1¼ cups green tomatoes, peeled
   and pureed (or mashed)
2 cups grated carrots
1 cup chopped walnuts or pecans,
   toasted

Preheat oven to 350°. Grease three 8" round cake pans.

In a medium bowl, whisk together the flour mix, xanthan gum, Egg Replacer, baking soda, salt, cinnamon, ginger, and sugar.

In the bowl of your mixer, beat the eggs slightly. Add the oil and tomato puree. Beat slowly while adding the dry ingredients. Beat only until incorporated. Stir in the carrots and nuts. The batter may seem quite thin.

Spoon into the prepared pans and bake for 30–35 minutes or until a tester comes out clean. Remove from pans and cool on racks before putting together with your favorite frosting. A cream cheese frosting is the usual one with carrot cake. *Makes 20–24 servings.*

*Nutrients per serving: Calories 340, Fat 20g, Cholesterol 45mg,
Sodium 290mg, Carbohydrates 38g, Protein 3g, Fiber 1g.*

Angel Food (Revised)

This old favorite with our GF flours can look and taste like those you made before diagnosis. Remember the secrets of angel food: the mixing bowl for the egg whites must be free of any oil and the whites themselves free of any speck of yolk.

⅓ cup potato starch
⅓ cup cornstarch
⅓ cup powdered sugar
1 teaspoon dried lemon peel
   (optional)
12 large egg whites

2 tablespoons water
½ teaspoon salt
1¼ teaspoons cream of tartar
¾ cup sugar
1 teaspoon vanilla (optional)

Preheat oven to 375°. Have available a large angel food pan with removable bottom.

Sift together 4 times the flour, cornstarch, and powdered sugar. Add lemon peel (if used).

In the bowl of your mixer, whip the egg whites, water, salt, and cream of tartar until foamy. Slowly add the sugar while beating until soft peaks form. Fold in the flour mix, a little at a time. Add the vanilla (if used) and spoon into the cake pan. Cut through the batter with a knife to eliminate any air bubbles.

Bake for 35 minutes. Reverse pan immediately when taken from oven and stand on legs or tubular center until cool. Drop the cake, reversed, onto the serving plate and frost with whipped cream or your favorite frosting, if desired. *Makes 12–16 servings.*

Nutrients per serving: Calories 80, Fat 0g, Cholesterol 0mg,
Sodium 110mg, Carbohydrates 19g, Protein 3g, Fiber 0g.

---

*E*ggs separate best when cold, but must be brought to room temperature to whip for angel food cakes.

---

232   The Gluten-free Gourmet Cooks Comfort Foods

Featherlight Chiffon Cake

325° or 350°

Here is another old favorite that has had a makeover with the "new" flours. The Featherlight Mix turned out the best cake I've made from this recipe—although other mixes have been suggested. Try this new, light chiffon next time.

2 cups Featherlight Mix
1½ cups sugar
1 tablespoon baking powder
1 teaspoon salt
½ cup vegetable oil

7 eggs, separated
¾ cup orange juice
2 teaspoons grated orange rind
½ teaspoon cream of tartar

Preheat oven to 325°. Have on hand a large tube pan, or a 9" × 13" oblong cake pan. Do not grease the pan.

In the mixer bowl, whisk together the flour mix, sugar, baking powder, and salt. Make a well in the center and add the oil, unbeaten egg yolks, orange juice, and rind. Beat on low speed until blended. Turn the mixer to high and beat 5 minutes.

In a large bowl, beat the egg whites and the cream of tartar with an electric mixer until they form very stiff peaks. Pour the batter mixture gradually over the whipped whites, gently folding with a rubber spatula until just blended.

Pour the batter into the tube or oblong pan. Bake the tube pan for 65 minutes, the oblong pan for 45–50 minutes. *Makes 16–20 servings.*

*Nutrients per serving: Calories 170, Fat 6g, Cholesterol 25mg,
Sodium 65mg, Carbohydrates 160g, Protein 2g, Fiber 0g.*

A foam (angel, sponge, and chiffon) cake is done when you touch the top lightly and it springs back.

Rinehart Family Prune Cake 350°

Janet sent me this recipe, writing, "I hope you can adapt it for gluten free. I'd love to be able to eat it again!" Using the Four Flour Mix, I prepared a rich cake with a flavor between plum pudding and spice cake.

Note: *Some prunes are soft and can be cut without cooking.*

CAKE:
1 cup cooked dried prunes
2½ cups Four Flour Mix
2 cups sugar
1½ teaspoons xanthan gum
2½ teaspoons Egg Replacer
  (optional)
1 teaspoon cinnamon
1 teaspoon cloves
1 teaspoon nutmeg
½ teaspoon salt

1 cup vegetable oil
4 eggs
1 cup buttermilk
2 scant teaspoons baking soda
1 cup chopped walnuts or pecans

GLAZE:
1 cup (2 sticks) butter or margarine
1 cup sugar
½ cup buttermilk
½ teaspoon baking soda

Preheat oven to 350°. Grease a bundt or tube pan well and dust with rice flour.

Cook the prunes (if they aren't soft), drain, and cool. (Remove any pits.) Chop slightly.

In the bowl of your mixer, blend the flour mix, sugar, xanthan gum, Egg Replacer (if used), spices, and salt. Make a hole in the center and add the oil. Mix well. Add the eggs, one at a time, beating after each addition. Add the buttermilk and baking soda and beat until smooth. Stir in the prunes and nuts.

Spoon the batter into the prepared pan and bake for 1 hour or until a tester comes out clean. Reverse immediately onto the cake plate.

To make the glaze: Melt the butter in a small saucepan. Add the sugar, buttermilk, and baking soda. Bring to a boil; boil for 1 minute. Brush immediately onto the warm cake, letting the glaze soak in over the whole surface. Cook before serving. *Makes 20–24 servings.*

*Nutrients per serving: Calories 340, Fat 20g, Cholesterol 55mg,
Sodium 260mg, Carbohydrates 40g, Protein 4g, Fiber 1g.*

Banana-Nut Cake 350°

Moist and flavorful, this cake is a sure winner.

1 cup plus 2 tablespoons Featherlight Mix	One large ripe banana, mashed
½ rounded teaspoon xanthan gum	3 tablespoons buttermilk
1 teaspoon baking powder	1½ teaspoons lemon juice
½ teaspoon baking soda	¼ cup (½ stick) margarine
1 teaspoon Egg Replacer (optional)	⅔ cup sugar
¼ teaspoon salt	2 eggs
	1 teaspoon vanilla
	¼ cup chopped pecans or walnuts

Preheat oven to 350°. Grease an 8" round cake pan.

In a medium bowl, whisk together the flour mix, xanthan gum, baking powder, baking soda, Egg Replacer (if used), and salt.

In a small bowl, add the buttermilk and lemon juice to the mashed banana.

In the bowl of your mixer, cream the margarine and sugar. Add the eggs, one at a time, beating until smooth and fluffy. Add the vanilla. Add half the dry ingredients and half the banana mixture. Beat just until smooth. Repeat with the second half. Beat about 1 minute. (Don't overbeat.) Stir in the nuts and spoon the batter into the prepared pan. Bake for approximately 30 minutes or until a tester comes out clean and the edges of the cake separate slightly from the pan. Cool before serving topped with whipped cream and fresh banana slices or with your favorite icing. *Makes 6–8 servings.*

Nutrients per serving: Calories 240, Fat 9g, Cholesterol 55mg, Sodium 290mg, Carbohydrates 38g, Protein 3g, Fiber 1g.

A creamed cake is done when a tester (purchased wire or wooden toothpick) comes out clean. If wet and sticky, bake a few minutes longer and test in another spot.

Banana-Pineapple Cake

350°

Moist and full of flavor, this cake should please all your cake-eating friends. It keeps well and tastes better the second and third day.

1 cup teff flour (ivory)	1 cup vegetable oil
2 cups Featherlight Mix	1¾ cups sugar
2 teaspoons xanthan gum	4 eggs
2 teaspoons Egg Replacer	1 teaspoon vanilla
1 teaspoon gelatin	2 cups diced bananas
1½ teaspoons baking soda	(about 3 bananas)
2 teaspoons baking powder	1 cup chopped pecans
1 teaspoon salt	One 8-ounce can crushed
2 teaspoons apple pie spice	pineapple with juice

Preheat oven to 350°. Line three 8" round cake pans with wax or parchment paper and grease, or grease a 9" × 13" oblong cake pan.

In a medium bowl, whisk together the teff flour, Featherlight Mix, xanthan gum, Egg Replacer, gelatin, baking soda, baking powder, salt, and spice.

In the bowl of a mixer, beat the oil and sugar until light. Add the eggs, one at a time, beating after each addition. Beat in the vanilla. With the mixer on low, blend in the dry ingredients but don't beat hard. Stir in the bananas, pecans, and pineapple with juice until well blended.

Spoon the batter into your prepared pan(s) and bake the round cake pans for 25 minutes or the oblong pan for 40–45 minutes or until a tester comes out clean. Cool before frosting. This cake almost shouts for a buttercream or cream cheese frosting. *Makes 20–24 servings.*

Nutrients per serving: Calories 270, Fat 13g, Cholesterol 35mg, Sodium 210mg, Carbohydrates 36g, Protein 3g, Fiber 2g.

Three Gingers Pound Cake

Take pleasure, as well as comfort, in a modern-tasting, old-fashioned pound cake. This tastes best if you can use butter.

1 cup Featherlight Mix
½ cup teff flour (ivory preferred)
1 scant teaspoon xanthan gum
1 teaspoon baking powder
½–1 teaspoon ground ginger to
 taste
¼ teaspoon salt
⅔ cup (1⅓ stick) butter or
 margarine

1⅓ cups sugar
½ tablespoon grated gingerroot
1 teaspoon vanilla
3 eggs
½ cup milk or nondairy
 substitute
2 tablespoons finely chopped
 candied ginger

Preheat oven to 350°. Grease a 9" × 5" loaf pan and dust with rice flour.

In a medium bowl, whisk together the Featherlight Mix, teff flour, xanthan gum, baking powder, ginger, and salt.

In the bowl of your mixer, beat the butter, sugar, gingerroot, vanilla, and eggs on low speed until well blended; turn the mixer to high and beat for 5 minutes. On low speed, beat in the dry ingredients alternately with the milk. Fold in the candied ginger.

Spoon the batter into the prepared pan and bake for 60–65 minutes or until a tester comes out clean. Cool for 10 minutes in pan before removing to a rack to cool completely. Serve plain, with whipped topping, or top with fruit. *Makes 12 servings.*

Nutrients per serving: Calories 270, Fat 12g, Cholesterol 80mg, Sodium 200mg, Carbohydrates 39g, Protein 3g, Fiber 1g.

---

*T*he oven must be preheated for all baking unless the recipe says differently.

Devil's Food Cake 350°

The devil's food cake was originally created to contrast with angel food, and this certainly does with its rich, dark chocolate flavor. Whether made with bean flour or with a combination of Featherlight Mix and teff, this comes out with a fine, springy texture that keeps well.

¾ cup boiling water
1 cup cocoa powder
¾ cup buttermilk
1 cup Featherlight Mix plus ¾ cup teff flour or 1¾ cups Four Flour Mix
1 scant teaspoon xanthan gum
1 teaspoon baking powder
1 teaspoon baking soda

½ teaspoon salt
2 teaspoons Egg Replacer
1½ cups brown sugar
½ cup mayonnaise
1 egg plus 1 egg white
1 teaspoon vanilla
3–4 drops red food coloring (optional)

Preheat oven to 350°. Grease a 9" × 13" oblong cake pan and dust with rice flour.

Into the boiling water, whisk the cocoa powder. Let cool slightly before adding the buttermilk.

In a medium bowl, whisk together the flour mix, xanthan gum, baking powder, baking soda, salt, and Egg Replacer. Set aside.

In the bowl of your mixer, beat the brown sugar, mayonnaise, eggs, and vanilla until light. Add the food coloring (if used). Beat in the cocoa mixture. Add the dry ingredients and beat only until well blended. (The batter may seem thin.)

Pour the batter into the prepared pan and bake for 25–30 minutes or until a tester comes out clean. Cool before frosting with your choice of frostings. Both chocolate and buttercream go well with the rich taste. *Makes 15–18 servings.*

Nutrients per serving: Calories 180, Fat 7g, Cholesterol 15mg,
Sodium 210mg, Carbohydrates 26g, Protein 3g, Fiber 1g.

Cream Cheese Pound Cake 300°

A very different version of the ever popular pound cake that uses light cream cheese for part of the shortening. This is great eaten plain but also wonderful under crushed fruit or berries. This may also be made with all Featherlight Mix.

2 cups Featherlight Mix	2½ cups sugar
½ cup sorghum flour	¾ cup buttermilk
1 rounded teaspoon xanthan gum	3 whole eggs
½ rounded teaspoon baking soda	3 egg whites
½ cup butter	1½ teaspoons vanilla extract
One 8-ounce package cream cheese (⅓ lightened is preferable)	1½ teaspoons almond extract

Preheat oven to 300°. Coat a bundt pan with nonstick spray or grease it well.

In a medium bowl, whisk together the flour mix, sorghum flour, xanthan gum, and baking soda.

In the bowl of your mixer, beat the butter, cream cheese, and sugar until light and fluffy. Beat in the buttermilk. Add the eggs and egg whites one at a time, beating well after each addition. Add the extracts and beat well. Slowly beat in the flours until well mixed.

Pour the batter into the bundt pan and bake for 1 hour and 15 minutes or until a tester inserted into cake comes out clean. Cool in the pan for 10 minutes before turning out onto the serving plate. Cool cake completely before cutting. Serve plain or with a fruit or sauce topping. *Makes 16–20 servings.*

Nutrients per serving: Calories 288, Fat 9g, Cholesterol 240mg, Sodium 55mg, Carbohydrates 5g, Protein 5g, Fiber 0g.

A cream cake is always made by beating the fat and sugar together until fluffy. This traps air to help leaven the cake and make it tender.

Chocolate Pecan Cupcakes

Montina, bean flours, and sweet chocolate make a perfect marriage in this cupcake, which all my tasters have agreed is a "keeper." I added pecans but if your family doesn't like nuts, they are optional. Eat plain or frost with icing of your choice.

2 ounces sweet chocolate	1 teaspoon Egg Replacer
¼ cup water	½ cup (1 stick) butter or margarine
1¼ cup Four Flour Mix	1 cup sugar
¼ cup Montina flour	2 eggs
1 scant teaspoon xanthan gum	½ teaspoon vanilla
¼ teaspoon salt	½ cup buttermilk
1 teaspoon baking soda	3 tablespoons chopped pecans
1 teaspoon baking powder	(optional)

Preheat oven to 350°. Fill sixteen 2" muffin cups with paper liners and spray with vegetable shortening spray.

Combine the chocolate and water in a microwaveable bowl. Microwave at defrost until a smooth sauce forms, testing every 2 minutes. Cool. If you don't have a microwave, heat water and chocolate in a pan on the stove over low heat.

In a medium bowl, blend the flour mix, Montina flour, xanthan gum, salt, baking soda, baking powder, and Egg Replacer.

In the bowl of your mixer, cream the butter and sugar. Add the eggs, beating well after each addition. Add the cool chocolate mixture and vanilla. Mix well. Add the dry ingredients alternately with the buttermilk until well blended. Remove the bowl from the mixer and stir in the pecans (if used).

Spoon the batter into the muffin cups. Bake approximately 23 minutes or until a tester comes out clean. Remove the muffins in their liners from the pans when they are cool to touch. Cool before frosting with your favorite icing or serve plain, if desired. *Makes 16 cupcakes.*

Nutrients per serving: Calories 310, Fat 17g, Cholesterol 55mg, Sodium 160mg, Carbohydrates 32g, Protein 6g, Fiber 1g.

Light White Icing

For a creamy appearance and ease of handling, nothing beats the confectioners' sugar icing. This one has some shortening for extra body and keeping quality. For a creamy color, use Butter Flavor Crisco; for a pure white, use white shortening.

1½ pounds confectioner's sugar
⅓ cup shortening
2 teaspoons vanilla

⅓ cup boiling water
Pinch of salt (to taste)

In a chilled bowl, whip the confectioners' sugar, shortening, and vanilla. Add enough boiling water to make the icing fluffy and smooth. Beat well. Add salt to taste. *Makes about 1½ cups icing.*

Nutrients per serving (2 tablespoons): Calories 116, Fat 2g, Cholesterol 0mg, Sodium 8mg, Carbohydrates 18g, Protein 0g, Fiber 0g.

VARIATIONS:

COFFEE ICING: Replace the boiling water with extra-strong coffee.

CHOCOLATE AND COFFEE ICING: Add ⅓ cup cocoa powder to the confectioners' sugar and replace the boiling water with extra-strong coffee.

LEMON-LEMON ICING: Replace the vanilla with fresh lemon zest and the water with hot lemon juice. (For a lighter lemon taste, use lemonade in place of lemon juice.)

MAPLE ICING: Change flavoring to maple and replace 2 tablespoons of the water, before boiling, with 2 tablespoons maple syrup.

Lighter Cream Cheese Frosting

Although lighter, this frosting still has the flavor and texture of your old cream cheese frosting.

One 8-ounce package reduced-fat
  cream cheese
2 tablespoons butter
1 teaspoon lemon juice

1 teaspoon orange or lemon zest
½ teaspoon lemon flavoring or
  vanilla
3 cups confectioners' sugar

In the bowl of your mixer, beat cream cheese, butter, lemon juice, zest, and flavoring until smooth. Beat in the confectioners' sugar, 1 cup at a time, until frosting is a good spreading consistency. Add additional sugar if needed. *Makes approximately 2 cups frosting.*

Nutrients per serving (2 tablespoons): Calories 100, Fat 3g, Cholesterol 10mg, Sodium 100mg, Carbohydrates 17g, Protein 1g, Fiber 0g.

If a 2-layer cake is made into cupcakes, count on 24 to 30 of the smaller cakes.

Whipped Cream Frosting

Ever had your whipped cream frosting start to weep or run just when you served your cake? With this trick you can have whipped cream that stands up for a couple of days.

1 packet unflavored gelatin	2 or 3 cups whipping cream
¼ cup cold water	Sugar to taste

Dissolve the packet of gelatin in the cold water in a small glass or metal bowl. When dissolved, place the bowl in warm water to soften the gelatin until it will pour into the cream. Place the gelatin and cream in the mixer and whip to firm peaks. Add sugar. Frost your cake and keep it refrigerated until serving. If any is left, return to refrigerator. *Makes approximately 1 quart frosting (enough for top and sides of a large cake).*

Nutrients per serving (2 tablespoons): Calories 110, Fat 10g, Cholesterol 35mg, Sodium 15mg, Carbohydrates 1g, Protein 6g, Fiber 0g.

---

*A*lmost any cake can be made into cupcakes. Bake at the same temperature as the cake recipe calls for but reduce the time by one-third to one-half.

Flourless Cookies

This is a new and wonderful variation of the original flourless cookie in my first book and is still a favorite food. The vanilla white chips can be changed to chocolate, butterscotch, or peanut butter.

Note: *Always use a processed commercial nut butter such as Skippy or Jif.*

1 cup brown sugar	1¼ teaspoons baking soda
1 cup peanut butter	1 teaspoon vanilla
2 eggs	¾ cup vanilla (or white) chips

Preheat oven to 350°. Grease cookie sheets or line (ungreased) with parchment paper or teflon pan liners.

In the bowl of your mixer, blend the brown sugar and peanut butter. Add the eggs and mix to blend. Spoon in baking soda and vanilla and mix about 1 minute. Pour in vanilla chips and blend by hand.

Drop cookies 1 heaping teaspoonful at a time on cookie sheets, leaving 1½" between them to allow for spreading. Bake 8–11 minutes. Remove with a wide spatula to cool on racks. *Makes 3 dozen cookies.*

Nutrients per cookie: Calories 80, Fat 5g, Cholesterol 35mg,
Sodium 25mg, Carbohydrates 8g, Protein 2g, Fiber 1g.

Peanut Butter Biscotti

The hint of peanut butter and the crunch of peanuts make these cookies excitingly different.

1 cup chopped peanuts, toasted
1½ cups GF Mix
½ cup sweet rice flour
¼ teaspoon salt
1 teaspoon xanthan gum
1 tablespoon baking powder
1 teaspoon Egg Replacer
1 teaspoon unflavored gelatin

¼ cup butter or margarine
3 tablespoons creamy peanut
  butter
½ cup sugar
3 eggs
1 teaspoon vanilla
¾ cup vanilla chips, chopped

Preheat oven to 350°. Toast the chopped peanuts for 4–5 minutes. Remove nuts and raise heat to 375°. Lightly grease a cookie sheet.

In a medium bowl, combine the flour mix, sweet rice flour, salt, xanthan gum, baking powder, Egg Replacer, and gelatin.

In the bowl of your mixer, beat the butter, peanut butter, and sugar at medium speed until well blended. Add eggs, one at a time, beating well after each addition. Beat in vanilla. Gradually add the dry ingredients, beating only until the dough is smooth and will form a ball in the hand. Stir in the peanuts and vanilla chips.

Divide the dough in half, shaping each piece into a 9" × 1½" log and then flattening it to ¾" thick and 3" wide. (An easy way is to form the dough into the log with your hands and then place it on the cookie sheet to flatten.) Bake 15–18 minutes until the edges are lightly browned. Cool for 10 minutes.

Bake at 375°. Cut each log on an angle across the width into ¾" slices. Lay slices, cut side down, on the cookie sheet and bake 8–10 minutes. Turn over and bake an additional 7–10 minutes. *Makes 3 dozen biscotti.*

Nutrients per cookie: Calories 110, Fat 6g, Cholesterol 20mg,
Sodium 65mg, Carbohydrates 12g, Protein 3g, Fiber 1g.

Three-Layer Lemon Bars 350°

An outrageously delicious lemon bar with a new flour. This must be kept in the refrigerator but does last for several days. For many this thick crust will be tasty, but if you desire, the ingredients can be cut by ⅓ to achieve a thinner one.

CRUST:

1½ cups Featherlight Mix

1 teaspoon xanthan gum

⅔ cup teff flour (ivory)

½ cup confectioners' sugar

1½ teaspoons grated lemon rind

½ teaspoon salt

¾ cup (1½ stick) butter, melted

CREAM CHEESE LAYER

1 cup lemon yogurt

Two 8-ounce packages cream
   cheese

2 tablespoons Featherlight mix

1 egg

3 tablespoons granulated sugar

LEMON LAYER:

3 eggs

1⅓ cups granulated sugar

3 tablespoons Featherlight Mix

1 teaspoon baking powder

2 teaspoons grated lemon rind

⅓ cup fresh lemon juice

Preheat oven to 350°. Grease a 9" × 13" baking pan.

Crust: In a medium bowl, whisk together the Featherlight Mix, xanthan gum, teff flour, confectioners' sugar, lemon rind, and salt. Add the melted butter and stir well. Press the dough into the bottom of the prepared pan.

Cream cheese layer: In the bowl of your mixer, beat the yogurt and cream cheese at medium speed until combined. Turn speed to high and beat until smooth. Add the flour mix, egg, and sugar and beat at medium speed until combined. Increase speed to high and beat until smooth. Pour over the crust in the baking pan.

Bake for 20 minutes and then add the lemon layer.

Lemon layer: In the bowl of your mixer, beat the eggs and sugar on medium until combined. Add the flour mix, baking powder, lemon rind, and juice and beat until smooth. Return to oven and bake 30 minutes or until the top is light golden and set. Cool in pan to room temperature before refrigerating for at least 1 hour. Cut into bars. *Makes 24 servings.*

Nutrients per bar: Calories 236, Fat 12g, Cholesterol 67mg,
Sodium 130mg, Carbohydrates 29g, Protein 5g, Fiber 1g.

Raspberry and Pecan-Topped Shortbread 350°

In this special cookie, the familiar old favorite, shortbread, is spread with raspberry jam and topped with a pecan-caramel crust. These will be cut into squares and crosswise into triangles, for a different and more modern look on the cookie tray.

BASE:
¾ cup toasted pecans
1½ cups Featherlight Mix
½ teaspoon (rounded) xanthan gum
¾ cup (1½ sticks) butter or
    margarine
⅔ cup brown sugar
1 scant teaspoon vanilla

TOPPING:
3 tablespoons Featherlight Mix
¼ teaspoon salt
¼ teaspoon baking soda
2 eggs
½ cup brown sugar
1 teaspoon vanilla
1 cup chopped pecans, toasted

MIDDLE LAYER:
⅓ cup seedless raspberry jam

Preheat oven to 350°. Line an 8" × 12" oblong baking pan with foil, leaving extra inches over the side to use as handles for removing. Grease the foil well.

Base: In a food processor, finely grind the pecans with the flour mix and xanthan gum.

In the bowl of your mixer, beat the butter, brown sugar, and vanilla at medium speed until creamy. Add the flour-nut mix at low speed until a soft dough forms. Spoon the dough into the prepared pan and smooth evenly to about ¼" thickness. Bake until the edges are golden (about 20–22 minutes). Cool.

Spread the jam evenly over the cool crust.

Topping: In a small bowl, whisk together the flour mix, salt, and baking soda. In the bowl of your mixer, beat the eggs, sugar, and vanilla at medium-high speed. Turn the mixer to low and beat in the flour mixture until just blended. Pour in an even layer on top of the jam and sprinkle with the chopped pecans.

Bake until the center is completely set and the top is golden (25 minutes). Cool in the pan before lifting the shortbread from the pan with the foil handles. Peel off all foil and cut into 15 squares and then halve the squares on the diagonal. *Makes 30 cookies.*

Nutrients per cookie: Calories 150, Fat 9g, Cholesterol 25mg, Sodium 80mg, Carbohydrates 17g, Protein 1g, Fiber 1g.

*A*lways read the ingredient list before you start to bake and have all ingredients handy. Rice or bean based flours do not accept substitutions as well as wheat flour does.

New Oatmeal Cookies with Quinoa Flakes 375°

This cookie with quinoa flakes can be made with raisins and nuts or just with raisins. For another flavor, check the variation below.

1¾ cups Featherlight Mix or Four
    Flour Mix
1 scant teaspoon xanthan gum
1 teaspoon cinnamon
1 teaspoon baking powder
¼ teaspoon baking soda
1 cup butter or margarine
1 cup brown sugar

½ cup white sugar
2 eggs
2 cups quinoa flakes
1 cup light raisins
1 cup chopped walnuts or pecans,
    toasted (optional)

Preheat oven to 375°. Lay out 2 cookie sheets. Leave ungreased or cover with teflon liners.

In a medium bowl, whisk together the flour mix, xanthan gum, cinnamon, baking powder, and baking soda.

In the bowl of your mixer, beat the butter and sugars until creamy. Beat until well incorporated. Break in the eggs and beat until smooth.

Still using the mixer, blend in the flour mix. Remove from the mixer and incorporate the quinoa flakes, raisins, and nuts (if used) until smooth. Drop by heaping teaspoonfuls on cookie sheets and bake for about 10 minutes or until the edges are golden. *Makes 4 dozen cookies.*

*Nutrients per cookie: Calories 90, Fat 4g, Cholesterol 12mg,
Sodium 46mg, Carbohydrates 13g, Protein 1g, Fiber 1g.*

VARIATION:

OATMEAL-CHOCOLATE CHIP COOKIES: Exchange the raisins for chocolate chips.

Chewy Quinoa Cookies

350°

Quinoa flakes, butter, and brown sugar. You couldn't ask for a tastier combination. These cookies keep well and are actually better after a few days.

Note: Quinoa flakes may be purchased in the cereal section of natural food stores.

½ cup (1 stick) butter or
   margarine
1 cup brown sugar
¼ cup Featherlight Mix or rice
   flour

1 teaspoon vanilla
1 egg white
¼ teaspoon salt
1½ cups quinoa flakes
½ cup finely chopped walnuts

Preheat oven to 350°. Grease 2 baking sheets or line with parchment paper or teflon liners.

In the bowl of your mixer, cream the butter and brown sugar. Beat in the flour mix and vanilla. Add the egg white and salt and beat until smooth. Stir in the quinoa flakes and walnuts.

Pinch out tablespoon-sized bits of the mixture and roll into 1¼" balls, spacing them on the cookie sheets about 3" apart. Press them into ¼"-thick rounds with a glass bottom dipped in sugar. Bake for about 11 minutes. Let cool for 1 minute before removing to cool on the rack. *Makes 2 dozen cookies.*

*Nutrients per cookie: Calories 80, Fat 5g, Cholesterol 10mg,
Sodium 70mg, Carbohydrates 10g, Protein 1g, Fiber 0g.*

---

*M*eringues made in damp weather may fall and come out limp.

Oatmeal Cookies Deluxe

350°

The oatmeal called for here is quinoa, but the cookies come out tasting as if you used Irish oats. (Use them if you can get the oatmeal without contamination.)

2 cups Featherlight Mix
½ teaspoon xanthan gum
1 teaspoon baking powder
½ teaspoon baking soda
1 teaspoon cinnamon
½ teaspoon salt
¾ cup (1½ sticks butter or margarine)
¼ cup vegetable shortening

1 cup white sugar
1 cup brown sugar
¼ cup honey
2 eggs
1 teaspoon vanilla flavoring
2½ cups quinoa flakes (or oatmeal)
1 cup raisins
1 cup chopped pitted dates
1 cup chopped walnuts

Preheat oven to 350°. Grease 2 cookie sheets or line with teflon sheets.

In a medium bowl, whisk together the flour mix, xanthan gum, baking powder, baking soda, cinnamon, and salt.

In the bowl of your mixer, beat the butter, shortening, and both sugars until light and fluffy. Beat in the honey, eggs, and vanilla. Gradually beat in the flour mixture. Stir in the quinoa flakes, raisins, dates, and nuts.

Drop by tablespoons onto prepared sheets, leaving space for the cookies to spread. Bake for about 10 minutes. Cool 5 minutes on sheets before removing to a flat surface covered with wax paper to cool completely. *Makes about 5 dozen cookies.*

Nutrients per serving: Calories 120, Fat 4g, Cholesterol 20mg, Sodium 60mg, Carbohydrates 20g, Protein 1g, Fiber 1g.

Christmas Cherry Fruit Drops

Use these cookies, filled with candied cherries, crisp rice cereal, and vanilla drops, as a large part of your Christmas cookie tray. The recipe makes 6 dozen that handle and keep well.

Note: *If you don't have the sorghum flour, increase the Featherlight Mix by ½ cup.*

2 cups Featherlight Mix	3 eggs
½ cup sorghum flour	2 cups crisp rice cereal
1 scant teaspoon xanthan gum	1 cup walnuts, chopped
1 teaspoon baking soda	½ cup red candied cherries, chopped
½ teaspoon salt	
1 cup (2 sticks) butter or margarine	½ cup green candied cherries, chopped
¾ cup granulated sugar	
½ cup brown sugar	1½ cups white vanilla chips, divided
1 teaspoon vanilla extract	

Preheat oven to 350°. Grease a cookie sheet or line with teflon liners.

In a medium bowl, whisk together the flour mix, sorghum flour, xanthan gum, baking soda, and salt.

In the bowl of your mixer, beat together the butter and sugars until creamy. Beat in the vanilla, then eggs, one at a time, beating well after each addition. With the mixer on low, slowly add the flour mixture, beating just until blended. Remove the bowl from the mixer and, with a spoon, stir in the cereal, walnuts, cherries, and 1 cup of the chips.

Drop by rounded teaspoonfuls onto the cookie sheets, 1" apart. Bake 10–11 minutes until slightly browned. Transfer to cooling rack and repeat with remaining dough.

When all the cookies are finished, place them on wax paper. Melt the remaining chips in the microwave on medium and transfer to a sandwich bag with ⅛" cut diagonally across one bottom corner. Pipe 2–3 narrow lines across the cookies for decoration. When cooled, the cookies can be stored in a covered container for 1 week or frozen for several months. *Makes 6 dozen cookies.*

Nutrients per cookie: Calories 100, Fat 6g, Cholesterol 17mg,
Sodium 80mg, Carbohydrates 12g, Protein 1g, Fiber 0g.

Frosted Mincemeat Cookies 375°

The hint of mincemeat and the flavor of teff blend in these great drop cookies that look festive enough for any party with their coffee-flavored frosting and pecan-studded top.

COOKIES:
1 cup teff flour
2 cups Featherlight Mix
1¼ teaspoons xanthan gum
½ teaspoon salt
1 teaspoon dried lemon peel
1 cup shortening
1½ cups sugar

3 eggs
1⅓ cups mincemeat

FROSTING:
3 cups confectioners' sugar
3 tablespoons cold coffee
½ cup melted butter or margarine
66 pecan halves

Preheat oven to 375°. Line 2 cookie sheets with parchment paper or teflon liners.

In a medium bowl, whisk together the teff flour, Featherlight Mix, xanthan gum, salt, and lemon peel.

In the bowl of your mixer, beat the shortening and sugar at medium-high speed until light and fluffy. Beat in the eggs one at a time, mixing well after each addition. Reduce speed to low and gradually add the flour mixture until just combined. Stir in the mincemeat.

Drop by tablespoon onto the prepared cookie sheets, leaving 2" between cookies. Bake 12 minutes or until golden brown. Cool the cookies for 1 minute on sheets before removing to wire racks to cool completely.

For the frosting, beat all the ingredients in a large bowl on medium speed until smooth. Spread 1 rounded teaspoonful on top of each cookie. Swirl toward the edges but don't cover completely. (The frosting should resemble a small rug in the center.) Top this with one of the pecan halves. *Makes 5½ dozen cookies.*

Nutrients per cookie: Calories 98, Fat 4g, Cholesterol 9mg,
Sodium 52mg, Carbohydrates 14g, Protein 1g, Fiber 0g.

Hawaiian Dream Drops

A cookie flavored with dreams of Hawaii! This vanilla chip cookie is a happy flavor change from the old-fashioned chocolate chip from which it originated.

1¾ cups Featherlight Mix
½ cup sorghum mix (or use 2¼ cups Four Flour Mix instead of the above flours)
½ teaspoon xanthan gum
1 teaspoon baking soda
1 teaspoon salt
1 cup (2 sticks) butter, softened
¾ cup granulated sugar

¾ cup brown sugar
2 teaspoons pineapple flavoring
2 eggs
½ cup shredded coconut
½ cup chopped macadamia nuts
2 cups (12 ounces) white vanilla chips
½ cup chopped candied pineapple or golden raisins

Preheat oven to 375°.

In a medium bowl whisk together Featherlight Mix, sorghum flour, xanthan gum, baking soda, and salt.

In the bowl of your mixer, cream the butter and both sugars. Add the eggs one at a time, beating well after each addition. Blend in the pineapple flavoring.

Gradually beat in the flour mixture. Remove the bowl from the mixer and stir in the coconut, macadamia nuts, vanilla chips, and pineapple.

Drop the dough by teaspoonfuls onto ungreased baking sheets. Bake 9–11 minutes until golden brown. Let the cookies cool 2 minutes before removing from the sheet to cool completely. *Makes about 5 dozen cookies.*

Nutrients per serving: Calories 120, Fat 7g, Cholesterol 25mg, Sodium 105mg, Carbohydrates 15g, Protein 1g, Fiber 0g.

Frosted Fudge Fingers

These are for chocolate lovers. They really do taste like fudge. This has a thick icing for special occasions (holidays). For a thinner one, cut the frosting ingredients by one-third, or, if you wish, omit the frosting altogether.

COOKIES:
¼ cup teff flour
½ cup Featherlight Mix
½ teaspoon xanthan gum
½ teaspoon baking powder
⅓ teaspoon salt
⅓ cup butter or margarine
2 ounces unsweetened chocolate squares
1 cup sugar

2 eggs
1 cup chopped pecans, toasted

FROSTING:
¼ cup butter or margarine, melted
2 cups confectioners' sugar
2 tablespoons cream or nondairy substitute
1½ teaspoons vanilla

Preheat oven to 350°. Line an 8"-square baking pan with foil, allowing several inches to hang over on 2 sides for handles. Grease the foil.

In a medium bowl, whisk together the teff flour, Featherlight Mix, xanthan gum, baking powder, and salt.

Melt the butter and chocolate in a microwavable bowl on medium until melted (1½–2 minutes). Pour into the bowl of your mixer and beat in the sugar and eggs on medium-high speed about 2 minutes. Reduce speed to low and beat in flour mixture until just combined. Pour into the prepared pans. Fold in the pecans.

Bake until just set in the middle and sides begin to pull away from the pan (25–30 minutes). Cool completely in the pan.

For frosting, beat the butter, confectioners' sugar, cream, and vanilla in your mixer on medium speed until smooth. Reduce speed to low and beat until fluffy.

Lift the chocolate layer out of the pan. Peel off the foil and transfer to a flat surface lined with waxed paper. Spread the frosting evenly over the top of the cookie base. Let stand until frosting is firm and then cut into 3½" × 1" bars. *Makes 2 dozen bars.*

Nutrients per serving: Calories 235, Fat 13g, Cholesterol 45mg,
Sodium 150mg, Carbohydrates 30g, Protein 2g, Fiber 19g.

Best Ever Cheesecake Bars

350°

Have a cookie and a small bite of cheesecake at the same time. This recipe was so good, my tasters persuaded me to add it to the book.

Note: *Calories and fat content can be lowered by using a lightened cream cheese.*

CRUST:

¾ cup (1½ sticks) butter or margarine

⅔ cup brown sugar

2 cups GF Mix

1 teaspoon xanthan gum

1 cup walnuts, finely chopped

FILLING:

Two 8-ounce packages cream cheese

½ cup sugar

1 teaspoon vanilla

2 eggs

Three 2.1-ounce Butterfinger bars, crushed

Preheat oven to 350°.

Crust: In the bowl of your mixer, beat the butter and sugar together until smooth and fluffy. On low speed, blend in the flour mix and xanthan gum. Add the nuts until just incorporated. Reserve 1 cup of the crust mixture and press the rest of it in the bottom of an ungreased 9" × 13" pan. Bake for 10 minutes. Cool slightly.

Filling: Wipe out the mixing bowl and beat together the cream cheese and sugar until smooth. Add the vanilla and eggs. Beat about 2 minutes. Fold in the crushed candy and spoon over the crust. Sprinkle the reserved cup of crust mixture on top.

Bake for 30 minutes or until the cheesecake layer is set. Cool to room temperature before cutting. Store in the refrigerator. *Makes 16 bars.*

Nutrients per bar: Calories 400, Fat 26g, Cholesterol 81mg, Sodium 116mg, Carbohydrates 35g, Protein 0g, Fiber 1g.

---

*W*hen cutting cheesecake, use a sharp, straight-edged knife and dip it in hot water and wipe dry after each cut, or try unflavored dental floss.

Brandied Peach Cheesecake
(No Bake, Egg-Free)

No book of comfort foods would be complete without cheesecake. This one takes the old-fashioned Jell-O pudding soaring to heavenly heights. Use a crumb, cereal, or graham cracker crust. (See pages 265–267 for crusts.) The recipe calls for 4% (whole) milk to get the firmest set; otherwise the cheesecake may be soft.

One 9-inch GF crust

CAKE:

One 8-ounce package cream
    cheese

1½ cups 4% milk

¼ cup apricot brandy

One 3.75-ounce package instant
    vanilla pudding mix

TOPPING:

One 10-ounce package frozen
    peach slices, defrosted

¼ cup raspberry jelly

2 tablespoons apricot brandy

In the bowl of your mixer, blend the cream cheese with ½ cup of the milk until smooth. Add the rest of the milk, the brandy, and the pudding. Beat slowly until smooth. Pour into the crust and chill for 1 hour or more.

Top with the peach slices arranged in circles. Heat the jelly and brandy in a small saucepan and drizzle over the peaches. Chill well before serving. *Makes 6–8 servings.*

*Nutrients per serving: Calories 280, Fat 12g, Cholesterol 40mg,
Sodium 310mg, Carbohydrates 34g, Protein 4g, Fiber 1g.*

Cheesecakes have been made for centuries. In the second century, the first basic recipe was offered by a Greek living in Rome.

Linfield Cheesecake

I was experimenting with this tropical-flavored cheesecake when a committee from my alma mater joined me at my condo. They were its first tasters and declared it a "keeper," so we all agreed the cake should be named for the college.

CRUST:
1 cup flaked coconut
¼ cup chopped macadamia nuts
2 tablespoons butter or
    margarine, melted

FILLING:
Two 8-ounce packages cream
    cheese (light okay)
1 cup sugar

3 tablespoons GF Mix
3 eggs
1 cup sour cream (light okay)
3 tablespoons lemon juice
1 teaspoon vanilla
¼ teaspoon pineapple or almond
    extract
One 8-ounce can crushed
    pineapple, drained well

Preheat oven to 350°. Grease a 9" springform pan.

Crust: In a small bowl, combine the coconut and macadamia nuts. Stir in the butter and press onto the bottom of the prepared pan. Bake for 10 minutes. Cool.

Filling: In the bowl of your mixer, beat the cream cheese and sugar until smooth. Add the flour mix and beat well. Add the eggs, beating on low until just combined. Add the sour cream, lemon juice, and flavorings; beat until just blended. Remove the bowl from the mixer and stir in the drained pineapple with a mixing spoon.

Pour the filling over the crust. Bake 50 minutes or until the center is almost set. Cool and refrigerate for 4 hours or overnight. To serve, top each piece with a dab of whipped cream or nondairy substitute and decorate with a slice of peeled kiwi fruit (or your choice of other tropical fruit). *Makes 12 servings.*

Nutrients per serving: Calories 510, Fat 35g, Cholesterol 120mg, Sodium 220mg, Carbohydrates 43g, Protein 8.5g, Fiber 1g.

Lemon Buttermilk Pie

This comfort food is a pie from my childhood. With plenty of butter and buttermilk from her home churning, all Mother needed was a lemon to make a custard pie with a strong lemony taste. Team the filling with any pie or tart shell you choose. (I like the Featherlight Vinegar Pastry on page 264.) This also makes an excellent filling for a layered cake.

One unbaked 9" pie shell	3 eggs
1½ cups sugar	1 teaspoon vanilla
¼ cup (½ stick) butter or	1 teaspoon lemon juice
margarine	1 tablespoon grated lemon peel
2 tablespoons GF Mix	1 cup buttermilk

Preheat oven to 350°.

In the bowl of your mixer, beat the sugar, butter, and flour mix until well blended. Beat in the eggs, one at a time, beating well after each addition. Blend in the vanilla, lemon juice, and peel. Add the buttermilk and beat. Pour into the prepared crust and bake for approximately 40–45 minutes or until the filling is puffed and the top is brown. Cool before serving. *Makes 6–8 servings.*

Nutrients per serving: Calories 240, Fat 8g, Cholesterol 95mg, Sodium 115mg, Carbohydrates 41g, Protein 4g, Fiber 0g.

---

*I*f you lower the fat in a cheesecake recipe by using lower-fat cream cheese, be sure you substitute with a block cheese, not the tub type (unless it is the soy cream cheese).

Caramel Custard-Pecan Pie

400°–300°

Here you have the old favorite pecan pie with a lighter custard base. Because this pie filling is still quite rich, I prefer to pair it with the simple Featherlight Vinegar Pastry (page 264).

One unbaked 9" pie shell
1 egg, well beaten
3 egg yolks, beaten
1 cup sugar
1 cup brown sugar
1 tablespoon Featherlight Mix or
   GF Mix

1 tablespoon cornmeal
¼ teaspoon salt
¼ cup butter or margarine,
   softened
½ cup chopped pecans
1 teaspoon vanilla
1 cup milk or nondairy substitute

Preheat oven to 400°.

Combine the eggs, white sugar, brown sugar, flour mix, cornmeal, salt, butter, pecans, vanilla, and milk. Pour into the pie shell. Bake for 15 minutes. Reduce oven temperature to 300°. Bake for another 45 minutes or until the center does not jiggle. Cool before serving. *Makes 6–8 servings.*

Nutrients per serving: Calories 320, Fat 14g, Cholesterol 125mg, Sodium 160mg, Carbohydrates 47g, Protein 4g, Fiber 1g.

Chess Pie

350°

Probably few of my readers will remember this old-fashioned farm favorite. I found it to be even tastier than I remembered since I used the Quick and Easy Nut Crust (page 265) for added flavor.

Note: *If you don't have the grits, white cornmeal may be substituted.*

One unbaked 9" pie shell
1 tablespoon quick grits
1¼ cups sugar
½ cup (1 stick) butter or
  margarine (melted and cooled)

4 eggs, beaten slightly
1 tablespoon white vinegar
⅛ teaspoon salt
1 teaspoon Vanilla, Butter & Nut
  flavoring

Preheat oven to 350°.

In a mixing bowl, blend the grits and sugar. Stir in the cooled butter, eggs, vinegar, salt, and flavoring. Pour into the prepared pie crust. Bake 45 minutes or until the top is set. Cool completely before serving. *Makes 8 servings.*

Nutrients per serving: Calories 346, Fat 19g, Cholesterol 138mg, Sodium 169mg, Carbohydrates 40g, Protein 4g, Fiber 0g.

---

*F*or an attractive top pie crust, brush lightly with milk or nondairy substitute and sprinkle with sugar before baking.

Peach Pie with Streusel Topping

400°–350°

This recipe calls for peaches but works equally well with apples, blackberries, or pears.

CRUST:
One Featherlight Vinegar
    Pastry crust (page 264),
    unbaked

FILLING:
3 tablespoons chopped pecans
1½ pounds frozen peach slices,
    thawed
¼ cup granulated sugar

3 tablespoons cornstarch
¼ teaspoon ground allspice

STREUSEL:
½ cup rice flour
½ cup brown sugar
1 teaspoon cinnamon
6 tablespoons (¾ stick) butter or
    margarine
¾ cup chopped pecans

Preheat oven to 400°.

Fill a 9" pie plate with the pastry and flute the edge decoratively.

Sprinkle the 3 tablespoons of pecans over the pastry.

Slice the peach sections, if they are not already sliced, to about ¼" and place in a bowl. In a small bowl, whisk together the sugar, cornstarch, and allspice and gently toss this mixture with the peaches. Spoon the fruit into the crust, mounding slightly in the center.

In the same bowl mix together the rice flour, brown sugar, and cinnamon. Work the butter in with a pastry blender (or your fingers) until medium-sized crumbs form and the whole feels slightly moist. Toss in the pecans and mix again. Sprinkle this streusel over the pie.

Bake for 10 minutes at 400°. Reduce heat to 350° and bake another 65 minutes or until the filling bubbles around the edge. Let cool 1 hour before serving. Serve with whipped cream or nondairy topping or ice cream. *Makes 8 servings.*

*Nutrients per serving: Calories 489, Fat 27g, Cholesterol 28mg,
Sodium 277mg, Carbohydrates 61g, Protein 6g, Fiber 4g.*

Pecan Bites

These bite-sized bits of pastry and filling were created to show celiacs that we really can have prize-winning pastry. They were such a hit at a food show that I've included them in this book. With the filling of pecan pie, they can grace a cookie tray anytime, but if you want the perfect Christmas treat, substitute the mincemeat filling from The Gluten-free Gourmet *(page 203).*

One recipe Featherlight Vinegar Pastry (page 264), unbaked	½ cup brown sugar
6 tablespoons liquid egg substitute	½ teaspoon vanilla
	1 tablespoon butter or margarine, melted
½ cup dark corn syrup	¾ cup finely chopped pecans

Preheat oven to 400°. Grease the cups of 24 miniature muffin tins (1¾" size) with vegetable oil spray.

Make up the pastry and roll out in 3" circles. (I use a glass.) Snip ½" cut into one edge and using this as overlap, place the pastry shells in the muffin cup. Repeat until all 24 are filled.

In a medium bowl, beat the egg substitute. Add the corn syrup, sugar, vanilla, and melted butter. Stir together until blended. Fold in the chopped pecans and fill the pastry shells by spooning 1 dessert spoonful into each. Bake 30 minutes. Cool 10 minutes before removing to tray. *Makes 24 bites.*

Nutrients per bite: Calories 145, Fat 7g, Cholesterol 10mg,
Sodium 36mg, Carbohydrates 10g, Protein 1g, Fiber ½g.

Featherlight Vinegar Pastry

450°

This recipe first appeared in The Gluten-Free Gourmet Makes Dessert *and has proved so popular as an extra-tender, never-fail crust that I felt I should include it again for the pies in this volume.*

2¼ cups Featherlight Mix
1 rounded teaspoon xanthan gum
½ teaspoon salt
1 tablespoon sugar (or to taste)
¾ cup shortening

1 tablespoon rice vinegar (or other)
¼ cup liquid egg substitute or
   1 egg, beaten
4 tablespoons ice water
Sweet rice flour for rolling

In a medium bowl, blend the flour mix, xanthan gum, salt, and sugar. Cut in the shortening until coarse crumbs form. In a small bowl, beat the vinegar and egg substitute together with a fork. Add the ice water.

Stir the wet ingredients into the dry ingredients with a fork and keep blending until the dough forms a ball. Work a little with your hands to obtain a smooth texture. Cover and refrigerate for 30 minutes or more before rolling out.

Divide the dough in half and roll out on waxed paper or plastic wrap dusted with sweet rice flour. (I roll these on my kitchen counter since I have a lot of room there.) Use as much of the sweet rice flour as needed to work easily. Place the dough in a 9" pie tin. (If you're using plastic wrap, carry the dough on the wrap to the pie tin, then invert the dough into the pan.) Bake as directed for the filling used.

For a baked single crust, prick the pastry with a fork on sides and bottom. Bake the crust in a preheated 450° oven for 10–12 minutes or until slightly browned. Cool before filling. *Makes enough pastry for a 9" 2-crust pie or 2 pastry shells.*

Nutrients per serving (⅙ crust): Calories 170, Fat 90g, Cholesterol 15mg, Sodium 105mg, Carbohydrates 19g, Protein 1g, Fiber 0g.

VARIATION:

SPICED PASTRY: Add ¼ teaspoon cinnamon and ¼ teaspoon nutmeg to dry ingredients. Substitute iced orange juice for the ice water.

Quick and Easy Nut Crust

425°

This crust is as easy as the name promises and is very tasty. Use it for such creamy fillings as chess or custard pie to spark up the smooth, bland taste.

1 cup of almond meal	1½ tablespoons cream or
¼ cup powdered sugar	nondairy substitute
2 tablespoons chilled butter or	
margarine	

In a food processor, blend all the ingredients until the dough clumps together in a ball. Chill 15 minutes before rolling the dough out in a circle on a board covered with plastic wrap. Transfer to a 9" pie pan with the plastic, reversing into the pan.

If the pie is to be baked, fill and bake at the temperature recommended for the filling. For precooked fillings, bake the crust at 425° for 8–10 minutes.

Nutrients per serving (⅙ crust): Calories 175, Fat 15g, Cholesterol 13mg, Sodium 30mg, Carbohydrates 9g, Protein 4g, Fiber 5g.

---

*F*or a 2-crust pie, always use a glass or dull metal pie pan. Shiny ones will cause the bottom crust to turn out soggy.

Graham Cracker Crust

375°

If you've tried the graham crackers on page 227, you know how easy it is to have them on hand for this old favorite. Use the almond meal for an extra-special crust (as in the cheesecake on page 257).

1½ cups finely crushed GF
   graham crackers
¼ cup almond meal (optional)

4 tablespoons (½ stick) butter or
   margarine, melted

Place the cracker crumbs in a 1-gallon plastic bag. Add the almond meal (if used). Pour in the melted butter and blend together by working the bag with your hands until all the crumbs are moist. Pat the mixture into and up the side of a 9" pie tin. Bake as directed for the filling used.

If the filling is already cooked, bake the crust in a preheated 375° oven for 6–8 minutes. Check after 6 minutes to prevent the crust from browning too much. Cool before filling. *Makes one 9" pie shell.*

Nutrients per serving (⅙ crust): Calories 166, Fat 12g, Cholesterol 21mg, Sodium 256mg, Carbohydrates 15g, Protein 1g, Fiber ½ g.

Absolutely Sinful Cereal Crust

This crust is so rich, it is truly sinful. Use it for any open-faced pies, whether they be fruit, pumpkin, or custard cream, but be prepared to cut the pieces smaller than usual. Try this also for cheesecake.

Note: *If macaroon coconut (a fine grind) is not available in your store, use flaked or shredded coconut and chop finer in a food processor.*

3 tablespoons butter or
   margarine, melted
⅔ cup brown sugar
1 cup GF rice flakes, crushed

1 cup GF cornflakes, crushed
⅔ cup macaroon coconut
⅔ cup walnuts, ground fine

Stir together all the ingredients. Line a deep 9" greased pie tin with the mix, patting well up the sides. Or pat into a 10" springform pan for cheesecake. Bake as directed for the filling used.

If the filling is already cooked, bake in a preheated 375° oven for 6 minutes or until the crust is slightly browned. Cool before filling. *Makes one (deep) 9" pie crust or one 10" cheesecake crust.*

Nutrients per serving (⅛ of crust): Calories 220, Fat 11g, Cholesterol 10mg, Sodium 180mg, Carbohydrates 31g, Protein 3g, Fiber 1g.

*I*n making a cheesecake dairy-free, use the 8-ounce tub of Tofutti (soy) cream cheese as a replacement for the 8-ounce brick of dairy cream cheese.

Fruit and Dumplings

A wonderfully easy hot dessert made on top of the stove when fruit is plentiful. I suggest huckleberries, blueberries, loganberries, or blackberries. Even juicy peaches can be used with the sweet dumplings.

3–4 cups fresh or frozen and thawed berries or fruit

1 cup water (or enough to cover fruit)

1½ cups sugar (or to taste)

1 tablespoon lemon juice

One recipe Dumplings (page 228)

Place the berries, water, sugar, and lemon juice in a 4-quart saucepan (with a lid) on the stove. Bring to a gentle boil.

Meanwhile, make the dumplings. Drop the dough by small spoonfuls onto the boiling fruit sauce. Cover, reduce heat to simmer, and cook without peeking for 20 minutes.

Serve hot in small bowls with the fruit sauce spooned over the dumpling. Top with heavy cream, whipped cream, or ice cream. *Makes 8 servings.*

Nutrients per serving: Calories 310, Fat 6g, Cholesterol 25mg, Sodium 320mg, Carbohydrates 64g, Protein 2g, Fiber 5g.

Lemon Pudding Cake

350°

If you're craving the taste of lemon, try this easy cake with lemon sauce made in one pan.

½ cup sugar

3 tablespoons GF Mix

1½ teaspoons grated lemon
   peel

3 tablespoons lemon juice

2 tablespoons melted butter or
   margarine

2 eggs, separated

1 cup milk or nondairy substitute

⅛ teaspoon cream of tartar

Preheat oven to 350°. Butter a 1½-quart casserole or baking dish.

In a mixing bowl, whisk the sugar and flour mix. Add the lemon peel, juice, and melted butter. Mix well.

In a small bowl, whisk the egg yolks and blend in the milk. Stir into the lemon mixture.

In the bowl of your mixer, beat the egg whites with the cream of tartar until moist peaks form. Gently fold the whites into the lemon mixture.

Pour the batter into the prepared pan and bake 35–40 minutes or until the top springs back when lightly touched. Serve warm, scooping down to the bottom to include the pudding that has formed under the cake. *Makes 4–5 servings.*

*Nutrients per serving: Calories 243, Fat 10g, Cholesterol 127mg,
Sodium 133mg, Carbohydrates 34g, Protein 6g, Fiber 0g.*

Banana and Rum Topping

A simple microwave topping that dresses up ice cream or frozen yogurt: a microwave version of Bananas Foster.

4 tablespoons butter or margarine
⅔ cup brown sugar
2 tablespoons rum

2 firm bananas, sliced
GF vanilla ice cream, frozen yogurt,
   or frozen soy ice cream

Combine the butter and brown sugar in a 4-cup microwave safe bowl. Microwave on high, uncovered, for 1½–2 minutes or until slightly thickened, stirring twice. Add the rum and sliced bananas. Microwave on high 1–1½ minutes or until heated through.

To serve, place 2 scoops ice cream in serving dishes and top with the hot banana sauce. *Makes 4 servings.*

Nutrients per serving: Calories 390, Fat 17g, Cholesterol 70mg,
Sodium 150mg, Carbohydrates 53g, Protein 3g, Fiber 3g.

Ice Cream Sandwiches with Chocolate Crust 375°

When asked what I missed on the GF diet, I admitted that the only ice cream treats I couldn't resist were the cookie sandwiches with ice cream filling. Now I don't have to miss them anymore.

COOKIES:
1½ cups Four Flour Mix
1½ teaspoons xanthan gum
½ cup cocoa powder
¾ teaspoon salt
½ teaspoon cinnamon
½ teaspoon baking soda (scant)
¾ cup (1½ sticks) butter
1 cup brown sugar
½ cup sour cream

⅓ cup ripe banana (mashed)
1 tablespoon instant coffee
   (optional)
1 tablespoon water
1 teaspoon vanilla

ICE CREAM:
1 quart of purchased GF ice
   cream in freezer (vanilla or
   French vanilla)

Preheat oven to 375°. Grease 2 baking sheets or cover with teflon baking liners.

In a medium bowl, whisk together the flour mix, xanthan gum, cocoa powder, salt, cinnamon, and baking soda.

In the bowl of your mixer, beat, on medium speed, the butter and the sugar until smooth and creamy. Beat in the sour cream, mashed banana, the coffee (if used) dissolved in the water, and vanilla. Turn the mixer to low and gradually beat in the flour. The batter will be thick.

Drop on the prepared sheets by heaping tablespoons, leaving about 3 inches between cookies. Spread the dough to form thick circles. Bake, one pan at a time so the bottoms don't burn, for about 9–11 minutes. Using a spatula, carefully flatten the hot cookies before removing them to cool. This recipe should make 30 cookies.

When the cookies are cold, match them by size and prepare the fillings, three at a time, by spooning, one dipperful per sandwich, the frozen ice cream onto waxed paper, then folding it and pressing with the hands to the round cookie shape approximately ½" thick. Remember to store the ice cream in the freezer when you are not dipping into it. Working quickly, make up the 3 sandwiches and place each in a small sandwich bag and into the freezer. Continue until all are finished.

When the ice cream sandwiches are frozen hard, place them in two 1-gallon freezer bags (7 or 8 sandwiches to a bag) and refreeze for up to 3 weeks. *Makes 15 sandwiches.*

Nutrients per serving: Calories 100, Fat 6g, Cholesterol 15mg,
Sodium 115mg, Carbohydrates 12g, Protein 1g, Fiber 0g.

Pecan-Pumpkin Roll

375°

I've put many rolled desserts in other books, but this new one is special with the pecans baked into the outside and the flavor of teff with the pumpkin and spice. This can be made a day ahead to save time on the day of the party or special dinner.

CAKE ROLL:
½ cup Featherlight Mix plus
   ¼ cup teff flour or ¾ cup Four
   Flour Mix
½ teaspoon xanthan gum
1 teaspoon baking powder
1 teaspoon Egg Replacer
3 teaspoons pumpkin pie spice
½ teaspoon salt
3 eggs
1 cup sugar

1 teaspoon lemon juice
⅔ cup canned pumpkin
1 cup chopped pecans

FILLING:
One 8-ounce package cream
   cheese
¾ cup powdered sugar
1¼ cups nondairy whipped
   topping

Preheat oven to 375°. Cut wax paper to fit an 11" × 16" jelly roll pan. Grease the pan well; place the paper in the pan and grease the paper.

In a medium bowl, whisk together the flour(s), xanthan gum, baking powder, Egg Replacer, pumpkin pie spice, and salt.

In the bowl of your mixer, beat the eggs and sugar until light. Mix in the lemon juice and pumpkin. Add the dry ingredients and mix well. Spoon into the prepared pan, spreading well so the batter is even. Sprinkle with the nuts. Bake for 15 minutes.

Cool 10 minutes before turning out onto a clean, flat-textured tea towel that has been sprinkled with powdered sugar. Remove the paper and roll up (from the short side) in the towel, folding some of the towel over the cake at the beginning. Let cool.

Unroll and spread with the filling, made by combining the cream cheese, powdered sugar, and whipped topping. Roll without the towel and seal in foil. Refrigerate until serving. *Makes 8 servings.*

*Nutrients per serving: Calories 180, Fat 2½ g, Cholesterol 80mg,
Sodium 75mg, Carbohydrates 38g, Protein 4g, Fiber 1g.*

Mixes, Dressings, Salsas, Creams

The recipes in this catch-all chapter include mixes (used in some of the recipes), salad dressings, creams (which can be made either dairy or nondairy), chutneys, and salsa. You can buy salsas and chutneys at the grocery, but they are never as spirited as those made at home with fresh ingredients.

The Creamed Soup Base is an absolute necessity for many of the casserole and meat dishes that call for a can of cream soup. The Cheese Mix for Macaroni is a dream come true. Since we can now buy good GF macaroni at health food stores (Tinkyada brown rice pasta, for example), with this base mix we can have that old favorite macaroni and cheese anytime we desire.

Creamed Soup Base

This base is a time-saver when a recipe calls for a can of creamed soup. I always keep some by my stove so that it is now as handy for me as canned soups used to be. A few tablespoons of this dry mix plus water or stock (see directions below) and you can have cream of chicken soup, mushroom soup, tomato soup, cheese soup, shrimp soup, or a cream sauce or gravy.

Note: *For vegetarians, there are some vegetable soup bases on the market. For the lactose intolerant, I suggest using the powdered baby formula Isomil (soy) or Pregestimil (corn) instead of Lacto-Free nondairy dry powder for the best flavor.*

1 cup dry milk powder or
   nondairy substitute (see note)
1 cup white rice flour
2 tablespoons dried minced
   onions

½ teaspoon pepper
½ teaspoon salt
3 tablespoons GF powdered soup
   base (chicken or vegetable)

Combine all ingredients and mix well. Store in an airtight container on your pantry shelf. *This mix is the equivalent of 8–9 cans of soup.*

*Nutrients per serving: Calories 140, Fat 4g, Cholesterol 15mg,
Sodium 170mg, Carbohydrates 21g, Protein 5g, Fiber 0g.*

CREAM OF CHICKEN SOUP: In a small saucepan, blend 3–4 tablespoons of the base with ¼ cup cold water. Add 1 cup hot or cold water (or chicken stock) and cook over medium heat, stirring until the soup thickens. Use 3 tablespoons for thin soup, 4 for thick soup.

CREAM OF MUSHROOM SOUP: Follow the instructions for Cream of Chicken Soup, using the liquid from one 4-ounce can of mushroom bits and pieces as part of the water (reserving the mushrooms). After the soup thickens, add the mushrooms.

CREAM OF TOMATO SOUP: Follow the instructions for Cream of Chicken Soup, using one 5.5-ounce can of V8 juice as part of the liquid.

CHEESE SOUP OR SAUCE: Follow the instructions for Cream of Chicken Soup, using ¼ cup of the base. Add ¼ cup extra water. Stir in ½–⅔ cup grated cheddar cheese before removing from the stove.

SHRIMP SOUP OR SAUCE: Follow the instructions for Cream of Chicken Soup. Use an 8-ounce bottle clam juice plus the ¼ cup water and add one 4½-ounce can broken shrimp (drained) or ½ cup cut-up, cooked shrimp before removing from the stove.

TASTY CREAM SAUCE: Melt 1 tablespoon butter or margarine in a small saucepan and add 1 teaspoon chopped chives or 2 thinly sliced green onions before putting in the soup base. Add 1¼ cups hot water and cook as directed for Cream of Chicken Soup.

TO USE IN A CASSEROLE: If your casserole (scalloped potatoes, etc.) calls for canned soup and is to be baked over 1 hour, just tumble the Creamed Soup Base with the ingredients and pour on 1¼–1½ cups hot water.

Biscuit Mix

Store a canister of this handy mix in your refrigerator for biscuits or pot pie toppings in minutes. Put the directions for mixing on the container so you won't have to refer back to the cookbook.

4 cups plus 3 tablespoons
  Featherlight Mix
3 tablespoons baking powder
2½ teaspoons baking soda
2½ teaspoons salt

¼ cup sugar (or to taste)
½ cup dry buttermilk powder
3 tablespoons Egg Replacer
  (optional)
1 cup less 1 tablespoon shortening

In a large mixing bowl, whisk together the dry ingredients. With a pastry blender, cut in the shortening until no lumps appear. Store in a 2-quart container in the refrigerator.

TO MAKE BISCUITS: Preheat oven to 400°. To 1¼ cups mix, add 1 egg (or ¼ cup liquid egg substitute) beaten with ¼ cup water. Handle gently and roll out on rice floured board. Bake for 12–15 minutes. *Makes 8 biscuits.*

TO TOP STEWS OR CHICKEN PIES: To 1¼ cups mix, add 1 egg (or ¼ cup liquid egg substitute) beaten with ⅓ cup water. Stir to moisten and drop by spoonfuls onto the hot stew or pie. Bake at about 350° for 20–25 minutes or until the biscuits are done. *Makes 8 biscuits.*

*Nutrients per biscuit: Calories 130, Fat 6g, Cholesterol 25mg,
Sodium 320mg, Carbohydrates 18g, Protein 2g, Fiber 0g.*

Cheese Mix for Macaroni

Make up this mix and have it ready any time you're hungry for macaroni and cheese. Once you cook the macaroni, all it takes is a few more minutes and you have the same dish as the one prepared from that blue-and-yellow boxed mix. And this version is gluten free!

2 cups dry milk powder
1¼ cups grated cheddar or
    Parmesan/Romano cheese
½ cup GF Mix

1 teaspoon paprika
½ teaspoon mustard powder
¼ teaspoon pepper
½ cup margarine or butter

Combine all dry ingredients in a medium bowl. Cut in the margarine and work with your fingers until it is in fine granules. Store in the refrigerator in a container with the directions for macaroni and cheese (see below) taped to the outside. *Makes 5 cups mix.*

TO MAKE MACARONI AND CHEESE: Cook 1½ cups macaroni. In a medium saucepan, combine 1 cup mix, ½ cup milk, ½ cup water, and ¼–½ teaspoon salt. Cook, stirring, until the mix comes to a boil. Continue cooking for 2 minutes. Drain the macaroni and stir in the sauce until coated. *Makes 2–3 servings.*

Nutrients per serving: Calories 580, Fat 40g, Cholesterol 120mg, Sodium 840mg, Carbohydrates 32g, Protein 25g, Fiber 0g.

Devonshire-Style Cream
(With Changes for Dairy-Free)

In today's "low-fat" culture, this might be culinary heresy, but I still drool over the thought of cream so thick it clots on the jam on my scone. This imitation might please others who, like me, crave an old-fashioned treat at tea or luncheon.

3 ounces light cream cheese or
  Tofutti nondairy cream cheese
1 teaspoon sugar

1 cup heavy cream or ¾ cup
  nondairy creamer

Have all ingredients at room temperature.

In a medium bowl, beat the cream cheese and sugar on medium-high speed until light and fluffy. Add the cream and beat until stiff peaks form. Cover and refrigerate for several hours or overnight. Serve with scones or biscuits. *Makes almost 2 cups.*

Nutrients per serving: Calories 25, Fat 2½ g, Cholesterol 10mg,
Sodium 20mg, Carbohydrates 0g, Protein 0g, Fiber 0g.

Mock Crème Fraiche
(With Changes for Dairy-Free)

This mock crème fraiche contains less fat than the original. Use it in recipes that call for the real thing or as filling for fruit tartlets or to spread on biscuits and scones.

1 cup heavy cream or ¾ cup nondairy creamer

One 8-ounce container nonfat sour cream or nondairy sour cream

¼ cup sifted confectioners' sugar

In a large bowl, beat the cream, sour cream, and confectioners' sugar until soft peaks form. Refrigerate, covered, for several hours for flavors to meld. *Makes about 2 cups (32 tablespoons).*

Nutrients per tablespoon: Calories 30, Fat 2½ g, Cholesterol 10mg, Sodium 5mg, Carbohydrates 1g, Protein 1g, Fiber 0g.

Fruit Salsa

A delicious topping for poached or grilled chicken or fish. If not used immediately, this will keep for several days in the refigerator.

½ cup finely diced mango
½ cup finely diced papaya
2 tablespoons diced red onion
2 tablespoons chopped macadamia
  nuts

1½ tablespoons lime or lemon
  juice
¼ teaspoon salt

Combine all ingredients in a small bowl. Serve immediately or cover and refrigerate for several hours or overnight. Spoon 2 heaping tablespoons over each serving of hot chicken or fish. *Makes 4–6 servings.*

Nutrients per serving (including 3-ounce chicken breast): Calories 164, Fat 3g, Cholesterol 72mg, Sodium 210mg, Carbohydrates 6g, Protein 6g, Fiber 1g.

Cranberry-Pineapple Chutney

This chutney can be used either with meat dishes or with curry. It's perfect for those who love cranberries. Like all chutneys, this keeps well in the refrigerator for several days.

½ cup fruit vinegar (raspberry, wine, or apple cider)
¾ cup sugar, divided
2 tablespoons grated gingerroot
½ teaspoon chopped garlic
1 teaspoon dried orange peel
¼ cup chopped walnuts or pecans
¼ cup finely chopped red onion
¼ teaspoon cayenne pepper
One 10-ounce package fresh cranberries (frozen fresh okay)
One 8-ounce can pineapple, crushed (in syrup)
½ teaspoon salt

In a medium-sized saucepan (not aluminum), combine the vinegar, ½ cup of the sugar, gingerroot, garlic, orange peel, nuts, onion, and cayenne pepper. Simmer, uncovered, 10 minutes.

Add washed cranberries, pineapple with syrup, and salt. Return to simmer and cook 15 minutes more, stirring occasionally. Remove from heat and stir in the remaining ¼ cup sugar. Cool to serve. *Makes 8 servings.*

Nutrients per serving (¼ cup): Calories 103, Fat 0g, Cholesterol 0mg, Sodium 147mg, Carbohydrates 27g, Protein 0g, Fiber 1g.

Orange and Plum Chutney

We can buy many chutneys at our regular grocery stores, but this one is so tasty, I'm including the recipe so you can prepare it to accompany rice or meat dishes.

1 cup water	6 red plums, pitted and cut into
⅔ cup sugar	½" cubes
6 tablespoons wine vinegar	1 orange, grated for zest and then
1 tablespoon grated gingerroot	peeled and cut into ½" cubes
1 clove garlic, minced	¼ teaspoon ground cinnamon

In a 2-quart saucepan, bring the water and sugar to a boil. Stir until the sugar is dissolved; add the vinegar, grated gingerroot, garlic, and half the plums and orange. Boil 5 minutes.

Add the other half of fruit, the orange zest, and cinnamon. Cook about 12 minutes at a gentle boil. Cool to serve. Refrigerate for other meals. Keeps about 1 week. *Makes 2 cups.*

Nutrients per ¼ cup: Calories 109, Fat ½ g, Cholesterol 0mg, Sodium 3mg, Carbohydrates 25g, Protein ½ g, Fiber 1½ g.

Quick Hollandaise Sauce

Use this sauce on fish or vegetables to "tart" up the meal.

½ cup mayonnaise   1 tablespoon lemon juice
1 egg   ¼ teaspoon prepared mustard

In a small microwavable dish, beat together the mayonnaise and egg. Add the lemon juice and mustard. Microwave on medium, uncovered, for 1¼–1¾ minutes or until slightly thickened, stirring twice. Serve warm. *Makes ¾ cup.*

Nutrients per serving (2 tablespoons): Calories 35, Fat 4g, Cholesterol 10mg, Sodium 25mg, Carbohydrates 0g, Protein 0g, Fiber 0g.

Thousand Island Dressing

This old-fashioned dressing is making a comeback. It is excellent on Crab or Shrimp Louis, topping the simple wedge of lettuce that has again become stylish, and on Reuben Sandwiches (page 189). The recipe was published in the Seattle Times *by the Kathy Casey Food Studios, Seattle, and is reprinted here with permission.*

2 hard boiled eggs, finely chopped
⅓ cup chopped black olives
3 tablespoons fresh lemon juice
1½ cups mayonnaise
½ cup Heinz tomato-based chili sauce

½ teaspoon black pepper
½ teaspoon Tabasco (or to taste)
1 teaspoon Worcestershire sauce
⅓ cup sweet pickle relish
1 tablespoon grated onion

In a medium bowl, mix all the ingredients together. The dressing can be stored in a covered container in the refrigerator for up to 1 week. *Makes 2¾ cups.*

Nutrients per serving (2 tablespoons): Calories 200, Fat 22g, Cholesterol 40mg,
Sodium 330mg, Carbohydrates 5g, Protein 0g, Fiber 0g.

Hint-of-Orange Dressing

Try this dressing for a hint of orange on your potato or pasta salad. It is especially good on the Chicken Pasta Salad on page 115.

Note: If you can find dairy-free mayonnaise and tofu sour cream, you may use them for a dairy-free salad.

½ cup mayonnaise
½ cup sour cream
2 teaspoons grated orange peel
2 tablespoons milk or nondairy
  substitute

1½ teaspoons orange juice
  concentrate
2 tablespoons orange juice
Salt to taste

In a small bowl, combine all the ingredients. Mix well before blending with your favorite potato or pasta salad. The dressing can be safely stored for several days in the refrigerator. *Makes 1½ cups.*

Nutrients per serving (2 tablespoons): Calories 90, Fat 10g, Cholesterol 15mg, Sodium 100mg, Carbohydrates 1g, Protein ½g, Fiber 0g.

Chicken or Turkey Sausage

Many stores now carry some form of chicken or turkey sausage, but I usually make my own by buying the leanest ground meat I can find and adding my own seasoning (to taste) from a mix purchased at the meat department of my local grocery. (These mixes are not on display; ask the meat cutters if they have some.) This assures me that I get no extra filler or fat and the seasoning is gluten free. The usual ratio to make sausage is: 2 level teaspoons of seasoning per pound of ground turkey, chicken, pork, or venison. Adjust the seasoning to suit your own taste.

Nutrients per serving (¼ pound): Calories 190, Fat 14g, Cholesterol 75mg, Sodium 980mg, Carbohydrates 27g, Protein 14g, Fiber 0g.

Where to Find
Gluten-Free Baking Supplies

Today, with Internet ordering and neighborhood health stores carrying more gluten-free flours, mixes, and even baked goods, this section is not as necessary as it was when I started. But, for many, a large amount of our baking needs will have to be special-ordered through one of the following suppliers who feature gluten-free flours and the necessary specialty items such as xanthan or guar gums.

All the new flours featured in this book (amaranth, quinoa, millet, teff, Montina) are so unusual they haven't reached many of the regular markets. Although the garfava bean and sorghum mix (Four Flour Blend) and the Featherlight Mix are sold in some health food stores and by many of the celiac organizations, they have to be special-ordered by those who live too far from these outlets. Bear in mind that it's still cheaper for cooks to order the flours separately and make their own mixes unless convenience is a major factor.

You will notice this list has grown with the addition of many companies listing fully baked GF products to make life simpler and easier. And don't worry about the taste for almost all the companies offer goods that compare well, or even better than, foods made with gluten flour.

ALPINEAIRE FOODS (shelf-stable dehydrated soups and meals): 4031 Alvis Court, Rocklin, CA 95677; phone (800) 322-6325 or (916) 824-5000. Accepts orders by mail, phone, or fax. Some products can be found in grocery or sporting goods stores. Write or phone for a full product list.

AMAZING GRAINS (Montina flour and baking mixes for bread, muffins, and brownies): 405 Main St. S.W., Ronan, MT 59864; phone (877) 278-6585, fax (406) 676-3537, e-mail: Penny@montina.com. Web site: www.montina.com. Takes orders by phone, fax, mail, e-mail, or web site.

ANCIENT HARVEST QUINOA (whole-grain quinoa, quinoa flour, quinoa flakes, and pastas [made with corn/quinoa]): Quinoa Corporation, P.O. Box 279, Gardena, CA 90248; phone (310) 217-8125, fax (310) 217-8140, e-mail: quinoacorp@aol.com. Web site: www.quinoa.net. Orders accepted by phone, mail, or web. Some products can be found in health food stores and some groceries. Call or write for a price list.

AUTHENTIC FOODS (baking mixes for pancakes, bread, cakes, and veggie burgers; Garfava flour; Bette's Four Flour Blend; brown and white rice flour; tapioca starch, potato flour, potato starch, and many other GF flours; xanthan gum; maple sugar; vanilla powder; and other flavorings): 1850 West 169th St., Suite B, Gardena, CA 90247; phone (800) 806-4737 or (310) 366-7612, fax (310) 366-6938. Web site: www. authenticfoods.com or www.glutenfree-supermarket.com. Accepts orders by phone, mail, fax, or Web. Write, call, or visit the web site for a complete product list. Some products can be found in health food stores.

THE BAKER'S CATALOGUE, a wholly owned subsidiary of The King Arthur Flour Company, Inc. (rice, tapioca, and potato starch flours; xanthan gum; gluten-free mixes; baking tools and pans): P.O. Box 876, Norwich, VT 05055; phone (800) 827-6836, fax (800) 343-3002. Web site: www.BakersCatalogue.com. Accepts orders by phone, fax, mail, or web. Please request a free Baker's Catalogue.

BEAVER CREEK BAKERIES (soy, sorghum flours, cookies, and bars): P.O. Box 430, N. Main St., Clarksville, IA 50619; phone (888) 566-5431 or (319) 278-4345, fax (319) 278-4661, e-mail: sales@beavercreekbakeries.com. Web site: www.beavercreekbakeries .com. Phone or e-mail for a full product list.

'CAUSE YOU'RE SPECIAL CO. (gluten-free, casein-free mixes for cakes, cookies, breads, muffins, biscuits, pancakes, pizza crusts, and pastry; plus rice, potato starch, and tapioca starch flours, xanthan gum): P.O. Box 316, Phillips, WI 54555; phone (toll-free) (866) 669-4328, fax (603) 754-0245; Web site: www.causeyourespecial.com. Accepts orders by mail, phone, fax, or Web. Some products may be found in health food and specialty grocery stores.

CELIMIX PRODUCTS [Nelson David of Canada Ltd.] (baking mixes, soups, gravies, cookies, crackers, pastas, and more): 66 Higgins Ave., Winnipeg, Manitoba R3B 0A5, Canada; phone (886) 989-0379. Write or phone for an order form.

CYBROS, INC. (breads, rolls, cookies, white rice, and tapioca flours): P.O. Box 851, Waukesha, WI 53187-0851; phone (800) 876-2253, fax (262) 547-8946. Accepts orders by mail, phone, or fax. Products can also be found in health food stores and are sold by some celiac organizations. Write or phone for an order form.

DIETARY SPECIALTIES (baking mixes, dry pastas, snacks, and main dishes to heat and serve): 1248 Sussex Turnpike, Unit C-2, Randolph, NJ 07869; phone (888) 640-2800, fax (973) 895-3742. Write, phone, or fax for a full product list or visit the Web site: www.dietspec.com.

DIXIE LEGUMES PLUS, INC. (lentil soups, chili, casserole, and salad mixes): P.O. Box 1969, Tomball, TX 77377; phone (800) 233-3668, fax (281) 516-3070. Web site: www.dixiediner.com. Accepts orders by phone, mail, or fax. Some products can be found in health food and gourmet stores and specialty supermarkets. Call for a free catalog.

EL PETO PRODUCTS LTD. (strictly gluten-free manufacturer and distributor of fresh-baked products, baking mixes, soups, pastas, gluten-free flours, cookbooks, snacks, and crackers; bean, rice, quinoa, millet, and other GF flours milled specially for them at The Mill Stone): 41 Shoemaker St., Kitchener, Ontario N2E 3G9, Canada; phone (800) 387-4064, fax (519) 743-8096, e-mail: elpeto@golden.net. Web site: www.elpeto.com. Order by phone, fax, mail, or e-mail. Some products can be found in regular markets and health food stores.

ENER-G-FOODS, INC. (vacuum-packaged breads, rolls, buns, pizza shells, doughnuts, cookies, granola bars; dry mixes, cereals, and flours; xanthan gum; methocel; dough enhancer; almond meal; tapioca, bean, rice, and other gluten-free flours; and Bette Hagman's flour mixes; Egg Replacer; Lacto-Free; and cookbooks): P.O. Box 84487, Seattle, WA 98124; phone (800) 331-5222, fax (206) 764-3398. Accepts orders by phone, mail, fax, or secure web site: www.ener-g.com. Phone for a catalog of their long list of products, which are also available in health food stores and specialty markets.

ENJOY LIFE FOODS (kosher and free of all common allergens: bagels, snack bars, cookies, and more): 1601 N. Natchez Ave., Chicago, IL 60707; phone (773) 889-5070 or (toll free) (888) 503-6569 (50-ENJOY), fax (773) 889-5090. Takes orders by phone or fax. For more information or to find a store near you, phone or visit the Web site: www.enjoylifefoods.com.

FOOD FOR LIFE BAKING COMPANY, INC. (baked bread and muffins, pastas): P.O. Box 1434, Corona, CA 92878-1434; phone (800) 797-5090, fax (909) 279-1784, e-mail: info@foodforlife.com. Web site: www.foodforlife.com. Order by mail. Write or phone for a complete order form. Products can be found in the frozen food sections of specialty and natural food stores under the Food For Life name.

THE FOOD MERCHANTS (polenta and polenta pastas): Quinoa Corporation, P.O. Box 279, Gardena, CA 90248; phone (310) 217-8125, fax (310) 217-8140. Web site: www.quinoa.net. Accepts orders by phone, mail, or Web. Some products can be found in health food stores and some groceries.

FOODS BY GEORGE (baked English muffins, pizza crusts, desserts, and main-meal items): 3 King St., Mahwah, NJ 07430; phone (201) 612-9700, fax (201) 684-0334. Anyone interested should write or phone for an order form. Fresh items often sold at celiac meetings in the New England area.

THE GLUTEN FREE COOKIE JAR (bread, bagels, cakes, cookies, and baking mixes): P.O. Box 52, Trevose, PA 19053; phone (215) 355-9403 or (888) GLUTEN-0, fax (215) 355-7991. Web site: www.glutenfreecookiejar.com. Accepts orders by mail, phone, fax, or web. Anyone interested should write or phone for an order form. Some products may be found in health food stores.

GLUTEN-FREE DELIGHTS, INC. (fresh-baked dinner rolls, bread, doughnuts, cookies, pies, pizza crust, and more): P.O. Box 284, Cedar Falls, IA 50613; phone (888) 403-1806. Web site: www.glutenfreedelights.com. Accepts orders by phone, mail, or Web site. Call for a brochure.

THE GLUTEN-FREE PANTRY, INC. (gluten-free mixes, crackers, cookies, pastas, soups, and baking supplies such as xanthan gum, guar gum, dough enhancer; a long list of gluten-free flours including white, brown, and wild rice, garbanzo bean, several corn flours, and more): P.O. Box 840, Glastonbury, CT 06033; phone (800) 291-8386 or (860) 633-3826, fax (860) 633-6853. Web site: www.glutenfree.com. Write or phone for a free catalog. Accepts orders by Internet, phone, mail, or fax. Computer-savvy people can also shop on-line.

GLUTEN-FREE TRADING CO., LLC (a store with over 750 shelf-stable gluten-free items ranging from baking supplies and flours through condiments, cookies, and pastas): 3116 S. Chase, Milwaukee, WI 53207; phone (888) 993-9933 or (414) 385-9950, fax (414) 385-9915. Phone, fax, or write for a catalog or visit the Web site: info@ gluten-free.net.

GLUTEN SOLUTIONS, INC. (offers 240 gluten-free products from 35 manufacturers): 737 Manhattan Beach Blvd, Suite B., Manhattan Beach, CA 90266; phone (888) 845-8836, fax (810) 454-8277. Web site: www.glutensolutions.com. Phone for an order form or order on-line. Some products may be found in Whole Foods markets.

GLUTINO (DE-RO-MA) (breads, bagels, pizzas, cookies, mixes, pastas, baked items, soups, dressing, pretzels, and gluten-free flours): 3750 Francis Hughes Ave., Laval, Quebec H7L 5A9, Canada; phone (450) 629-7689 or (800) 363-3438 (DIET), fax (450) 629-4781, e-mail: info@glutino.com. Web site: www.glutino.com. Carries top European lines: Dr. Schar, Bi Aglut, Glutafin, and Aproten. Call, fax, e-mail, or write for a catalog. Many items can be found in health food and grocery stores. Also sold through celiac organizations.

GRAIN PROCESS ENTERPRISES, LTD. (Romano, navy, chickpea, garbanzo-fava, and yellow pea flours, and other gluten-free flours including rice, buckwheat, millet, tapioca, potato, and arrowroot; xanthan and guar gums): 115 Commander Blvd., Scarborough, Ontario M1S 3M7, Canada; phone (416) 291-3226, fax (416) 291-2159, e-mail: karen@grainprocess.com. Write or phone for a product list. Takes orders by mail, phone, or fax. Some products can be found in health food stores.

KAYBEE GLUTEN-FREE PRODUCTS (mixes for bread, buns, muffins, cakes, cookies, pizza, and pierogi): P.O. Box 629, Cudworth, Saskatchewan S0K 1B0, Canada; phone and fax (306) 256-3424. Phone or write for an order form.

KING ARTHUR FLOUR: See BAKER'S CATALOGUE

KINNIKINNICK FOODS (breads, buns, bagels, doughnuts, cookies, pizza crusts, muffins, xanthan gum, guar gum; rice, corn, potato, bean, and soya flours; other baking supplies): 10940 120 St., Edmonton, Alberta T5H 3P7, Canada; phone (877) 503-4466 or (toll free) (877) 503-4466, fax (780) 421-0456, e-mail: info@kinnikinnick.com. Web site: www.kinnikinnick.com. Accepts orders by phone, mail, fax, or secure Web site. Offers home delivery of all products to most areas in North America. Some products may be found in health food stores and some in regular grocery stores in the alternative food section.

MRS. LEEPER'S PASTA (gluten-free/casein-free corn and brown rice pastas): 14949 Eastvale Road, Poway, CA 92064, phone (858) 486-1101, fax (858) 486-5115, e-mail: mlpinc@pacbell.net. Web site: www.mrsleeperspasta.com. Sold through health food stores and some gourmet sections in grocery stores under the Mrs. Leeper's label. Write or phone to inquire where products are distributed in your area. Mail orders will be filled for those living too far from stores handling these products. Will provide materials and samples to celiac support groups.

LEGUMES PLUS: See DIXIE-LEGUMES PLUS, INC.

MENDOCINO GLUTEN-FREE PRODUCTS, INC. (cake mix, bread mixes, pancake and waffle mix, general-purpose flour): P.O. Box 277, Willits, CA 95490-0277; phone (800) 297-5399, fax (707) 459-1834, e-mail: sylvanfarm@pacific.net. Web site: www.sylvanborderfarm.com. Products marketed under the Sylvan Border Farm label. Orders taken by phone, mail, fax, or e-mail. Write or phone for an order form. Some products may be found in health food and grocery stores.

MIMI & ME, INC. (gluten-free, lactose-free, casein-free kosher bakery desserts baked in a wheat-free bakery): P.O. Box 774, Lincroft, NJ 07738; phone (732) 758-9464, fax (732) 758-0041. Web site: www.miminme.com. Order by phone, fax, or mail. Shipped by UPS or USPS Priority. Write or phone for a brochure or order forms.

NANA'S KITCHEN (Spaetzle/Dumpling Board for making easy spaetzle or pasta): P.O. Box 2640, Oroville, WA 98844 or 2641 Mappin Court, Kelowna, BC V1Y 8H8, Canada: phone toll free (866) 868-2820, fax (250) 868-2817, e-mail: info@cooking withnana.com. Phone or e-mail for a brochure. Check the web site for more information: www.cookingwithnana.com.

THE REALLY GREAT FOOD CO. (mixes for breads, cakes, muffins, pizza, and more; cereal, snacks, soups, condiments, vitamins, and pasta; rice and tapioca flours; xanthan gum): P.O. Box 2239, St. James, NY 11780; phone (800) 593-5377, fax (631) 361-6920. Web site: www.reallygreatfood.com. Accepts orders by mail or phone. Call or write for a full product list.

RED RIVER MILLING COMPANY (sorghum [milo], mung, and garbanzo [chickpea] flours): 810 Cumberland St., Vernon, TX 76384; phone (800) 680-6904 or (940) 553-1211, fax (940) 553-1977. Accepts orders by mail or phone. Products also sold through Authentic Foods (see above) and celiac organizations. Company mills only gluten-free products.

MISS ROBEN'S (over 500 GF products: baking mixes, ready-to-eat products, cookbooks, pastas, ingredients, and baking supplies, including sorghum, bean flours, Bette Hagman flour blends, xanthan and guar gums, personal-care items, plus free technical baking support): P.O. Box 1149, Frederick, MD 21702; phone (800) 891-0083, fax (301) 665-9584, e-mail: info@missroben.com. Web site: www.missroben.com. Accepts orders by mail, phone, e-mail, fax, or web. Phone or write for a catalog.

SON'S MILLING (whole bean flour, sorghum, and other GF flours): 6820 Kirkpatrick Crescent, Victoria, BC V8M 1Z9, Canada; phone (250) 544-1733, fax (250) 544-1739. Accepts orders by phone, mail, or fax. Write or call for a complete list.

STERK'S BAKERY (new French bread, dinner rolls, bagels, gluten-free flour, baking mixes, and more): 3866 23 Street, Jordan, Ontario L0R 1S0, Canada, or 1402 Pine Ave. Suite 727, Niagara Falls, NY 14301; phone (905) 562-3086, fax (905) 562-3847. Accepts orders by mail or phone. Write for a free catalog.

TAD ENTERPRISES (rice, potato, and tapioca flours; xanthan and guar gums; bread mix, pizza crust, pasta): 9356 Pleasant, Tinley Park, IL 60477; phone (800) 438-6153, fax

(708) 429-3954, e-mail: tadenterprise@aol.com. Accepts orders by mail, phone, e-mail, or fax. Write for an order form for a complete list of products.

THE TEFF COMPANY (fine-milled teff flours, both ivory and brown, ground in gluten-free environment): P.O. Box A, Caldwell, ID 83606; phone (208) 455-0375, e-mail: teffco@earthlink.net. Accepts orders by mail or phone. Call for a brochure and more information.

TWIN VALLEY MILLS, LLC (sorghum flour): RR1 Box 45, Ruskin, NE 68974; phone (402) 279-3965, e-mail: sorghumflour@hotmail.com. Web site: www.twinvalleymills. com. Check the Web site for general information, on-line ordering, and retail outlets.

This list, offered for the reader's convenience, was updated at the time of publication of this book. I regret I cannot be responsible for later changes in names, addresses, or phone numbers or for a company's removing some products from its line.

Index

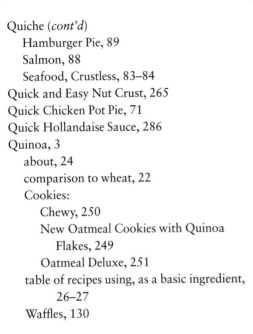

About the Author

BETTE HAGMAN, aka the Gluten-Free Gourmet, was diagnosed as a celiac more than twenty-nine years ago. Since then she has written six cookbooks, each offering a multitude of delicious wheat- and gluten-free recipes—what she calls a "prescription for living." She is a writer, lecturer, and twenty-nine-year member of the Gluten Intolerance Group (GIG). Hagman lives in Seattle.